SOBRIETY WITHOUT END

By

FATHER JOHN DOE
FATHER·RALPH PFAU

Hazelden
Center City, Minnesota 55012-0176
1-800-328-9000 (Toll Free U.S., Canada, and the Virgin Islands)
1-651-213-4000 (Outside the U.S. and Canada)
1-651-213-4590 (24-hour Fax)
http://www.hazelden.org

ISBN-13: 978-1-61649-474-2
ISBN-10: 1-61949-474-3

TABLE OF CONTENTS

ADJUSTMENT

"Having had a spiritual awakening...."

Today the world is filled with anxiety. The world itself is in the throes of a universal "anxiety neurosis." Every civilized nation is desperately seeking peace even to a frantic race for armed superiority to guarantee peace; every family is demanding security; every soul is seeking not only security, but also serenity —peace of mind, peace of soul.

On the other hand, contradictory as it may seem, few—very few ever seem to find this object of universal seeking. In fact people—most people—seem to end with more unsolved problems; more anxieties; more tensions; more "nerves"; and with less peace of mind and soul as time goes on. To fully realize this "pursuit of the modern mirage" and this endless searching without surcease or solution, we but have to call to mind the billions of tons of "peace pills," tranquilizers, barbiturates, and almost innumerable other types of sedatives which are annually consumed; we have only to witness the endless queue wending its way to the psychiatrists, to the sanatoria, and to the asylums; we have only to sit for a spell in any doctor's office or clergyman's study and listen to the pitiful tales of frustration, fear, and hopelessness; nor must we overlook the increasing number of those who failing to find peace of mind are stumbling off the cliff of despair as a tragic ending to their confused thinking and living.

And then we all ask again and again: why—why—why? Must it be so? Is there no true and solid path to peace of mind and soul? Has the world so changed? Have people so changed? Has God changed? Is peace of mind and peace of soul possible in this modern, hectic chaotic world?

It is not only possible—it is simple both to understand and to achieve—*if we want to!* But the achievement of this "consummation devoutly to be wished" is dependent upon four things which make its attainment possible.

1. *We must seek and work toward true "peace" and not confuse the terms which writers often use in a very broad sense—*

5

peace of mind, peace of soul, peace of heart, happiness and contentment.

2. We must quit *trying to change the world, people, God and His eternal laws.*

3. We must *change us.*

4. We must seek all this *from God.*

As we shall see in our discussion on The Serenity Prayer, the terms used above all have very distinct and different meanings. The term *peace* means "absence of conflict." Therefore *peace of mind* means having no *mental conflicts; peace of soul* means having no *moral or spiritual conflicts;* and *peace of heart* means having no *emotional conflicts. Happiness* means the state wherein we *have what we want.* "I finally got *what I have been wanting so long* and now I am *perfectly happy!" Contentment* has still another connotation—it means *satisfied with self;* self-contained.

But any or all of these "states" are difficult to maintain in human nature. We might possibly achieve one or the other *occasionally,* but seldom does one remain for long in life in any of them. *Life is like that*—and *we are not going to change it.* It has been that way ever since sin entered the world and since fallen human nature began to influence life and living, and it will be thus as long as man lives on this earth with that fallen human nature.

So it is that most people are chasing a *"will-o-the-wisp."* We are desperately trying to achieve and to maintain for always peace of mind, peace of soul, peace of heart—happiness and contentment, first trying to "lasso" one and then the other; at times all five. But eventually we end up with conflict, and disappointments, and suffering, and frustrations, and sin, and emptiness.

There is only one possible permanent solution to our frantic seeking. That is to change our sights and instead of trying so desperately to have all these "transient" states, to set our sights and our prayers on the one and only state which can be permanent and a state which will eliminate perhaps none of the above, but *will condition us against any and all eventualities.* This state too is a state of *"peace"*—the *"peace which surpasseth all under-*

6

standing," and comes only from God through prayer and practice.

This is brought about as stated above by *accepting* instead of trying to change *the world, people, God* and *God's laws;* by working day in and day out to *change us*—our *attitudes, habits, and actions;* by humbly beseeching God—day in and day out—for this *peace which surpasseth all understanding* and which is a state of being able to be *undisturbed in spite of conflict or suffering or disappointments or sin or anything that might cross our path.*

We know of no *exact* word expressing this condition. The nearest is the word used by members of Alcoholics Anonymous: *Serenity.* But it is not only alcoholics who are frantically seeking this serenity. *All humans* have it as the object of their living although so few seek it from its source; in the only manner in which one can attain it; from the only One Who can give it: *God.*

Through all ages, men have attained this serenity—this *peace.* But all who have attained it, did so by exactly the same process although under different names and for different reasons. Sad to say, most people seek it sincerely only after all else has failed: as witness the alcoholic. It is brought about only through a *complete change of personality* and to a point where *everything* in life takes on a new meaning and a "new look"—including God.

In the middle ages this *change* was called a *"conversio mores"* which literally meant a *complete change of customs and habits.* Religion has always called it a *"true conversion"* although religion itself is not necessarily involved as we shall see. Again, they meant a *complete change of the person* in relation to religion. Alcoholics Anonymous calls it a *"spiritual awakening"* as a result of taking the twelve steps suggested by the A.A. program. They, too, in this mean a *total change toward life and living: towards one's self: towards one's neighbor: and towards one's God.*[1] Psychiatry has given this change in man the impressive name of *"adjustment,"*—to *life and living and God.* And the average man of the street has a name for it too. It is *"growing up."*

But whether we label it *conversion* or *awakening* or *adjustment* or what have you, one thing is sure it is an absolute pre-

---

[1] For this reason so many in Alcoholics Anonymous fail to attain true serenity. They have never fully and sincerely taken *all* of the steps.

requisite to the attaining of serenity or true *peace*. Nor does it make any difference what *format* we use to effect this change, we *must experience certain fundamental interior convictions* whether we accomplish the change as an alcoholic along the path of the Twelve Steps or as a neurotic along the lines of one of the psychiatric therapies or as a sinner along the Exercises of Saint Ignatius or some other way. And these are the basic *"convictions"* which must be brought about in every one who hopes to some day have *serenity* or *true peace*.

1. There must be *petition*. We must seek help—either human or divine. This happens when the alcoholic seeks A.A. or becomes willing to accept help. It happens when the neurotic seeks the doctor or advisor and becomes willing to use his advice and directives. It happens when the sinner seeks his God, and becomes willing for Him to forgive and to save. Actually in all these cases it is the *"dawn of humility"*—the realization that *no one ever goes through life no matter who he may be without someone's help; that no one is sufficient unto himself.* It is evidenced in the cries of countless sinners down through the ages: "O God, that I may *see!*" It is the first step in the solution of all problems of life. *"Seek* and you will find."

2. Having sought help and guidance, brings *recognition*. We are able with the help of someone else to *see our problem as others see it; as God sees it; objectively.* In short we *recognize* it *as a problem*. In the alcoholic this happens when *he honestly recognizes his problem as alcoholism,* instead of all the many and varied other problems which he had always placed first in necessity of solution. In the neurotic it is the recognition of his problem as one of nerves; and in the sinner the recognition of his problem as one of sin.

3. Presuming honesty, recognition demands *admission*. Perhaps for the first time we *honestly and completely without reservation admit* that *we* have a problem. In the first step the alcoholic achieves this admission of honesty: "We admitted we were powerless over alcohol; that our lives have become unmanageable." The neurotic achieves this conviction when he *accepts* the advisor's verdict that the fact that he has a neurosis. The sinner

8

does so when he in the words of the prodigal son cries: "I have sinned against God and my father." All have *begun to accept responsibility*.

4. With the acceptance of responsibility comes in alcoholic, neurotic and sinner *contrition* for all the errors and mistakes and sins of the past, but *not self-pity*. We begin to be *sorry* for what *we have done to others* instead of what we had always *blamed* others for. We *were responsible*. We *are sorry*.

5. And being sorry, we immediately have a *volition* to avoid these same mistakes in the future. We become *willing* to make amends, and to *do differently*. All A.A.'s will recognize these changes taking place along the twelve steps.

6. And then, and then only comes the *"versio"* the *conversion*. We are *different* in our *attitudes toward life, toward ourselves, toward others, toward God*. Why? Because in the process of *turning* we looked *inside (introversion)* and saw both our failings and our talents and abilities; we looked outside *(extroversion)* and saw the potentialities of our fellowman's help and of God's help; and we then *changed;* we *converted,* we had an *awakening,* we *adjusted* by accepting what we *could not change;* by changing what *we could change;* and we continually sought help to know the difference.

7. With this beginning of the "new" man, there comes a necessity of a *continuation* of these attitudes and of a continued *practice* of all the *principles which we learned in the process*.

8. And then, and then only will we enjoy the *fruition*—the *peace beyond understanding*, the serenity every human is seeking, but alas so few finding.

In our volume *Sobriety and Beyond* we tried to analyze in detail the various steps suggested to the alcoholic in his pursuit not only of *sobriety* but in his attaining of the area *beyond sobriety* which gives this serenity. Towards the end of the book we saw that en route the alcoholic learned that there were certain "principles" which if *practiced* day in and day out would maintain this serenity. In the following pages we have endeavored to analyze all of these principles to help the sincere alcoholic—or any sincere

9

person seeking serenity—*continue his sobriety—his serenity*—for all the days of his life.

We know from experience that these principles "work"; not only for the alcoholic but for *any human being who wants a solution of their problems and who wishes to achieve and maintain serenity*. They were not written in the king's library nor in the halls of justice. They were begotten in the hearts of thousands of alcoholics who had for so long tried to "reach out beyond the sordidness, the deceit, the folly, the ignorance, the immorality, the sham, the materialism, and the hypocrisy of this world to grasp that elusive something which spells kinship with the lovely, the beautiful and the Divine in life." They are phrased in very ordinary language by a very ordinary guy, so the very ordinary guy or gal may understand. And since the sobriety and the serenity we seek is something of the spirit, it is immortal. So it is fondly hoped that all who peruse these pages and meditate on these principles practicing them day in and day out will continue their sobriety not only until the end of their earthly sojourn, but into eternity; that their sobriety and serenity will be in truth

Sobriety Without End!

PRINCIPLES AND PRACTICE

". . . and practice these principles in all our affairs."

In our college days, we attended a school which was surrounded by people of German descent. The townsfolk mostly all spoke German, our professors all knew German, and all of the workers at the College spoke German. And so in such an atmosphere, one could hardly help picking up at least a few choice German expressions. Some we made our own: "ya," "nein," "was ist das" and other similar, but simple phrases. However there was one axiom that always fascinated us. Why, we do not know, but its phraseology, its sequence, and its almost resonant quality seemed always to cause it to stand out above all of the rest. It has an English counterpart and translation, but such never seemed to carry the depth of meaning as did the precise phrasing of the German which even in its absolute literal translation is far more meaningful in our language than the English axiom.

In German this phrase is: "Die übung macht den meister." The English axiom is: "Practice makes perfect." The English literal translation would be: "Continuing repetition makes the master." We feel "practice" denotes experiment, whereas "übung" means a little bit more and means to "repeat" and to "repeat" and to "repeat" the *same* identical action, word, phrase or what have you, not necessarily until it is "perfect,"—for "perfect" is too idealistic—but a "continuing repetition" until one has the ability to automatically repeat it at will or until one is "master" of said action, word, phrase, etc., under any circumstances and in any situation. So to become the master of anything it is necessary to repeat and repeat—day in and day out—hour in and hour out—and, if necessary, minute in and minute out. All else can but beget mediocrity.

All of us have known at times famous people either personally or through reading about them. Always there have been the very few of every field of endeavor who have "mastered" their work or art or sport. And it is precisely this "mastery" that makes them stand out above all others in their field of endeavor.

All of us, too, have had the experience of realizing that some such artist, or musician, or sports figure has suddenly faded from the spotlight and has been relegated back again to the ranks of the mediocre or even into oblivion. It is then that we ask ourselves, why? What happened to cause such to fall from fame?

It was one such great violinist who gave the insight into what was behind these "failures" when he made the following statement: "If I fail to *practice* one day, I shall notice the difference in my playing; if I fail to practice two days, my family will notice the difference in my playing; if I fail to practice three days, my public will notice the difference in my playing."

Why such failures? What happened? They quit *practicing*. They either gradually or suddenly discontinued that constant repetition that made them masters, and which was necessary to maintain the mastery once acquired. "Repeat and repeat and repeat, day in and day out, hour in and hour out and, if necessary, minute in and minute out."

The above fact was behind the seemingly endless and, to us, foolish repetitions of our school lessons. It is the reason behind the success of a few who achieve the "top" in any profession. It is behind those very, very few who *stay* at the "top"— who remain "masters" in their field of endeavor.

And do you know something? It is that same almost startling truth that is behind those who achieve and maintain *mastery* in A.A.—not masters of drinking, but masters of sobriety—which means maintaining complete, total sobriety under every circumstance and in any and every situation. It is the truth behind those few in A.A. who achieve and maintain serenity and happiness and peace of mind in spite of the changing vicissitudes of life and in the face of any and all obstacles. It is the truth behind those many who have now gone for A.A. through the portal of death—sober and happy, and courageously meeting their final curtain call. Not necessarily perfection; but mastery.

And do you know something else? It is also the above truth that is the missing factor in all of those A.A.'s who were sober or at least "dry" for awhile, or for a few years, or even for many years and who then suddenly "slipped" into the oblivion of drinking again. What happened? Why do A.A.'s slip? Why does the old-timer in A.A. often disappear from our ranks? All of these questions can be answered by the same answer—the same identical truth: *They quit practicing.* They "learned" A.A.; they "learned" the twelve steps; they "learned" all about alcoholism and the alcoholic. But they *quit practicing all of those things they learned.* They seemed to have forgotten that all of the twelve steps are necessary for obtaining sobriety and happiness; and that *all* of the *twelfth step* is necessary for *maintaining sobriety and happiness*—for *retaining* the *mastery in sobriety.* They never learned, or they forgot, or they never accepted the truth that to *"practice these principles in all of our affairs"* means to *repeat and repeat and repeat—day in and day out, hour in and hour out,* and, if necessary, *minute in and minute out* those *principles* we learned in A.A. in *all of our affairs,* i.e., in *every* area of living:

> In our home life.
> In our social life.
> In our business life.
> In our financial affairs.
> In our spiritual life.
> In our emotional life.
> In our physical life.
> In our thought life.
> In our A.A. life.

All slippees, all unhappy people in A.A., all unhappy people —period, have never begun to, or have not continued to apply, the most important part of the whole program for continued sobriety and happiness:

"To practice these principles in all of our affairs."

What principles have we learned in A.A.?

We do not here refer to those underlying truths and principles with which most of us have been familiar prior to joining A.A.,—the principles of justice, the ten commandments, etc. We refer to the *application of these same age-old truths to the alcoholic problem* and to the alcoholic. The principles that "worked" for the alcoholic; all the "how" of using the truths many of which we already knew, but which we seldom used or used wrongly or badly; the principles we, as alcoholics, *need* to use in our living, if we ever hope to achieve—not perfection—but *mastery* of living *as alcoholics, masters of sobriety.* And *sobriety,* total sobriety, means not only freedom from alcoholic indulgence, but also peace of mind, contentment, happiness, peace of soul, *adjustment to life,* to *reality,* to *God's will and man's presence.*

DECISIONS

"On the plains of desolation there bleach the bones of countless millions who at the very dawn of victory sat down to wait—and waiting died!"

There is nothing in human life more devastating to human nature than the habit of or the inability to make up our minds when problems and potentials come along in our daily living. Nor is this destructive force present and doing its damage only when these problems and/or potentials are in our conscious thinking. Experience has taught us that as long as a problem which presses for solution is *unsolved*, it is tearing at our whole personality *even though we may at the moment not be consciously thinking of the problem.* And the more we permit indecisive mental habits to take hold, the more does its damage flow over into our every day thinking, feeling, acting and living.

One of the first by-products of indecision is *procrastination,* which simply means the habit of always *"putting off for the morrow."* Being unable or unwilling to solve the situation confronting us we ever so gradually pick up the habit of just putting it aside for another day. And as we learned in our discussion of *action,* to-morrow is never. And so problems increase, grow in size, and grow for themselves a thicker and thicker armor ever more and more resisting solution. This only feeds procrastination. And it isn't long until we have a well rooted habit of *procrastination.*

Another by-product of *indecision* is *neglect of work,* and failure to meet obligations. We can't or don't make up our minds —we put off for tomorrow—we *just don't do it.* And so our work goes undone—our obligations go unfulfilled.

Then comes the damage to our emotions : *tension, irritability, anxiety and depressive moods.* These are all the end-result of that constant and repeated irritation and conflict going on inside : *"Maybe I will, maybe I won't; maybe I can and maybe I can't; maybe I should and maybe I shouldn't."*

From all this stems an *over-tired body.* And day after day, we seem to feel always so tired even though on the surface we seem not to be over-tiring ourselves. We are not conscious of that continual expenditure of energy going on day in and day out— either in our conscious or in our sub-conscious minds—*making up our minds!*

And *spiritually,* the soul itself makes little or no progress toward God nor in the practice of virtue, *because we can't make up our minds!*

And as a secondary result there comes that familiar old habit of excuses. In no other way can we meet a new day unless we dig up an excuse to cover the neglect of yesterday and to-day which came from our *habit of indecision.*

On the other hand *most problems of life would be solved and all problems would be fifty per cent less burdensome, if we would only make up our minds once and for all to make up our minds day in and day out as the problems arise;* if we could only bring ourselves to acquire the *habit of decision.*

Now let's take the word *decision* itself. It comes from two Latin words; "de"and "cidere," which mean literally *"to cut in half."* And we know from the experience of the race that most problems are *actually halved* once there has been a full decision.

Let's take a look at history and see first the results of in-decision; and then we shall take a look-see at the results of decision.

It was way back in the beginning of the human race that we find indecision coming into the picture and wreaking its ravages. It happened when Eve—the first woman—was confronted by the serpent. After telling the serpent that Almighty God had for-bidden them to eat the fruit of a certain tree in paradise; and after the serpent had countered with a beautiful piece of rational-ization—she *hesitated;* for she evidently had never *made a full decision* to serve God and *only God* irrespective of what or who might endeavor to make her waiver in this service. So she hesi-tated; she "saw that the fruit was delightful to behold"; she doubted God; she believed the serpent; *she ate the fruit.* It is the story of every sinner since that time and is prima facie evidence that such a sinner (we speak of serious or willful wrongs, not of the daily faults and failings which are part and parcel of human nature) has not yet *made up his mind that God comes first;* that His laws are immutable regardless of circumstances, place and association. And so it is: God commands; the serpent (or circumstance) denies; we doubt God, believe the serpent—and we sin.

Then there is the well-known story of Lot's wife. When fleeing from Sodom and Gomorrha, although merely "exercising the ordinary prerogative of womanhood!" she *hesitated*—and we know from the bible story, she was turned into a pillar of salt. She couldn't make up her mind or *hadn't* made up her mind that what God had told them was absolutely true.

Moses was chosen to lead the Israelites out of bondage and into the Promised Land. Everything went along fine until he was asked by Almighty God to strike the rock and told that from the rock would flow water for his water-starved people. Then it was that Moses *hesitated*: lack of faith and trust caused *indecision* and because of this the privilege of actually leading his people into the Promised Land was denied him. It is quite evident that he had *never made up his mind* that *anything* which God commands or directs *must be reasonable and true* albeit many times necessitating the miraculous.

Another outstanding example of indecision in history is Pilate who condemned Christ. As we read this story we see evidence all along the trail of *Pilate's inability to make up his mind.* At one time he would be about to absolve Christ; at another to condemn Him. In the end *he was sure he should absolve,* but *fear* of the disfavor of Caesar—which had caused all of his indecision—caused him to rationalize that merely by "washing his hands" he could side-step his obligation as judge. And so this he did and to the Jews he said: "You have a law; go and judge Him by it." And so although disavowing any responsibility, he still was the one responsible for Christ's crucifixion. And so it is that today—nineteen hundred years later—although Christianity has spread throughout the entire world, Pilate is only remembered "as the one who condemned Christ."

Augustine was for many years a very great sinner—but

often-times we wonder whether *indecision* was not at the base of and the real reason for his long delay in converting to God. Let's listen to one of his prayers—then form your own judgment: "O God, give me the grace of purity, *but not yet*"!

On the other hand we find that history is full of examples of great men who achieved success in their fields of endeavor *because they were men of decision.*

The history of Roman conquests, right or wrong, shows that these great ancient warriors were successful in their wars because they were men of decision. Read the Gallic wars which so many high school pupils must slave through in translations, and there above everything else we see that Caesar was able to and as a matter of fact did *make decisions*—important decisions—even in the heat of battle.

And still in the years of the past, Augustine who as we mentioned above was a man of indecision and sinned for so many years, by that same token became a saintly man and an outstanding doctor of theology *once he made up his mind to serve God*—no matter what the cost, nor what any thing or anyone might try to prevail upon him to change his course. Remember the story?

Augustine was walking up and down in his garden late one afternoon (probably trying to make up his mind about something and not being able to do so). Suddenly there came a voice saying softly, "Take and read, take and read." Augustine glanced toward his table and there noticed a bible. He picked it up, opened it and the first words to meet his eyes were: "Not in rioting and drunkenness, not in chambering and impurities . . . but put ye on the Lord Jesus Christ and make not provision for the flesh in its concupiscences." And then once and for all Augustine finally made up his mind; and aided by grace *decided* once and for all to serve God rather than his flesh. *A full decision!*

In the modern era we have many outstandingly successful men, but invariably we find as part and parcel of their success the ability to make decisions.

One of these men was the late Franklin Roosevelt who four times was elected president of the United States. All through his career there stands out one quality which undoubtedly enabled him to achieve and to accomplish—the ability to make decisions—day in and day out. Particularly do we see this in evidence in his early years in the White House. For it was during those crucial years following the depression that we see Mr. Roosevelt making world shaking decisions, and with finality. Whether we be Democrat or Republican,—whether we like and admire Mr. Roosevelt or not,—whether we agree with his decisions or not, there can be no question that he *was successful* in being President. (He got there four times!)

Then there is General Douglas McArthur who without question is one of the outstanding military men of the age in which we live. Read the history of the second world war—from Bataan and back to Bataan again—and there we see outstanding in his career and successful victory in the far East, the ability to make decisions, even to that now famous statement early in the war when leaving the Philippines: *"We will* return!" He had made up his mind!

Our President, General Dwight Eisenhower, who along with McArthur and as Supreme Commander in Europe during the second world war, was successful in leading our forces to ultimate victory, was a man able to make *decisions* for the entire armed forces.

Mr. Churchill, one of the greatest diplomats of all times, in his memoirs of the war gives evidence of being, perhaps even above his other outstanding qualities, a *man of decision.*

Even Mr. Harry Truman, when he *"made up his mind to give 'em hell,"* went out and got himself elected President!

And good old Satchel Page who was still pitching and winning ball games to a ripe old age, says in his recipe for his longevity in action: "Never hesitate and look around, someone might be catching up with you."

Take a good look around almost any A.A. group. Who are the ones who *have* serenity; who *have* taken all the steps; and who *have* all that the program promises—*the members who once again in their living have acquired the habit of decision and who have achieved the ability to make up their minds.*

The habit of decision is acquired again in the very same manner in which we picked up the habit of indecision—by *practice*. It was perhaps many years ago when we were first faced with a problem about which we couldn't or didn't make a decision. And then there was another time—and another—and another, until we became victims of indecision. So it is that now by the same process we replace this habit by the habit of decision. And we do it simply *by making decisions*—day in and day out; first one, then another—and another—and another, until again we have the *habit* of decision.

This is not the same as *action*. It is rather the *trigger of action*. It is like the shooting of the gun. The actual firing of the bullet is the action, *but the pulling of the trigger is the decision.*

Now comes the question, "How is a decision arrived at in the human personality?" Let's take an example. Let's take an example of the greatest Person Who ever lived—Christ. And let us take the example of His agony in the garden of Gethsemane. The problem was the carrying of the cross and His ultimate Crucifixion. The question, should He do it. So He goes into the garden and in prayer and meditation He *learns the facts of the problem.* And these facts were: the sacrifice was necessary; it was His Father's Will that He do it. Then immediately comes the decision: *not My Will but Thine be done;* and then the action: He went to His apostles and said, "Come, the hour has come; let us go." To summarize: He learned all the knowable facts; He weighed them in the light of reason and God's Will; He *made His decision.*

Then another outstanding example which is excellent for analysis is the time when Mary, Christ's Mother, was told that she was to be the Mother of the Redeemer. What did she do? She first *learned the facts.* Would her vow be preserved? She was assured that it would. Was it God's Will? It was. Then immediately came her decision: "Behold the Handmaid of the Lord; be it done to me according to Thy Word." Again, she learned all the knowable facts; she weighed them in the light of reason and God's Will; *she made her decision.*

With all due reverence, how would a person of indecision have acted under the same circumstances?

In Christ's place, he too probably would have learned all the facts, *but then he would have started "shooting angles"*: "But isn't there some other way? *Must* I do it now? Couldn't we put it off until the next Pasch?" Excuses, excuses, excuses!

Then there would be the indecisive woman in place of Mary. What would she have done? She probably would have learned the facts, but immediately would have followed this discovery with "But *I'm* not worthy. Surely God doesn't want *me*?" And would there possibly be that old standby: "But, what will people say?" Excuses, excuses, excuses!

And in both cases: "Let me think it over and I'll let You know later, God!"

A full decision means making up our minds once and for all without *any reservations*—without any "if's," "and's" or "but's." A half-decision is no decision. This is the primary reason that so many fall off the first step of the A.A. program. "Alcoholic? Well, maybe I am; then again maybe *I'm* not." There is no such thing as being a "little alcoholic"! We either are—or we aren't.

This factor was dramatically brought out when A.A. was first introduced to Indianapolis. It seems that the one who founded A.A. there had read the Saturday Evening Post article and had written to New York for further information. He had been "dry" for several years, but unhappy about it. It also happened at the same time that an A.A. member from Cleveland had written to New York for the names and addresses of inquirers so he could call on them on his sales route. He received the name of the fellow from Indianapolis. He arrived there on a Sunday afternoon. He went to the inquirer's home and there found him sitting with his family—now all grown. Immediately he spoke out: "Hello, Mr............, I understand you're an alcoholic!"

"Well, now, a-a-a-," stammered the surprised gentleman, "Maybe I am, and maybe I'm not."

"Make up your mind, Mister," bluntly spoke his visitor, "You *either are or you aren't"!*

And another A.A. group was conceived and brought into being.

Such a full decision can be made as an *over-all* decision

29

regulating daily routine occasions so that whenever the circumstance or question or problem arises, we have *already made our decision*. The reason we "stick our necks out" so often is because we wait until the occasion arises to make our decision—and many times we give in against our better judgment. Let's take an example.

So many become over-taxed with twelfth step activity because they let the decision go until the occasion arises—and they always give in and finally become over-burdened to their own detriment. The wise man—the man of decision—makes up his mind *once and for all*: "this is the maximum time I can give to twelfth step activity and keep my own serenity and be sure of my own sobriety. *Any* over that is out." Then when it happens, the decision is *already* made; the answer is "No." And so with many daily routine recurrent problems and occasions. An *over-all* decision will prevent frequent, "Should I or shouldn't I? Well, guess I better."

The writer has found this so very necessary and useful in his travelling and speaking. He has made a decision once and for all relative to many problems presenting themselves at every stop. So when they do arise, the answer is already decided. One example: Once our schedule is made and the itinerary begun, no more invitations are taken to speak en route. We learned the hard way that otherwise we ended up with many talks, no work done, dead tired and returning home with a combination of over-tiredness and over-burden of put-off work. So we made a decision— once the itinerary is begun, no more talks *no matter who asks*. The answer already is "No." And now we have reasonable schedules: a time to talk, a time to rest, a time to keep abreast with our office work.

In the spiritual life, writers called this a "Rule of Life," i.e., over-all decisions *regulating all the daily difficulties before they happen*. Such can be extended to cover *all* of our activities in all of the various phases of life.

Now, what are the obstacles to acquiring the habit of decision? What are the causes of indecision in human life?

In our opinion they are four basic causes or obstacles, with many minor contributory causes here and there:

1. *Fear of failure*—Most people of indecision have an exaggerated fear of failing and an exaggerated need of being always successful. We find this present in practically every alcoholic. That is what made us *perfectionists*. We couldn't bear to fail; we couldn't bear to have anything less than the perfect, the best. But at the same time we couldn't bring ourselves to expend all the time, patience, and energy necessary for this perfection, this success. So we were *afraid* to make a decision. Wasn't it Franklin Roosevelt who made that famous statement in the depth of the depression: "The only thing we have to fear is fear"? Again the bugaboo of the alcoholic—*fear*.

This begins to dissipate itself in the sincere alcoholic when he comes to A.A. and sees all those who *have succeeded*. And then it is that he begins to reason to himself "What others have done, I can do." It was the daily thought of Augustine after his conversion: "Others have, why not I." From this comes the influence of the Divine, and we say to ourselves, "What I can not do, *we* can." And then a decision—*we will*. This is what happens to most of us in the first three steps. Read 'em over, chum!

2. *Refusal to accept reality*—From childhood we have been pampered and spoiled and protected from having to face reality and problems or to shoulder responsibility. As a result we became dreamers, procrastinators and perfectionists. As a result the inability or the unwillingness to make decisions lest a decision would bring us face to face with reality; lest a decision would force responsibility upon us; lest a decision would force us to take the time and to have the patience and willingness to expend the energy necessary for perfection.

They tell us that Mr. Walt Disney is a perfectionist, but one who has the patience, ability, and is willing to work at reaching perfection in his work.

Ourselves? We wanted a short-cut!

3. *Lack of divine faith and trust in God*—As we indicated above in passing, from being helped by other human beings we then proceed to a new faith and confidence in the Divine. We

learned that self-confidence is fine—as far as it goes, but that there are and always will be circumstances and problems in life wherein self-confidence is not enough. We need Divine help. So from an awakened or a renewed faith in God we again begin to "trust"; to believe that He not only *can* but *will*. It was the daily motto of the saints: "God will provide." Our difficulty is failing to realize that in all of our actions so very much depends upon God—we have only to do that which in us lies. From this comes that age-old dictum: "Whoever does what he himself is able to do of himself, *God will not deny the grace.*" Let us always remember *ours is only the foot-work;* it is God Who gives the success or permits the failure.

4. *Pride and stubbornness*—How many times we knew what we should decide to do; we even at times *wanted* to decide it; but *we bogged down in indecision because of what someone might say, or think!* We were *too proud* to make a decision. Again we were repeating inside the words of Pilate who knew so well that Christ was innocent: "But what will Caesar say?"

Or at times we are just too stubborn to give in. We know what should be our decision; again we may even *want* to make it; but *because certain people we dislike are involved in some way or other,* we hold back—we're stubborn—we can't make up our minds.

5. *Weak human nature*—As Saint Paul so eloquently puts it, "In my mind I serve the law of God; in my flesh the law of sin. The good that I will, I do not. The evil that I hate, I do. O miserable man, who will liberate me from the bondage of this death? The grace of God through Jesus Christ." And as a result with this interior conflict *(which will remain until we are dead!)* many times we hesitate, pulled back and forth by the desire for good and the tendency to evil—and we can't make up our minds! *But* with the help of God's grace *we can* establish the habit of *decision.*

Now let's see how this works out practically in the various areas of living.

1. *In the home*—How many problems in the home are never solved, *because husband and wife or mother and father have never made up their minds mutually to solve them!* There simply

is *no meeting of minds.* After all, the family is the basic social *unit,* and the decisions must be made as a *unit,* and the first prerequisite for that is that there be a *mutual meeting of minds* between the mother and father or the husband and wife. We would have no need for the endless advice and articles on *"How to adjust to the emotional life of your husband (or your wife),"* or *"How to adjust sexually,"* or *"How to solve marriage problems,"* if only husband and wife would learn that very basic principle of *all* adjustment, namely that there *first* must be a *meeting of minds,* which is nothing more nor less than *mutual decisions.* But when the one does not *know* the other's mind, there is hesitation, there is indecision, there are more problems.

So many come to the writer with so-called "marriage problems" and our *unqualified advice is always: both husband and wife should together consult a competent advisor and there in the presence of each other make their decisions on the advisor's counsel.* Then there is a *meeting of minds,* and a *unified decision,* and amazingly, in the face of this, *most problems* even *serious ones* are solved, and many times very easily solved. And this meeting of minds enables husband and wife to *make decisions as a unit without suspicion,* or *doubt,* or *fear*—the three most common forerunners of all family problems.

Again, how many today still do not own their own home *simply because they have never made up their minds to get started.* Always it has been "We're gonna make up our minds *sometime"*—and that "sometime," my friend, means *never!*

2. *In business*—Like the ones above, how many still have no better job than they had five, ten, twenty years ago although they had always *intended* to get a better job. But they never *made up their minds* to go out and find one. They will—*sometime;* which still means *never!*

Who is the successful salesman in business? He is the one who when he starts his day, or week, or month, has *made up his mind* and therefore he *knows upon whom he is going to call, what he has to sell,* and precisely *what he is going to say about what he has to sell.* This man ends his day, or week, or month with successful sales. But the man of indecision? He is going to call

33

on *lots* of customers, and is going to sell them *lots* of things, and is going to tell them *lots* of things about his product. He doesn't exactly know whom he is going to call on, or what he is going to say, or what he is going to sell—because he hasn't made up his mind yet,—*but he will* as he goes along. So he calls on several—then time out for a short one!

3. *In our emotional life*—How many tensions, nervous upsets, jitteriness, sleeplessness and what have you are directly a by-product of indecision! The subconscious is *loaded* with undecided problems, stuck there because we couldn't make a decision. Emotionally it is like Fibber McGee's closet. Could we expect anything but tension? And how many nights do we not lie awake batting a problem back and forth or even because of unsolved problems of which we may even not at the moment be conscious. But they are still there—unsolved—and taking their toll emotionally and causing sleeplessness etc., day in and day out. How many times do people not have anxieties, and depressions, and the jitters, and restlessness because of an unsolved problem albeit now forgotten or forced out of their consciousness. And so we have more problems for the psychiatrist—because *we couldn't or didn't make up our minds!*

4. *In our mental life*—Procrastination, forgetfulness, excuse-making, mental conflicts,—all these come along in the wake of the habit of indecision. There is no better mental hygiene existent than a well established *habit of decision!*

5. *In our physical life*—It is amazing how long it takes to tire the body itself, *if* there are no emotional and mental factors causing over-tiredness. But many wear out physically so quickly, are over-tired most of the time, *because of their habits of indecision.* And psychosomatic medicine today tells us that not only over-tiredness, but innumerable other sicknesses of the body stem from or are complicated by *indecisions.* What a difference in any serious illness between the one who *has made up his mind he wants to get well;* and the one who *can't or won't make up his mind he wants to get well*—sometimes he wants to get well, and again sometimes he wants to die—which he usually does!

6. *In our financial affairs*—The push-overs for salesmen are those who have never made a full decision as to just how much they can spend and just what they can afford to buy. So when the salesman shows them something attractive and quickly insists: "It is *only* five dollars a month" (for forty years!), they give in, they buy and it isn't long until they suddenly realize that they are over-burdened with payment plans. Then comes more indecision as to what to get rid of!

Even in gambling, the successful gambler is the one who can quickly make up his mind whether to bet or not to bet. A seasoned gambler can spot the hesitant guys a mile away.

It is a known fact that most people who "play the horses" lose. But it is a very little known fact that the reason so many lose is most of the time from human nature and the habit of indecision. Horsemen who know, tell us that there are many good "systems" on the market for playing the horses but most human beings most of the time are confronted with several other indications other than the system indicates (tips, hunches, etc.) and the average bettor then puts the system aside, bets his hunch, or tip or what have you—and he loses. Why? Because he had never made up his mind to *stick with his system irregardless* of hunches, and tips and the like. Systems are based on the laws of average which are immutable over a period of time; but a changing mind makes those laws very mutable in its choices when he becomes undecided and takes a chance on his "hunch." The writer once knew an avid horse follower who had a dozen systems down pat—and he attempted to use *all twelve* on every race! Of course he lost—consistently.

7. *In our spiritual life*—Why do so many fail to return to God or to progress spiritually? Because they have never made up their minds to do so. Remember the story of Augustine? We referred to it in passing above. We mentioned how for many years he failed to convert to God, because of indecision. On the other hand we find that *once Augustine made up his mind* on that fateful afternoon in his garden, he not only converted to God, but became a very saintly man and one of the greatest theologians of all ages. Let's look at the story again:

It all happened towards evening. Augustine was walking up and down in his garden (probably trying to make up his mind about a dozen things!) when he heard a voice saying: "Take and read; take and read." He looked around and there his gaze fell upon the bible. He took the volume, opened it and read there that now famous passage: "Not in rioting and drunkenness, not in chambering and impurities ... but put ye on the Lord Jesus Christ and make not provision for the flesh in its concupiscences." (Rom. xiii-13) And then it was that Augustine finally made a full decision. "Lord, what will You have me to do?" It was then that he made up his mind once and for all to serve God instead of his flesh. The rest is history. For Augustine that was the beginning of his real approach to God and to a saintly life. But we? We just can't make up our minds. And always our spiritual progress is rooted in that dim, hazy, far-off—tomorrow, we hope, maybe!

So few have a well established habit of prayer and meditation which is mentioned in the eleventh step simply because they have *never made up their minds exactly how and when* it is to be.

And many, so very many, still topple into serious faults and sins because they have never *made up their minds* to remove the *occasion* of their falls.

But we just can't bring ourselves to make that decision, can we? Sometimes we would like to; sometimes we wouldn't; so in practice we *don't!*

8. *In our A.A. life*—Still most slips stem from the inability or from the unwillingness to make *a full decision* in the very first step of the A.A. program. "Maybe I am and maybe I'm not," "Sometimes I think I am; then there are times when I think *I'm* not,"—*indecision.*

Why do so many still remain on the first step? They have never made up their minds to take *all* of the twelve steps.

And the third step proves to be such a bugaboo to so many because there again we meet head on with *"We made a decision. . . ."*

Why does a guy or gal first start missing meetings? He has never made up his mind that he not only does but always will need "insurance"; they have never fully decided that there simply is no graduation day in the A.A.—except death.

And many, many today put off for a long, long time attending their first A.A. meeting or seeking A.A., because they can't make up their minds.

Indecision!

As a child we were told many times: "The road to hell is paved with good intentions."

May we paraphrase, please?

The road to heaven—here and hereafter—and to serenity, and peace of mind and security and happiness and to total sobriety is paved with good and full decisions!

But you know something? *You* are the one who has to make up *your* mind!

THINK

*"With desolation in the land made desolate....
because there is none who thinketh...."*

Many times in the past we have endeavored to point out the extreme importance of *meditation*.[1] But we feel that perhaps the main obstacle to establishing the habit of meditation in many people is their inability to use their thinking processes correctly. We have been so used to "fast" thinking; "angle-shooting"; and rationalizing, that many have completely forgotten the art of true *thinking*. The truth of this fact and the need of its re-learning is evidenced in so many A.A. club rooms and meeting halls where we find in large letters, the little word: *Think!*

Undoubtedly many of the troubles and problems of the alcoholic stemmed from his refusal, willing or otherwise, to think. Because when we do not take time out to think, we can hardly ever *know* the truth or the circumstances or the over-all results which may stem from our actions. Undoubtedly the less of thought there is in a person, the more foolish decisions, the more foolhardy actions, the more problems and dire results.

However, this is nothing new, nor is it a product of the modern era alone. For way back in ancient times, it was Isaias who wrote "With desolation is the land made desolate because there is no one who thinketh in their heart." And in the Lamentation of Jeremias we hear the cry, "Jerusalem, O, Jerusalem, return to the Lord, Thy God." But they didn't stop to think. As a result they did not return until God by destroying Jerusalem "forced" man back to Him.

They tell us that there is such a thing as the *Drama of the Universe*. These historian-philosophers point out that since the beginning of man's life on earth there have been certain cycles, —cycles of man gradually departing from God and His Will and then a crisis and man's return to God. These cycles if we carefully read history will be found to fall into about a 500 year orbit. The

---

[1] Cf. Sobriety and Beyond, p. 285.

first such was terminated with the universal flood; then there was the destruction of Sodom and Gomorrha; the destruction of Jerusalem. Time will not permit listing all of them, but for our purpose it readily can be seen that in those years preceding the crises there could always be applied the words of Isaias: "With desolation is the land made desolate . . . etc." It is the same story over and over: Man serves God. Man gradually, ever so gradually, falls away from God. There is a crisis sent by God. Man returns to God. Then the cycle turns again and man ever so gradually forgets God. It is the *Drama of the Universe.*

Undoubtedly today according to all *thinking* men we are at the low arc of this cycle. There are so few "who thinketh in their hearts." When the crisis will come; what it will be; we cannot say. But there are glib albeit stupid writers today who try to pooh-pooh the idea of our age being so far from God and "prove" their contentions in condemning those who try to alert the present era to its danger by quoting words similar in warning from "hundreds of years ago." They then quite paternally tell their readers to ignore this big bad wolf of danger "because they already years ago said the same thing, and we're *still around.*" But they forget to tell or wantonly ignore the fact that pursuant to those expressed warnings of the sages through the years there *did* come the crisis; the flood, the destruction of Sodom and Gomorrha, the destruction of Jerusalem, etc. They forget to tell or were too stupid to be able to tell that today is a *new* danger; *another* age "who thinketh not in their heart."

But enough philosophizing. There is no question that today is one of the most talkative ages in history—not only because of the abundance of mechanical devices to diffuse our verbal barrages, but also because we have little inside our minds which did not come there from the world outside our minds, so that human communication seems to us a great necessity. There are so few listeners, although St. Paul tells us that "faith comes from hearing." And we might with due reverence to the apostle add on our own: "And is nurtured by *thinking* plus grace." *If the bodies of most of us were fed as little as the mind, they would soon starve to death.* Many otherwise good and pious individuals

44

wonder why they make little or no progress in their spiritual life in spite of daily and frequent vocal prayer. The real reason is that *they are spiritually—mentally starved.* They say hundreds of prayers, verbally—but they never regularly meditate and as a result they are attempting to live in a spiritual vacuum—a metaphysical impossibility. And so there is of necessity hyperactivity, restlessness, talkativeness,—and an over-emphasis on activity and movement. One's soul and body in this contradictory state of affairs is constantly attempting *rest in motion.* Whence such ridiculous remarks as "I went out to a party to *relax!*"; or for a drive (and in this traffic!), or dancing, or on a trip! Someone has said that the rocking-chair is a good symbol of our mentally-starved modern age—it enables one to sit in one place and still be on the go!

In their spiritual life, not even having stopped long enough to *know God* in honest thought and meditation, they again here resort to constant activity—verbal prayers, services, novenas,—by the dozen. Thus they cover up to themselves their true spiritual status which is in reality only built upon activity and not on God's Will. They merely *work* for God; they do not *love* Him. They hence do not want to be on the "outs" with God, just as a clerk does not want to be on the "outs" with his boss. And so, with so little *love* and *thought* operative in their arid and empty spiritual life, God's law and prayer are regarded as mere correctives, as something negative and restraining to their wishes. They ask of prayer that they keep from serious sin—that they will be enabled to restrain themselves *moderately* in their selfishness, in their intemperances, in their sins of the flesh: to the empty minds and hearts, their lies are only "white lies"; their drunks just a "couple of beers"; their sins of the flesh just a "little petting." Such souls have no real desire to know what God *wants* —they only wish to tell Him what *they* want,—so much, no more. For one finds out what *God* wants *only in thought and meditation.*

The core of being just "dry" is step one; the core of being "sober"is step eleven: and *that* is *thinking* in our hearts. And there can be no doubt that the one who is too busy to take time out to meditate and to think is just plain *too busy!*

Meditation ordinarily is taken to mean "thinking along spiritual truths." The dictionary says: "to think on, to revolve in one's mind, to contemplate truth, to search for truth." This is the broader scope of the term we are discussing at the present. It is the same process but has as its object not only spiritual truth, but *all phases of our life.* In other words, we want to learn what it means to *think*—to have the habit of thoughtfulness, and to reap the great rewards of such a habit.

The thinking mechanism of man has four possible paths, depending on the motivating factor, to the thought or the object which it seeks:

1. *Anxiety*—Whenever our thoughts are motivated by or are activated by *fear* we have anxiety. This is not true thinking. This is not thoughtfulness. It is very damaging to true thought and also to the whole personality.

2. *Imagination*—Here again we have no true *thinking.* The reason is that the *object* of my thought process is *false,* something *non-existent,* something *made up.* It is a great help in story writing, in fiction—but it has no place in meditation, in *thinking.*

3. *Analysis*—We used the term here to mean "self-analysis" as is commonly used in certain psychiatric therapies. Its object is the *subconscious* and is very dangerous to many; and should never under any circumstances be indulged in except rarely and with competent psychiatric help and direction.

4. *Meditation—thinking*—Here we have true thinking. Here the mind takes *truth* and thinks about it over and over again. Here the mind seeks *truth, facts*—it is *thinking,* it is *thoughtfulness.* It is a prerequisite for the solution of problems; for happy living; for sober living.

Think!

Now let us apply this principle to all of the areas of living.

1. *In the home*—One of the primary causes of trouble in the home is *thoughtlessness.* How many times we have said, alas too late. *"if I had only stopped to think!"* As the poet says:

"The thoughtless sentence, or the fancied slight,
"Destroy long years of love and estrange us;
"And o'er our souls there falls a freezing blight...."

46

We just didn't take time out to *think.*

Let's just take about five minutes out now; and let's analyze all those troubles in the home these past months. . . .

If we had only stopped to *think!*

Remember the old adage: "Always count ten"? We probably thought it was rather silly like we did a lot of the "old-ladies' axioms"; but it was merely trying to establish in ourselves the habit *of taking time out to think* before we spoke or acted. But like our attitude toward a lot of the truths of life, we rebelled. . . .

And we became, particularly in the home, *thoughtless,* and we hurt, and we had troubles, and we have problems. . . .

Think!

2. *In our business*—All rash business ventures usually come from a lack of thought. We should remember that sound judgment is always the result of *sound and sufficient thought.* Good and successful business follows good and sound principles. But only the one who takes time out to *think through* these principles and to *think through* each application of them is the successful businessman.

3. *In our finances*—We may not all be businessmen, but everyone has to handle some finance. (Unless we have relegated that to the better-half!) And the individual who usually ends up burdened with debt or a victim to foolish investments, is usually the one who never *thinks* when he *spends;* never *thinks* when he *saves;* and never *thinks* when he *earns.* So he spends, and saves and earns as he *feels* like spending, or saving or earning. A financial neurotic! And every now and again he goes on a *spending binge.* He just doesn't stop to *think.* And lo and behold, a dozen payments to meet, and only ten or eleven units of money to meet them. Enter the sheriff or repossessor!

But the *thoughtful* person *knows* how much he can spend, how much he can make, how much he can save—and how much he *must* save. Why? Because he took time out to figure all this out ahead of time, and has the habit of taking time out to think logically every time a new financial transaction or demand presents itself. He *is* the repossessor!

4. *In our emotional life*—The prelude to and the foundation of "Easy Does It" and relaxation is *thinking*. Thoughtlessness causes difficulties—difficulties cause tension—tension causes nervousness. Such then can't figure *why* they can't relax.

Sleeplessness is often caused by thinking things out after we retire for the night. We can avoid this if we *think things through when they present themselves*. Then it is a simple matter to lay everything on the side-table as we lay ourselves down to sleep, and they will not bother us at the early hours of dawn either. They will remain on the side-table until we pick them up again. It is all a matter of well established *habits of thinking*.

Nor does the thinking person "bark back" at critics, or irritating circumstances. Why? He can't. He has to take time out *to think* what he is going to say and *if* he is going to say anything.

Think!

5. *In our mental life*—All actions, good and bad, have their ultimate origin in *thoughts*. This is the reason that good mental hygiene is of utmost importance for happiness in life; and especially for happy sobriety. What is it we say: "Well, he isn't drinking, but his thinking is stinking and it won't be long until he's drinking." It is an inevitable sequence. Stinking thinking; thinking drinking; drinking. And whence does it stem? Why do we have "stinking thinking"? Simply because we have *no* thinking. We don't take time out to *think*.

Think!

6. *In our spiritual life*—*meditation!* The core of the spiritual life is *meditation*. The core of serenity and happiness is *meditation*. And as we saw above, meditation is simply *thinking* in the presence of God.

And let's be honest. Why do we still fall into serious sin? Why do we still neglect God and prayer? Why are we not more charitable to our fellowman? Why are we still big sinners, instead of big saints? We *don't take time out to think*—we don't *meditate!*

Again, let us look back over the past months. How many things we would not have done *if we had taken time out to think*.

48

And if we had a firmly established habit of meditation, we can be fairly sure that at least *most* of the time we *will* take time out to think.

We might even become a saint? *Think* so?

Think!

7. *In our social life*—If we took the time to think things through we would probably be very satisfied with our social status. For thought would give us the facts. And the facts would tell us that we are probably in exactly that social stratum that's best for us.

Whence do all the so-called "social amenities" come? Most of them are only a more exact expression of *thoughtfulness*. In fact a thoughtful person doesn't need to learn many social amenities. *He's got* the universal social grace that will fit every occasion: *thoughtfulness*.

Think!

8. *In our physical life*—It is the *thoughtful* person who takes care of his body realizing its value under God. He knows that abuse, for any reason, not only is wrong, but from a purely natural point of view is very damaging. Remember the oft repeated radio commercial: "Take care of your eyes, it is the *only* pair you will ever have." So if we just take the time to *think* this through, we will take care of our eyes. And so on for all the body. It is the only body we will ever have too, bud!

Psychosomatic medicine has proven time and time again the tremendous effect that *thinking* has on the bodily processes. But it is not *thoughtful*, relaxed, meditative thinking that affects the body—except as a marvelous tonic—; it is the *confused* thinking; the *fearful* thinking; the *imaginative* thinking, all of which again is not really thinking.

Think!

9. *In our A.A. life*—How many splits, and difficulties and frictions come from mere thoughtlessness. How many have never taken the twelve steps because they have never *thought over* the twelve steps. How many members, so-called, know so little about

the A.A. Book, albeit they may have read it even more than one time, simply because they have read it thoughtlessly, being preoccupied or being in a hurry. How few have ever *thought* through the big A.A. Book.

How many speakers make remarks which they would not have made had they stopped to think of the possible innuendoes contained therein or of those who might be hurt thereby, or take exception to, the remarks! "Well," we excuse ourselves, "we just didn't think."

Think!

And once again: *Think!* Because the habit of thinking is the difference between

Thoughtfulness and *thoughtlessness*
Meditation and *vocal prayer*
Peace and *conflict*
Dryness and *sobriety*

Think it over!

THE SERENITY PRAYER

*"God grant us the serenity . . . the courage . . .
and the wisdom. . . ."*

One of the first truths that become apparent to the thinking man is the inherent weakness of man's will and the need of a Power outside of himself—the need of God's help. He also soon recognizes the universal fact that in *all* problems there can only be two courses open: either *to change* and to *solve* the problem by action; or *to accept* and thus dismiss it from our conscious thinking. To remain in the middle—indecisive—will only produce more confusion, more problems, unhappiness. So the most important factor in approaching *all* problems is to know *when to change, and when to accept*—the *wisdom* to know the difference.

So it was that somewhere along the way in A.A. came the so-called *serenity prayer:*

"God grant us the serenity to accept the things we cannot change; the courage to change the things we can; and the wisdom to know the difference."

Whence did it come? We do not know. The writer has seen at least a dozen "proofs" of authorship, some dating back to the Old Testament. So we feel the only logical conclusion to be drawn relative to who is the author of this prayer is that we do not know. *Probably most people in history* who sought surcease from problems through the Power of God have used some like formula, because it asks for *all* that is necessary to solve *all* problems: either *accept* or *change* and to know *when* to do *which*. So in all probability many spiritual writers have somewhere in their writings a prayer similar to this and many such too could easily have been mistaken as having authored this specific form of prayer know as *The Serenity Prayer.*[1] But then it is of very little importance who authored it. Suffice it to say that it is an ideally worded prayer for the alcoholic or for anyone who wants to

---

[1] Often referred to erroneously as "The A.A. prayer." A.A. has no prayer, no form, no dogma, no rules. It is a prayer *used* by many A.A.'s, but *not* an "A.A. *prayer*."

honestly appraise and to sincerely try to solve their problems. So let's take it bit by bit and see just how this little prayer so exactly asks God for all we need in solving problems. Its words are very meaningful.

God—We are approaching One Who not only has all power, but, being *Our Father, wants* to use His Power on our behalf. For this reason St. Paul tells us *"If you have faith you can move mountains";* and again we read in the Scriptures: *"All things are possible to him who believes";* and *"Why are you fearful, O you of little faith."* God is God! He is *all-powerful;* He is *all-loving.* So, it is to such a One to Whom we address our petition:

Grant—We, in using this specific term, ask for an outright *grant: a gift regardless of merit or worthiness.* It is like to a *grant of land* which is ours *for the asking provided* we are willing to accept all the specifications. We have heard the words of Christ: *"Whatever"* we ask God in His Name will be given *no matter who we may be,*—the world's biggest saint or the world's biggest sinner. Wherefore *all* hesitancy and *all* questions of *unworthiness* should vanish, and with perfectly free access and assurance, we should ask Him to *"grant."*

Us—When Christ gave us the Lord's Prayer, which we shall analyze later in this volume, He always used *We—our—us* throughout the prayer. Never does He want us to use *I—my —me.* And in this He wants us to keep always in mind the necessity of excluding no one from our prayers; and also the necessity of *including* others *whenever* we pray. When we pray thus we are *practicing* "in word and in deed" *love* for our fellowman. Remember also in the Lord's Prayer: *"Forgive us as we forgive."* And so also here He will *grant* as we *grant;* He will *give* as we *give;* He will *hear* prayer in so far as *we* include others in *all* our prayers. *God grant us.*

The serenity—An ideally chosen word, yet one seldom fully understood by the user. *Serenity* means more than happiness, more than peace of mind, more than peace of soul, more than peace of heart, more than mere contentment. But it is possible for *serenity* to change for better or for worse all peace of mind, all happiness, all peace of soul, all peace of heart, all contentment, although actually it is a condition *outside* of all of them.

Let us first examine some of the expressions just referred to above:

Happiness is a result of having what we want; a result of having achieved what we set out to achieve; having no basic or serious unfulfilled desires *as of now*.

Peace of mind[1] means *absence of conflict* in the *mind;* no undecided serious problems; no concern; no worry; no *mental problems unsolved*.

Peace of soul means *absence of all moral conflicts,*—a state of soul wherein there is no serious habit of sin; no unforgiven serious sin; no sense of guilt in the soul. In short—no *unsolved moral problems*.

Peace of heart means *absence of all emotional conflicts*. This is the state when there are no "heartaches"; no unfulfilled emotional drives; no serious *conflict* of emotional desires within us. It rules out the feelings of intolerance; of unrequited love; of dissatisfaction with others' attitudes towards us as a person, or as a friend or as a loved one.

Contentment insinuates a sort of satisfaction with what we have. In contradistinction to *happiness, contentment* means there is an acceptance of the things we have, whereas *happiness* means having mostly what we want. When we are contented we negatively accept things as they are, although we don't like them. In short it means being *self-contained*.

But *serenity* is much more than all of these. It is always over and above them. It is preserved in face of and in spite of them. *Serenity* is actually *"That peace which surpasseth all understanding."* It is *an undisturbed state of the higher faculties of man's soul regardless of all and any other circumstances to the contrary.* It is the ability to remain *undisturbed* in *spite of* emotional conflicts being present either frequently or infrequently; in *spite of* whether we are happy or not; in *spite of* whether

---

[1] The dictionary defines *peace* as a state wherein there is an *absence of conflict*.

57

we get what we want or not; in *spite of* whether we are satisfied with ourselves and our circumstances or not,—*A peace which is above all understanding! Serenity!*

Ever see a little duck on the water? How undisturbed does it seem to be! Yet if we but look beneath the surface of the water we would probably see much commotion and its feet going for all they're worth. Perhaps this will help us to get the idea of *serenity. Undisturbed* in spite of *anything!*

We have our own pet little theory of serenity. Here is our definition: *Serenity* is the state from which *all fears*[1] have been eliminated with the exception of that filial love and reverential fear we have for God as our Father. In fact we feel that it is precisely through the acquiring of that filial love and devotion to God and His Will that in turn brings to us, from that same God *serenity*—that *peace which surpasseth all understanding.*

And so down through the ages we find people of every age who are *undisturbed;* who have *serenity* in spite of pain, or of disability, or reversals in life, or problems, or feelings, or hard work. Let one example suffice:

Christ on the cross: mental suffering, emotional stress, physical pain unimaginable to us—and yet *perfect serenity.* All we would have to do to sense this marvelous state existing in Christ at that time is to read and to ponder the words He spoke as He hung there for three hours one of which is: "Father, forgive them, for they know not what they do."

Mental conflict? Listen: "My God, My God, why hast Thou forsaken Me?"

Emotional conflict? Just a glance at Mary His Mother will tell us volumes!

Moral conflict? The sins of a *world!*

Physical pain? "I thirst."

Reversals? "And Judas went out and hanged himself with a halter." Then there are you and I!

---

[1] We do not mean here the very normal fear that arises on occasion of real danger. This is purely natural. Christ Himself had it in Gethsemane. We mean *'fears'* which *stifle action.*

Undisturbed—serenity—peace which surpasseth all under-standing!

God grant us the *serenity!*

To accept—Which means simply to say, "Yes, Father" to God in the face of circumstances, or people, which we cannot change, and *to mean it*. This in turn will dismiss it from our consciousness most of the time except when externally brought back to our consciousness. It means the willingness to do *God's will;* for *all* things that are, are God's will. So *to accept* means in short to say to God: "Okay, *I'll fit in*," and not try to force circumstances or people.

The things—A *thing* is rather all-inclusive. It leaves nothing out. It covers all the circumstances, inside and out; and all the people; and *all that exists*. It makes *no exceptions* therefore.

We—Again it is *we* not *I*.

Cannot—This refers to all things which we cannot change:

1. *Of our own power;* or

2. *With God's help;* or

3. *Because God's will or law makes it impossible to change* with *good conscience*.

Change—This means either by *elimination* or by *making different* so it no longer concerns us.

So, *God grant us the serenity to accept the things we cannot change....*

The courage—Courage has nothing to do with the feeling of fear. It is *not* the absence of fear as so many people wrongly suppose. Whenever the time comes that we have no natural feeling of fear arise on the occasion of a real danger, we will no longer be human. But *courage* means *valiant and determined action or determination in spite of fear*.

An example: The soldier is at the front. There is a charge by the enemy. He is *afraid*. He *fears* he might be killed. *But in spite of this* he fights on. He is *courageous*.

Perhaps the English word *fortitude* would be more to the point for analysis. Fortitude comes from two Latin words:

"forte" and *"do-dare"* which means to *do* bravely, or *"with strength"* which indicates that the *courageous* person is the one who is willing to do or does act *in the face of fear*.

So we are asking God to give us the willingness to do and the strength to accomplish whatever there is for us to do no matter what fear might beset us.

Again, we are asking more for what has to do with our will rather than our feelings. *God grant us the willingness to act always no matter what the obstacles or the fears.*

To change—Here again we have the word which means *to make different relative to us: to change.*

The things—Once more *all* things with *no* exception.

We—We—us—our; Not *I—me—my.* "When you pray, pray *thus: Our* Father..."

Can change—All those things are referred to here, people or circumstances, within or without, which *are able to be changed* either by *our own strength* or *with another's help* or *with God's special grace.*

God grant us the serenity to accept the things we cannot change; the courage to change the things we can; ...and

The wisdom—We have here in the world wisdom a very unique phenomenon. Its Latin counterpart is *"sapientia";* but then the English slang-word *"sap"* also has its origin in *sapientia.* Why? Because the "know-it-alls"; the "smart" fellows; the arrogant guys and gals started it. A *wise* person is usually the one who goes *contrary* to so-called popular, materialistic, modern trends. So the stupid crowd refers to them as *"saps."* Moses, Solomon, the Three Wise Men, Christ—all men of wisdom who *knew what truth taught and followed it* were called *"saps"* by their contemporaries.

So *wisdom* is not *knowledge.* Wisdom is *the ability to discern the truth and to find the correct course to follow all things being considered.* It is the ability to cut through all the thongs of knowledge and to discern the false from the true. In short it is knowing what to do with knowledge.

There are only two sources of wisdom in life; the one is *age;* the other is a gift of God. Youth, of itself, *cannot* have wisdom. They can get it *from God* as a gift,—whence all the various laws relative to the election or the appointment of someone to a position of responsibility. We also find that as a matter of course, most human organizations select an older person for such a position. Even our own United States demands that a President be at least 35 years old.

So if we want wisdom, it may come to us with age; it is *certain to come* as an answer to sincere and continued humble prayer. *God grant us the wisdom. . . .*

To know—This means to *be able to draw a definite conclusion;* to be *conscious of;* to *have the facts.* Which indicates to us that we should not sit back and *wait* for a blind fate, but that we should always try to learn what is the best course to take; the best decision to make; the correct action. How? By our *footwork plus grace in answer to prayer!*

The difference—The *difference* is *whether to act to change something;* or to *relax and accept things as they are.*

Practically speaking, here is a *lot* of the *wisdom to know the difference.* It is the basic knowledge in human nature which many, many times will let us know whether to accept or to change:

The experience of the race teaches us that

1—*Most things outside ourselves* (people, circumstances etc.) *we can not change;*

2—*Most of the things inside ourselves* (attitudes, knowledge, thinking etc.) *we can change.*

Or in short we have the oft-quoted axiom which is frequently heard around the A.A. groups: "Most of the time *we can not change others;* but we *can change ourselves.*"

God grant us the serenity to accept the things we can not change; the courage to change the things we can; and the wisdom to know the difference. . . .

Now let us see how this prayer can influence all of the areas of our living.

1. *In our home life*—In practicing the principles of the Serenity Prayer and using it efficiently we would as a general rule first and always *work on ourselves* seeking constantly to *change* ourselves so that we will constantly *improve;* and by the same token we will at the same time fully realize that *most* of everything and everybody else in the home we shall *usually* have to *accept* as they are.

Many problems between husband and wife stem from the one *trying to change the other,* instead of trying to adjust to and accept the other *as she or he is.* There is a constant stream of people coming to their priest, to their minister, to their doctor, to their psychiatrist or just to their friends who have one big complaint relative to their home difficulties. This is: "The *other one* won't do this; and the *other one* won't do that"! "Why don't she stop nagging"! Why does he always 'clam up'; why doesn't he say something"! Whereas the wise man decides that she is a woman, I can't change her, so she will tend to nag; I'll ignore it and not take issue. The wise woman will figure that he is a man, so he will tend to 'clam up'; I can't change him so I'll ignore it. Behold *two* people with serenity!

Although basically the human nature of *all* people, men or women, is the same, still there are also some very basic traits of man and woman which are very different. Some are irritating. But you know something? We "ain't a going to" change her (or him). So it is very stupid and certainly far from wisdom to try. So we *accept.*

And we can't change the husband or the wife for a new one either. 'Cause remember that there statement we made above about the Serenity Prayer and changing things? We said, that there are things *impossible to be changed because God's will or law forbids it.* Remember? Huh?

And then there are our children. We are not going to control them very much especially after they have entered the "teens." We can only work on *us.* We can give a *good example.*

We can give them opportunity to learn. *But we cannot force—we cannot legislate morality.* Force, threats and the like in the home *produce rebellion.* Kindness (not doting and pampering), understanding, encouragement and *love* are the things the children *expect* from their parents—and rightfully so.

And what if they get into trouble in spite of kindness, understanding, encouragement and love? Then that is beyond our responsibility—that is God's business. We have only the footwork even in dealing with those in our charge. But, funny thing is, *most kids who get* kindness, understanding, encouragement and love from their parents *won't* get into serious trouble. And the exceptions who do—well, that is just another thing we must *accept. . . .*

2. *In our social life*— Working on ourselves and accepting others as they are, makes us so much better citizens. Accepting the social circumstances in which we must live will throw out the possibility of being 'social-climbers"; it will eliminate dissatisfaction. And all along the path of life we won't be too concerned about all "those screwballs" we meet along the way! We will avoid that terrible frustrating habit of constantly trying to make everybody see things *our* way.

3. *In our business affairs*—The successful business man *accepts* competition instead of trying to eliminate or change it. It is the "gangster" who kills competition; or the communist.

4. *In our financial affairs*—We prudently work towards improving our state financially always ready to *accept* when reversal comes along. And when we must, we will *change* our spending habits to fit in with our income. And *wisdom* will also tell us to seek *competent* advice when investing, teaching us that solid investment is not necessarily a big gamble.

5. *In our emotional life*—We are alcoholic. As such we learned from A.A. that for the rest of our lives there would be certain types of emotional upset which we could not tolerate too frequently or for long. These upsets were: resentments, self-pity, conflict and the like. We learned that permitting these circumstances to come into our living too frequently or permitting

them to stay too long would ultimately and *automatically* set off that crave for alcohol over which we would not have control. We *cannot tolerate* these circumstances; we *must* change our habits leading to their repetition . . . or else!

We also learned the recurring cycles of depression, nervousness, sleeplessness etc., could be handled without conflict *by acceptance.* We learned that the solution of these circumstances lies in their *acceptance.*

We also *change* our habits of *rest;* we get *more.*

We avoid undue irritations by changing or accepting whatever circumstance might be causing irritation.

And all those "funny feelings," those "fear-feelings," those recurring "let-downs" we also *accept.* And you wanta know something? They'll leave *much* quicker!

6. *In our mental living*—We were all born with a certain "mental potential." This we cannot change. But, if we wish, we can *add* to the potential by knowledge, reading, and study. And we *can* enlighten it *by prayer.* But all the "screwy" thoughts that come along to *everyone;* the "bad" thoughts; the confusing thoughts can only be *accepted* and ignored. Spiritual writers for centuries tell us that there is only one way to handle unwanted thoughts; *ignore them.* They will leave sooner; and there will be no conflict set up. And when there is conflict there may be trouble. It is something like when an unwanted person rings the door-bell. The surest way of getting rid of him is *don't answer* the door—for if we do he *might* get a foot inside. And if we *argue* with him, even more so is he likely to remain and eventually get in. But if we simply remain quiet; accept his ringing; and ignore it, it won't be long until he leaves. So with all unwanted thoughts. Nor should we ever get the foolish idea that *we* are the only one who has such thoughts. We *all* do on occasion. It is merely the indelible stamp of fallen human nature.

7. *In our physical life*—The first step on the road to serenity in this regard is to *accept* the body God gave us,—defects and all. How much money is expended each year in *trying* to change

certain aspects of our God-given bodies! We of course do not intend to convey to our readers that it is wrong to try to change such—for example, to save our fast falling hair! Far from it. But the wise course is to be *prepared to fully accept* the fact when we learn we *cannot* save the falling hair!

Many people also refuse to accept the doctor's verdict in regard to certain illnesses. And although we think it but prudent to consult another doctor when there is question of a serious condition diagnosed by one already, it is very foolish and far from wisdom to *continue* to seek another doctor in the face of repeated verdicts. What such people are seeking actually is not advice, but *someone to agree with them* and to tell them they don't have the illness. They are refusing to *accept* the unchangeable or the inevitable.

A like type of refusal to accept is found in those who won't wear glasses, or hearing aids, or who won't take medicine. The woods are full of such people. How much they are missing in life. Too vain to *accept*. God grant us the serenity to *accept*. . . .

8. *In our spiritual life*—The Wisdom that is God tells us that in our spiritual life there are two very definite paths we must follow:

a—We must do our best *to change* all the serious sins and their occasion; *but* be prepared to accept them if in spite of all our efforts we fall again. (In the latter case we had better take another look at that pride of ours. "God gives grace to the humble; but resisteth the proud"!)

b—We must *accept* the recurrent faults and failings which are a part and parcel of fallen human nature and which will be recurrent until the day we die. At the same time we begin again anew each day to *improve* day in and day out, realizing that God will make us perfect on the day we perfect our humility—the two are in direct ratio.

We must also in our spiritual life change our habits of self-dependence into habits of God-dependence. "Of myself I am nothing; but I can do *all* things in Him Who strengthens me." Remember? "What I can not do, *we* can"!

65

And in most instances we would rid ourselves of serious sin and come so much closer to God *if* we would only *change* the circumstances which *inevitably* cause us to sin. There are *none* such which *cannot* be *changed*—*if* we only want to; if we are but willing!

And then sooner or later and soon at the latest we will come face to face with another circumstance which we *can not change; death*. It doesn't take much wisdom to know this; but true wisdom will also tell us to accept *now;* to be ever *ready* to accept *all* the circumstances which God may choose to send along with our death. The wise man does this *now*. He often tells God: "Whatever You send, in whatever way You decide, whatever kind of death *You* may choose for me, I'll accept." Such are *always* ready to die.

Finally, in the spiritual life, we must, if we are wise, *accept providence*. Whatever happens, whatever comes along, it is *God's* will and for *that* there is only *acceptance, acceptance, acceptance*—and again *acceptance*.

9. *In our A.A. life*—The first problem in A.A. is our alcoholism. We learn that there is *only* one thing to do relative to it: *accept it*. We are alcoholics. But let us not forget that the others in the group also are *still* alcoholic.

The group? We may either accept or we may change. It is not wisdom for a guy or a gal to *force* themselves to stay in a group from whom they get constant irritation. The group is for the individual and for his welfare. The idea that the individual is for the group is a bit "pinkish" in its philosophy. So if the group does not *help* an individual, then it is better and wiser for the individual to go to another (or form another) group. First things first—and *we* do come first.

In conclusion: He or she who prays day in and day out for the serenity to *accept* and the *courage* to *change* will certainly have their prayers heard and answered. And into such a one's life there will come and remain *always* true *serenity*. And oftentimes there will be *peace of mind;* and *peace of heart;* and *peace of soul* intermingled through and through with *happiness and contentment* because God *will grant us the serenity to accept the things we can not change; the courage to change the things we can; and the wisdom to know the difference.*

"Peace I leave you; peace I give you, not as the world gives peace..." but *"a peace which surpasses all understanding."*

HONESTY

"God grant us the grace to see ourselves as You see us; so that knowing ourselves and Your will, we will be enabled to carry it out."

The foregoing prayer has been used by the author many years as a prelude to all of his talks at the Retreats he gives throughout the country. And we do it because we feel in it we are asking for the most necessary quality of all sobriety: *honesty.* Furthermore we feel most emphatically after all of our years experience with ourself and thousands upon thousands of others that it is the "gist" of the whole A.A. program. And we do not hesitate to assure *any alcoholic,* no matter how low he or she may have sunk, that *if they can become honest with themselves,* they *will attain and maintain sobriety.*

The word *honesty* comes from the Latin: *"honestas"* which means a *"oneness"*—a oneness with truth. We are therefore honest with ourselves when we, in our opinions, attitudes and actions are *at one with facts.* We are honest with others when in communication with others either by *word or action* we are *at one* with the facts in our words or actions. All else is dishonesty with all of its varying connotations: double-dealing; excuse making; lying; putting on a "front"; deception or what have you.

As alcoholics we ended up the most dishonest of people; we ended up pathologically dishonest—the world's most accomplished liars. This quality is so very evident in the reaction in most of us when somehow it was first insinuated that we just might be an alcoholic. Oh, the blast that met this unsuspecting innuendo: *"Me* alcoholic? Impossible!"

This basic dishonest quality in a way "forced" us to put on a false front for others. We didn't dare let them know the truth. As a result there were the endless cover-ups, the innumerable excuses.

Even in the spiritual life of those who had even an iota of one, dishonesty permeated all we did. Our prayers themselves

73

became mere words if not a downright "lie." Remember? "O God, get me off this drunk and I'll *never* take another drink!" The big liars! We were not actually asking for the grace of sobriety; we were asking that God eliminate the "hurt." And so when the "hurtin'" stopped it was off to the races again!

The end result of all this in the alcoholic was a mess of confusion, distrust, jitteriness and all those other "circumstances outside normalcy" which beset him all the days of his drinking career.

So it was that before anything else, there was need of *honesty* before the alcoholic could even "begin to be sober." And *happiness—serenity* just don't exist without a basic *honesty.* It is like the grease on the axle; the ball-bearing in the wheel; the lathe in fashioning the wheel and the axle and the bearing, *it makes us fit life* so the normal conflicts and frictions thereof will not cause heat or destruction or be an insuperable obstacle.

History is filled with the examples of the difference between honesty and dishonesty. In the instances of the former, we find many examples of the success that inevitably follows the path of honesty; and in the instances of the latter, we see many examples of the dismal failure that just as inevitably follows the by-paths of dishonesty.

Let us look at some of the men and women whose phenomenal success may be attributed to the fact of their basic honesty.

First there is Saint Paul. His name was at the time Saul. He was a citizen of Rome. He hated Christianity and Christians. *But he was honest in his hatred.*

In the scriptural story we find him on his way to Damascus to brink back more Christians to be tortured and killed. He hated them. He, the scriptures tell us, "was *breathing vengeance*" as he rode along in his quest for human prey. He was not doing this because someone told him to; he wasn't doing it because of what someone might say if he didn't; he was not doing it as a practical joker; nor was he doing it out of downright human "cussedness." He was doing it. . . . "*breathing vengeance,*"—because he *hated* them and was in his persecution of them getting vengeance. He *honestly* hated them; and to *his*

74

mentality unilluminated by grace, he was doing what he thought he should do.

And then something happened. There was a brilliant flash of light and a sudden bolt of lightning and Saul was knocked in an instant off his horse onto the ground. *Honesty and the grace of God had met head on.* Saul was a proud man; he was a stubborn man; but he was an *honest* man. And when the grace of God comes head-on with such a person the pride and the stubbornness all melt into nothingness under the warming heat of the rays of grace. Grace is enabled to freely enter the mind and the heart of such *because there is no obstacle of a "closed-mind,"* or *of a "conniving heart,"* or *of a "bad will."* Honesty *is* good will. And what was it Christ said? *"Peace* on earth to men of *good will"—to honest* men.

And so when Saul was knocked to the ground and heard a voice saying, "Saul, Saul, why persecutest thou Me?" he immediately replied, "Who is it that I persecute?"

How different would have been the reply of the dishonest person! Listen: "Persecute? Whadya mean, persecute? Who's persecuting anyone? You must have the wrong guy!" Angles—lies—excuses—self-justification—*dishonesty.*

And going back to Saul, we find that because grace was permitted to enter into his heart and will, God led him on to become the Apostle to the Gentiles—the great Saint Paul,—*because he was honest.* Not necessarily did God choose him because he was honest, but having chosen him, grace was effective to the point of sanctity *because he was so honest.* Honesty is not a pre-requisite for being chosen by God for special tasks, but having been chosen it is the difference between grace being accepted and used, and grace being rejected and abused as witness: Judas.

Then there was Mary Magdalen. To quote Matt Talbot, "She was quite a gal." When her path and the path of Christ crossed she was a prostitute—just a common, ordinary prostitute. *But* she was an *honest* prostitute! We hasten to explain: There are two types of prostitutes! The one type is the woman who follows this degrading path for the sake of the money in it. She sells her body for the sake of the money paid to her—for no other reason. Actually she "loathes" the one she consorts with and all about it. But then there is another type. They are the minority. They indulge in prostitution for "the sake of the prostitution itself." They consort with men because they *want to do exactly that.* They are not prostitutes because of family background and difficulties; they are not indulging in prostitution because someone forced them into it; they are not selling their bodies for the paltry cash they receive for it; they are doing what they are doing *simply because they want to*—they love it. Odd, you say? Yes, but *honest.*

And so Magdalen was such—Magdalen was *honest.* She was a prostitute because she loved it; because she wanted just that.

And then something happened. Once more in the province of grace, *grace and honesty met head on.* Mary and Christ met face to Face. And she fell at His Feet fully admitting her condition, and she shed tears upon His Feet and she wiped them with her hair. Then grace pierced her "open" heart—that heart that was so prone to love in lust. And under the warming rays of that grace that same love stretched itself out and reached the pinnacle of the supernatural and she *"fell in love"* with Christ. And never more did the supernaturalized love leave her. In fact so great was Christ's love for her in return that He chose *her* to appear to after His Resurrection even before He appeared to Peter and the rest of the Apostles. *Why?* He Himself tells us when He told her: *because she had loved much."* Wrongly, yes,—but honestly.

And speaking of Peter—he is another excellent example of *honesty.* Honesty brought him to the courtyard. Dishonesty caused him to sin. But his basic honesty was the factor that enabled him to repent—when it met grace.

Let's look at what happened. Peter was a grand person. No education, no finesse, not a man of elegant words or phrases. He was a simple fisherman. But he was *honest.* So when the soldiers took Christ away, his honesty made him follow. He really loved Christ. He was really concerned about Him. He followed Him therefore *because he wanted to be near Christ,* not because he wanted to see the "show." He knew a sort of a dim, confused way that Christ was to suffer and die. However, without the full light of grace he was not fully clear about it. He knew he couldn't stop it as had been demonstrated when Christ healed the soldier's ear and told Peter to put his sword into the scabbard. But he went along because he honestly wanted to stay near Him to the end.

He even followed Christ into the courtyard. It was here a maid servant came along and accused him of being a Galilean and an accomplice of Christ. Then fear took over. And Peter, unaided by grace, and dogged by fear of the consequences, became for a moment dishonest. He lied. He swore to a lie. And then the cock crew. Just then, too, Christ passed and glanced at Peter. Again *grace and basic honesty met head on.* And Peter went out into the night and "wept loving tears." Peter, of the moment, was transformed by the grace of God into one of the most courageous of men when grace fully took over on the first Pentecost. Peter became the fearless head of the Apostles— *because he was honest.*

Augustine? Even in the depths of his sinning, Augustine showed a flash of his basic honesty when he prayed: "O God, give me the grace of purity—but not yet!" And so it was that, as we saw in our discussion of *decisions,* when the grace of God and Augustine met head on in his garden on that fateful afternoon— Augustine immediately asked "What will you have me to do," without an excuse, without questioning why and wherefore, without self-justification. And Augustine was led on to take his place among the elite of God as one of the greatest theologians of all times—because he was *honest.*

Now let us look at the other side of the picture. Let us take a few examples of history's well-known characters and see how *dishonesty* proved to be the reason for their failure.

First there is Judas. Judas was chosen to be one of the Apostles. His failure and suicide as a result of his *dishonesty* are sure proofs that God does not always choose anyone because of what they are. He chooses those He chooses simply because He wants them irrespective of their natural qualifications or lack of them.

77

The dishonesty of Judas was apparent long before his final act of despair. It shows itself in the episode with Magdalen. It was when she had broken the vial of precious ointment to anoint the Feet of Jesus. That irritated Judas. It irritated him to such an extent that he remonstrated by saying: "We could have sold the ointment and given the money to the poor." The big liar! He wasn't interested in the poor—*he was treasurer of the apostles!* So he was "miffed" because he was thinking of the "shekels' he might have gotten his hands on had she given him the ointment to sell.

And as with all such tendencies, Judas' dishonesty grew with passing time. It reached its pinnacle when he betrayed Christ with a kiss. He kissed his Friend—because he loved Him? An *honest* expression of friendship? No—but one of the blackest acts of dishonesty of all history. He kissed Him because it was the act that would point Christ out to His enemies. *And then and there grace and the depth of dishonesty met head on*... and with the heart sealed, and with the will bad, and with his soul shut tight against grace.... "He went out and hanged himself with a halter"! He committed suicide—because he was basically dishonest.

Then there's the old rascal Herod. In all of his pomp and power and glory he sent for Christ. Why? Because he wanted to help Him? No—but *only because he wanted a "show"*; he, the great Herod, must be in the act. He was dishonest.

Likewise Pilate. Did Pilate give Christ over to the Jews because he knew Christ was innocent? No—it was a good excuse to shun the responsibility of judging. Pilate *knew* Christ was innocent. So there was only one thing he could *honestly* do, and that was to acquit Him. But he was afraid of Caesar. What would Caesar say? So Pilate invoked an almost laughable law of the Jews to "get out from under it." He "washed his hands." And that—in his dishonest mentality—absolved him from blame!

Today? Christ's teachings have spread over the whole world. And Herod and Pilate? History only remembers them as those "who condemned Christ." Both of them had the great privilege of having Christ come to them. But their hearts and

78

minds and souls were shut tight against grace—because Pilate and Herod were *dishonest.*

Sodom and Gomorrha were two cities destroyed by God. Because they had sinned so terribly? We feel sure that many other cities down through history sinned as badly in so far as *what* they did. But Sodom and Gomorrha *justified their sins.* What was sin under the law of God they no longer considered sin. *Mass dishonesty!* And when grace spoke through God's prophets to these two towns,—it came head on with *dishonesty.* It only *hardened* their hearts. So God destroyed them. They were *dishonest.*

At the crucifixion of Christ, up on the summit of Calvary we can see dramatic examples of *honesty* and *dishonesty* side by side.

With Christ were also crucified two thieves. In those days criminals were frequently punished by crucifixion. Most of these men had been guilty not only of robbery and the like, but of more heinous crimes: murder, rape, etc. It was two such robbers that hung on crosses next to Christ—one on the right and one on the left.

The story tells us that the one on the left began to curse and blaspheme crying out to Christ to save Himself. But he wasn't too interested in Christ's safety. He was anxious to save his own hide. Seeing no move to do so on the part of Christ, he continued to curse and to blaspheme—a good indication of his disinterest in Him and a very good indication of his *dishonesty.*

But the thief on the right then spoke out. He condemned the other robber for his words and actions saying, "This man is innocent. We *deserve what we are getting.*" The exact truth! *Honesty.* And so again *grace and honesty meet head on.* And piercing the depth of the dying man's soul, he is moved to softly request of Christ: "Lord, remember me when you come into Your Kingdom." He asked for nothing more than a mere remembrance. He knew the heinousness of his own crimes. He felt unworthy of asking for more. But lo and behold he hears the most wonderful words ever spoken to a mere human being: "This day thou shalt be with Me in paradise." He became the first fruit of the Redemption—*because he was honest.*

The other guy? "He died blaspheming,"—because *he was dishonest.*

And all down through the ages, all of God's greats became greats *because they were honest.* On the other hand *many—many more than we ever realize*—although they might have been chosen for places of greatness in God's scheme of things *failed because they were dishonest.*

Look around the A.A. groups. Who are the ones who are sober and who have serenity? It is the ones who are *honest.* They are not necessarily the ones who *know* the twelve steps the best; they are not necessarily the "saints"; they may even be yet great sinners. But they are *honest. Honesty is the best policy!*

Then take a good look at all of the "slippees." What's wrong? They either *will not* be or *can not* be *honest.* Even in the A.A. Book we read in Chapter V that the ones who have the least chance of success in seeking sobriety are the ones who are "incapable of grasping a program of rigorous *honesty*"!

Again: we read in the A.A. Book *"willingness, honesty and open-mindedness* are essentials for recovery.... They are *indispensable."*

In the early days of A.A. there were no twelve steps; there was no big book: there was nothing but three axioms:

1. *Get honest with yourself (honesty)*
2. *Clean house (honesty)*
3. *Help others (honesty)*

And again the writer has never hesitated to make the statement without fear of valid contradiction: "If a person is *honest,* and *honestly tries,* he *will* stay sober."

Now let us see how this principle of *honesty* affects all of the areas of our daily living. Let us see how the practice of *honesty* day in and day out will not only bring happiness into our lives, but enable us to adjust successfully and surely in all of our living.

1. *In our home life—Honesty* would give all the members of the family the *facts.* And instead of every member of the family trying to bring out "what otta be," but "what can't be," all would work hand in hand to accomplish "what *can* be."

Quarrels, which are part and parcel of *every* home, would come and go without continuing rancor and resentments, because *honesty* would tell us that quarrels are solved the most quickly by *not making an issue*. So the husband and the wife have a spat. It's over. What causes the real trouble? When husband or wife keeps bringing it up—or "throwing it up." *Honesty* tells us that we are *all* human, and therefore liable to do mean little things *but* the truth is that such means little things *are not an indication of lack of love!*

Honesty would tell us to accept all the other members of the family *as they are;* and we would not spend the almost endless hours trying to *change* the others. Likewise it would tell us to *work on us,* because the truth of the matter of this human nature business is that we usually can't change others but we *can* change us. And it would also point out along these same lines *that the more we change us—amazingly, the more others begin to change in direct ratio.*

Honesty would tell us that *love* in the home means *giving* and not *demanding,*—love is sacrifice. It is the common experience of all clergymen, doctors, psychiatrists, judges and all who engage in counselling, that from all of the ones who come before them with family troubles, they always hear: *"he* won't do this; or *she* won't do that!" Never do we hear: "I haven't or don't do this or I haven't or won't do that." A husband constantly complains of his wife's "nagging"; a wife constantly complains of her husband's "clamming up." *Honest* appraisal of human nature would tell us that it is the nature of man to "clam up"; and that it is the nature of woman to "nag"—and there isn't much the other party can do about it but *accept it!*

How many, many troubles of the past every member of A.A. (honest member!) has finally come to realize were *their own fault* whereas he or she had for years been blaming others. And how much finer does not the husband of the wife appear to be *under the clear glass of honesty.*

Incompatibility! One of the commonest reasons alleged for divorce *usually* is a result of *dishonesty*—in courtship! Listen to the lies and cover-ups of two people who are courting and planning to marry:

"Why, I wouldn't want *him* to know it for anything!"

"Sure I have faults, lots of them, but I wouldn't want *her* to find them out!"

"Oh, I just *love* the things that you love; I just *love* books, and sports!" (She has actually never opened a book since grade school; has never before witnessed sports!)

"I am simply crazy about dancing, and parties, and people!" (He actually loathes dancing and parties and people!)

And then they get married! Emotion gradually disappears; friction develops; incompatibility!

"If I had known before I married you the kind of a person you are, I'd never have married you!"

And *why* didn't they know about each other? *Dishonesty!*

Love is blind or so they say; but *passion is deceived and* deceiving. *Honesty is the best policy.*

Then there are the children. One big reason so many children acquire *wrong* attitudes towards life is because of the inherent dishonesty of their parents. Pampering, or what Dr. Strecker of Pennsylvania University calls "Momism" is a form of dishonesty. In pampering, the parent attempts to lead the child to expect from life something that isn't there. They fail to give children an *honest* approach to life; to treat them and to teach them *what life inevitably will* teach them. The Scriptures themselves tell us: "Spare the rod and spoil the child." You know why? Because *life so often uses a rod* whether we like it or not. Honesty therefore will get the child used to what life will ultimately give. *Honesty is the best policy.*

2. *In our social life*—Honesty in our social life will first of all tell us that as members of society we have definite obligations *to* society. Therefore we will not tend so often to "side-step" these obligations; community interest, the common good, the need of our neighbor.

Honesty will also point out very clearly *who* our neighbor is. It will tell us that *all* people fall into this class because *all* people are children of God even as you and I. So, *honesty* will prevent us from discriminating against certain of the world's people because of their nationality, or because of their beliefs; or because of their color; or because of their social standing; or because of their poverty; or because of their wrongs done to us. Remember? "But I say unto you, *love* them who hate you: ... forgive your enemies." And then: "This is the greatest of the commandments ... that you love one another."

(Incidentally, it doesn't say *like* them. So if we cannot bring ourselves to *like* them; we can at least *love* them!)

Finally, *honesty* in our social relationships would keep us from becoming "social-climbers." We would never let on that we are someone we are not. Or to put it very facetiously: We wouldn't be the kind of a guy or gal who uses "nye-ther" when in reality we ain't had no education!

3. *In our business affairs*—It is the *honest* businessman who ultimately is the successful one. And this is particularly true in so far that a business man is *honest with himself*. There is no surer road to bankruptcy than through the short-cut of self-deception. It is always the sad plight of the man in business who is deceiving himself as to the true condition of his business.

Honesty is the best policy.

4. *In our financial affairs*—Not all of us are so situated in life as to be in business. But all of us do have some finance to take care of. And the one who gets into hot water is the one who is *dishonest* in appraising his financial status. Witness the one who is always living *above* his income; the one who has *more* payments to meet each month than he can afford; who buys things he will never need or use. Nor can we omit from this category the poor fellow or gal who always buys something *just because it is a bargain*. What are they going to do with what they bought? They don't know, but it *was* a bargain!

Honesty is the best policy.

5. *In our emotional life*—"And so we lied to get out of the lie we told to get out of the lie we told to get out of the lie we told ...." And this constant evasion of the truth and responsibili-

ty and reality causes nervous tension, and emotional fears, and an "acceleration of mind" endeavoring to cover up the dishonesties of yesterday. The person *who has nothing to cover up either from God or man is the one who is free from tension*—from emotional upsets and "nerves." *Fear* is at the basis of most emotional problems; but the one who is *honest* has *nothing* to fear!

Even the one who goes at "break-neck" speed "trying to please everyone" is dishonest. Truth tells us and the experience of the race proves it, that *no one can please everyone!* So honesty would tell us not to try. Honesty would suggest that we do the best we can with what we have and if in the process someone or other is not pleased or even "hurt," that is none of our worry.

It is amazing how many people keep themselves in an almost constant emotional "dither" just trying to please everyone. And you know something? Such people usually end up *displeasing* more people than if they hadn't tried nearly so hard.

Honesty is the best policy.

6. *In our mental life*—We used the term "acceleration of mind." It is quite a common phenomenon with most alcoholics and most nervous people. The "lay-awakers" are quite conscious of this process. You know whence it comes? It usually comes from "conniving" and "angle-shooting" in a frantic endeavor to get around the facts; in a foolish attempt to out-maneuver reality; in a constant effort to "out-think" the other fellow. It is part and parcel of the criminal mind and oftentimes is responsible for their indulging in dope-addiction. Actually it is simply a dishonest attempt to outsmart truth. Prudent planning knows nothing of this process; because prudent planning seeks *truth* and decides and acts and lives according to this truth it learns. But the "angle-shooter"; the "conniver"; the *dishonest* person *having had truth forced upon him,* constantly indulges in trying to side-step truth and reality and responsibility.

The *honest* person *relaxes* in meditation and peace of mind; the *dishonest* person *writhes* in mental conflicts and fears and "acceleration of mind."

Honesty is the best policy.

7. *In our physical life*—Much "sudden" sickness comes from the refusal to recognize or accept the symptoms—from *dishonesty*. The heart failures, the sudden break-downs, the pre-mature aging of many could have been avoided had such been *honest* with their doctors and themselves and done something about the symptoms which they at least "suspected" but did not admit either to their doctors or themselves.

There are three basic attitudes of people who go to the doctor for a check-up—two dishonest, one honest.

First there is the one who goes with a determination to convince the doctor that he is perfectly o.k. In this attempt he will use all kinds of evasions and false answers to get the doctor to tell him he is one hundred percent healthy. Many times he succeeds in deceiving the doctor; and himself. But he *can't deceive his* body. So sooner or later there comes the break-down or the heart attack or the sudden onslaught of old age before its time.

Then there is the fellow or gal who in their self-pitying hypochondria go to the doctor determined to convince him that they are not well. At least subconsciously they are endeavoring to get a "medically-attested-to" excuse for avoiding many of life's responsibilities. If they fail to convince the doctor, they will try to find an acquaintance who will agree that they are "ill." If they fail in this they will at least succeed in convincing themselves. They are dishonest. They are unhappy. They are *really ill,* but not with the illness they are "pampering." We call them "hypochondriacs." They "subsidize" many pharmaceutical houses!

And then we have the honest person who approaches his physician for a check-up. What is he looking for? He wants to know the *truth*. For only thus can he adjust to it in his living habits. Such a man *may* find himself with an ill body; but he will have a relaxed one—and he will have peace of mind and happiness in spite of his illness, for he *knows* and lives by the facts. *He is honest.*

Growing old gracefully is only another way of saying growing old *honestly*.

Honesty is the best policy.

8. *In our spiritual life*—There is no area of living in which dishonesty plays so much havoc, and in which *honesty* is such a needed factor for success, as in our spiritual life. In fact one of the primary reasons of failure in the spiritual life and of failure to progress spiritually lies in the *dishonest appraisal of self*. Most people either consider themselves worse or better than they really are. That's dishonesty. That's an obstacle to the grace of God.

Let's analyze this a bit closer.

Here is the fellow or gal who either has, in his deceiving self-pity, *more* faults than he really has; or still has faults when he thinks in the same self-pity that "after how hard I worked for so long" he should have freed himself of them. He gets nowhere. Why? He forgets or doesn't want to accept the fact that in the spiritual life the job of eliminating faults is ours *only in so far as the foot-work* is concerned. The success of eliminating them is entirely in the hands of God. When? When *He* chooses! And that, my friend, is usually on the day the sinner becomes *humble*—and that means *honest*. For humility is truth. And truth and honesty and humility have no truck with self-deprecation and self-pity.

Again, the one who deprecates himself often denies the having of certain talents the good Lord has endowed him with to *use* for his fellowman.. Admitting we have talent is not pride; it is the refusal to give the credit to Whom the credit is due that is pride. We all have talents—some very many talents—but they are *gifts* given not for *our* honor and glory but for the benefit of all those we come into contact with in life. To deny having these talents is *dishonest;* to deny they are gifts of God is *dishonest;* but to admit and to accept them and to use them and to give thanks to God for them is *honesty*. And you know what? It is often productive of sanctity! To refuse to use our talents on the pretext that it will make us proud is a beautiful excuse—for remaining a sinner!

We are what we are—full of faults and endowed with certain talents. That is *honesty*—that is humility. Who will deliver us

86

from the faults? Good will plus grace. What will enable us to use our talents successfully? Good will plus grace.

And where in the spiritual life do we learn *honesty?* Where will we find good will? Where will we obtain grace?

In *honest* prayer and meditation. Let's take a quick glance at the last half of the twelfth step: "... praying only for knowledge of His Will and the power to carry that out."

Honesty is the best policy.

9. *In our A.A. life*—Sobriety is the result of *honesty;* most slips come from *dishonesty.*

The biggest obstacle for most of us when we were first approached by A.A. was making that admission that we are alcoholic ... that our lives are unmanageable. *But* that is *honesty.*

In the early days of A.A. there were no twelve steps; there was no "big book"; there was no worked-out formula. The early members had only the three things to go on which we mentioned above. But all of these three axioms were a re-emphasis of the necessity of *honesty.*

The oft-used excuse given by those alcoholics refusing to attend A.A. is: "I'm not that bad; A.A. is just a bunch of drunks." *Dishonesty!* We find the same excuse given by many who attend no church: "It's just a bunch of hypocrites!" We tell both kinds: "You might as well go—there's always room for one more!"

Honesty is the best policy.

In concluding our discussion on honesty, we would like to throw out for thoughtful consideration the following:

The one who sins and knows and admits that he sins, can, and probably will merit grace—serenity—and salvation; but the one who sins and admits not that he sins hasn't got a chance— for he ain't got nothing to be saved from!

So there you have it.

Honesty is the best policy.

THE INVENTORY

"Made a searching and fearless moral inventory . . .
continued to take . . . inventory."

We saw in the preceding chapter that the "light to learn honesty" and the grace to become honest come as a result of the *honest* practicing of the eleventh step wherein it is suggested: *"We sought through prayer and meditation to improve our conscious contact with God as we understood Him praying only for His will for us and the power to carry that out."* But the footwork on our part necessary to achieve and maintain honesty is suggested in the fourth and the tenth step:

"We made a searching and fearless moral inventory of ourselves" (4); and *"We continued to take personal inventory and when wrong promptly admitted it."* (10)

The reason that the inventory is brought in twice in the twelve steps is because in the fourth step we work towards *achieving* attitudes on *honesty;* in the tenth step we work at *keeping* these attitudes.

In passing, we might remark that it has always been our opinion that the twelve steps are divided into three definite parts. Step one is the door; the entrance. Step two to nine inclusive is the readying of the alcoholic for living the program, for living adjusted to life. The tenth, eleventh and twelfth steps are the *living the program—day in and day out.* Steps one to nine we take only once, albeit we remind ourselves of the first one each day. But the tenth, eleventh and twelfth steps *are directives for sane, serene and saintly living presuming* we have already made the *adjustments* suggested in one to nine.

So with the inventory. In step four we take a general inventory—to clear the past and to recognize the present and to prepare for the future. Then we are finished with it, and day in and day out we take again and again the tenth step—the repeated inventory *lest we slip back into the mess we found in step four.*

An *inventory* and the need of one is nothing new. We feel quite sure that every successful person down through the ages took and continued to take an inventory. In fact *nothing* in life will continue to function on and on smoothly without an inventory. Let's look at some:

Business—The business man who takes no inventory soon goes bankrupt. So a successful business man takes a regular inventory and thus, and thus alone knows his business, his stock condition, his sales potentials, etc.

War—In war, in the armed forces, there is a constant check, a constant inventory as to material available, material in use, damaged material, men available, etc., etc. Even an inventory is attempted of the enemy potentials. Anything short of this would mean certain defeat.

Land—Few people who are prudent buy or sell land today without knowing exactly what *type* land it is. And this is learned through geological survey—an *inventory*. It is really the fool who sells all rights to land without knowing what the land potential is, the sub-soil, the subterranean soil, etc. And only a fool would buy without such knowledge.

In the quake areas of the world, a constant, repeated inventory of the sub-strata is taken—for security.

Machinery—The maintenance man would be useless if no inventory was necessary. But he is ever vigilant (if he is a good one) to check the wear, the gears, the oil, etc., etc.

Automobiles—To become practical and close to home we see that the person who gets the most trouble-free wear out of his automobile is the one who *checks* it regularly, who has a regular tune-up, who doesn't close his ears to noise and knocks. He "promptly" fixes them!

And in buying or selling the used car—how necessary is an inventory!

The home—It is the one who does not neglect to check at regular intervals *all* parts of his home that avoids the sudden onrush of "termites"; or the "sudden" fire from unnoticed rags, or papers, or oil which were responsible for the fire.

94

Finance—The importance of the need of an inventory in all things is remarkably brought into focus by the seemingly endless and detailed reports demanded regularly by both the banks and the bank-examiners. Might we not call the latter: *inventorians?*

And on and on—in everything without exception. Success— smooth operation—growth, all *demand* an *inventory* and one *regularly taken.*

How much more important for the human personality is such a regular inventory. That is *if* we hope to maintain *serenity —security—sobriety* and some day achieve *sanctity.*

Yet the alcoholic is the one most apt to neglect the taking of a regular inventory. We sometimes think this is a "hang-over" from the wonderful *"forgettery"* developed during the drinking days. In those days we didn't *dare* take an honest inventory. Something happened, and always our first reaction was "forget it!" Which we usually did—until it forced its presence on us again very dramatically during those endless hours of remorse after another binge.

The word "inventory" comes from the Latin "invenire" which means "to find." So when an inventory is taken it should be undertaken with the *intention* of *finding* all the facts about *us.* In the general inventory of the fourth step[1] we *look* for—we want to *find*—*all the facts about our past,* so that we can do something about them in the present. This is the general inventory. It is taken once. Let us concentrate more on the continued inventory of the tenth step. It is the one we should take again, and **again**, and again—and again.[2]

---

[1] Cf. *Sobriety and Beyond* or *The Golden Book of the Spiritual Side* in our interpretation of the Twelve Steps. There we have outlined a method of taking the general inventory in the fourth step.

[2] An *inventory* is not the same as *analysis.* Analysis attempts to uncover things in the "sub-conscious" mind of which the patient was perhaps not even conscious when it happened. The theory is that such happenings even though unconscious at the time, could still be influencing our thinking, feelings, etc., and will continue to do so until *brought to the conscious* understanding of the patient. On the other hand the *inventory* aims at bringing back to mind the *conscious* things we did in the past in order to now do something about them. The objective of *analysis* is the *sub-conscious;* the objective of an *inventory* is the *conscious*—i.e., things we are and were quite aware of doing or having done. An inventory is a wonderful catharsis for the mind and emotions; analysis is something that might cause much

We are not going to tell you *how* to take your inventory. We are not even going to tell you *how often* you should take your inventory. We are merely going to repeat what is *suggested* in the tenth step of the A.A. program; and then throw out for your perusal or rejection a couple of methods which experience has proven to be successful. And we will make two more little "suggestions":

1. Always be sure it is *our* inventory.

2. Always ask *God* for a little "hep," as they say in Texas, *before* taking the inventory.

The object of the inventory is to ascertain regularly just the exact status of affairs within our human personality. And for the alcoholic there is much more to look for and to check on than "wrong-doings" or sinful actions. We have several other sources of trouble than the purely moral. These are: *mental attitudes* and *emotional upsets and/or tensions* and *over-tiredness* Omitting or neglecting to keep these circumstances eradicated from our living might not cause us to lose our souls; but they might *cause us to lose our sobriety!* After all A.A. is not existing to save souls; it's job is only to *"wring them out"!* So in the inventory we look for wrongs and sins for the purpose of growing in the spiritual life and happiness; but we also look for these other danger signs *to sobriety.*

We might mention something too that is many times overlooked or misunderstood. The A.A. inventory is *not* the same as an *examination of conscience.* An examination of conscience looks for *sin;* the A.A. *inventory looks for anything that might be causing friction or conflict in the total personality.* This is the reason behind the much-wondered-at phenomenon of a fellow or a gal continuing to stay sober in spite of the fact of willful and repeated actions against the law of God. And this is the way of it: *if* a person can *kill their conscience* they can stay sober simply

---

mental damage unless in the hands of a prudent and expert psychiatrist. Most times it is not necessary for the alcoholic; and useless. Even the A.A. book says there should be a "minimum of analysis." The average alcoholic is usually *too* prone to be analytical. For this reason so many are apt to end in self-pity, or self-condemnation; or refuse to forgive self. We should never forget *we* are the first ones who must forgive ourselves.

by avoiding emotional and mental conflict, provided they have decided once and for all they can not drink. It is *not* the *actions of sin* that cause a slip; *it is the conflict of the conscience.* Likewise it is not the act of sex in the one who "plays around with another" which causes a slip; *it is the frustrations, fears* and *emotional tension set up by it* which causes the slip.

The method of taking an inventory? As we mentioned above, we are not going to tell you how you should take your inventory, but we will mention two methods which seem to have worked through the years.

First—The traditional method. This is a simple method but can become very monotonous and might prove to be burdensome to some and cause them to abandon their inventory altogether. It is the one that has been advised through the centuries, and is based upon the fact that whenever a human being improves in one factor of the soul, the rest will come along with that improvement. So spiritual writers have always advised: "Pick out your *biggest* fault; work on that and all the rest will come along."

There can be no question as to the validity and the effectiveness of such a method of taking our inventory. But remembering that the above advice was directed at sinners for the elimination of sins and faults, we would hesitate to recommend it to the alcoholic *without something added.* We would advise the same as the good spiritual writers do—for *spiritual* progress. But we would also advise for the alcoholic; "Also pick out your *biggest danger point to sobriety*—body, mind or emotions; and work on that and all the rest of this part of the human person will also come along." You see, the reason that the traditional advice was given is because the *soul is one.* It cannot be divided. So if one part improves; the whole soul will go along with it. *But* the *body* and the *soul can* be divided. Witness: One can have a *very healthy body;* and at the *same time* a *very sick* and *sinful* soul. *And* a person could become an heroic saint, and at the same time have a very sickly body, frequent emotional upsets, etc. *All these are partly from the body.* whereas *sin is always in the will—in the soul;* and likewise *virtue is always in the will—in the*

97

soul. But *sobriety* is in *both.* And alcoholism is a sickness of all three: body, mind and soul. Therefore the alcoholic, to avoid relapse, must take care of *all three.* *Let us never confuse sobriety with sanctity!* Even though we do know that we cannot have sanctity without sobriety; we *can* have sobriety—at least freedom from drinking—without sanctity. *Many do just that.*

So in taking our inventory along the traditional method let us always remember to *pin-point the biggest fault* in order to grow spiritually; but because we are alcoholics, let us also at the same time *pin-point our biggest danger-point* to a slip in order to grow in sobriety.

Secondly—The poker-chip method. This is a novel way of taking a regular inventory, but practical and effective. More than anything else it injects a little "interest" in this ordinarily drab inventory business.

It goes like this: Take one or more boxes of poker chips. Then take one at a time and write or print on it on one side one of your faults *and* as a reminder your biggest "slip-danger-point." As to the latter a few suggestions: depression, friction, over-tiredness, emotional tension, frustration, resentments, self-pity etc., etc.

Then your poker chip will look something like this. On one side it will have:

Anger

Resentment

Both the same thing? Well, hardly. Anger *leads* to resentment; but so will disappointment; frustration, etc. *Resentment,* as we shall see later in this volume in the chapter on "Resentments," involves the emotions, the mental attitudes, even the body on occasion.

Now we turn the poker chip over and print on the other side the *opposite* to the fault and a positive something that will tend to keep down the "emotional-danger-slip-point." So the other side of the poker chip number one will read something like this:

Kindness

An Act of Love

We will come back to this poker chip, but first let us finish the rest of them. And on each chip we print on one side one of our faults and one of our "danger-slip-points." On the other side we print the opposite of the fault and an appropriate action which will tend to keep this "danger-slip-point" under "wraps."

Then we place all the poker-chips in a box on our side table or somewhere handy, and *each day* we *blindly* pick one from the box. Having done this we then *make it a point to practice the suggested virtue and action at least once that day.*

For example, let us come back to chip number one. On one side we have *Anger—Resentment;* on the other side *Kindness— An Act of Love.* So if this is the chip we happen to pull out of the box today it means we will go out of our way to *practice an act of kindness.* We do not practice virtue nor grow spiritually by *avoiding sin;* but *by doing good, i.e.,* doing the *opposite virtue.* So we do not overcome a tendency to be angered by making up our minds *not* to get angry; we don't start out the day by keeping on saying over and over "I'm *not* going to get angry." (If we do that, we will!) So we *do* an *action of kindness to* someone.

The same holds true of our "danger-slip-point." On the chip we are discussing, it is *resentment.* So to take out a little insurance we will go out of our way to *do something for* someone to whom we are not obligated to do so. Or even better to do something for someone we don't particularly like.

But you say, "Isn't this the same as an action of kindness?" Well, yes—and no. An action of kindness means something done in a positive *kindly* manner. An action of love is to do something for someone, regardless of the manner. An action of love has to do with motive; an action of kindness has to do with its manner. For after all *anger* is something affecting the *manner* of our actions. "He spoke *angrily.*" Whereas on the other hand *resentment* is *deep* within; it deals with the inner emotions and the heart. *Love* is its only panacea.

Frankly we used these two examples to set your thinking process to working—and hard. You will be the one who benefits.

The poker chips? We do the same with whatever one we happen to select for that day. Well, it works—and it's interesting

99

—and when you're trying to differentiate and match all these virtues and faults and emotional upsets and what have you— you will have to do a powerful lot of thinking and meditating. And by the time you have all of your poker chips made up, you should have already progressed a long way along both the path of virtue and sobriety! And the *method* isn't so important—it's the doing it.

Now let us apply the principle of the *inventory* in various phases of our living.

1. *In our home life*—Perhaps the first practice which the principle of the inventory will point out to us in the home is that we should take *our own inventory* and not the rest of the family's.

But relating to all of the *material* sides of the home we will be enabled by an inventory to *know* our home *potential*. This will tend to veer us clear of over-burdening either the home with debts, etc., or of over-burdening the rest of the members of the family with chores and what have you which might be unnecessary and producers of friction. And as mentioned above we will, if we own our own home, take better care of that material part called a house but which to us will always be *our home*.

2. *In our social life*—Once more it might be wise if the principle of the inventory would continue to call to our minds the fact that it should always be *our* inventory and not the other fellow's. How much useless and even damaging and sinful gossip and criticism would be avoided!

And as Americans, an inventory of our native land will certainly emphasize the very great blessings of being an American. It will lead us to be *grateful* citizens. It will lead us to *help* our neighbor, for an inventory will show us those in need.

And an honest inventory of both the advantages and disadvantages of the other guy's or the other gal's position in life will probably send a feeling of deep appreciation and gratitude that God has placed us in the exact social circumstances which He has. If we could but look close enough, we feel that the beautiful green of our neighbor's grass would turn out to be a mirage—a reflection of our own unappreciated circumstances.

100

3. *In our business affairs*—There is little to add here. One of the most important parts to successful business is the inventory. And so necessary is it as one's business grows, that many go to great expenditure of money to install an elaborate IBM automatic system so they can constantly *know* their inventory.

An honest inventory of our own talents might also come in handy to convince us whether we are in the right business or not. Many fail because they undertake a business for which they are in no way fitted.

4. *In our financial affairs*—One of the most common "quirks" of human nature is the amazing way many seem to appraise their financial status. They do it this way: "If I have money in my pocket, I am 'flush.' " Even though they may have debts galore, they're "flush " and they spend freely. On the other hand if they don't happen to have much cash in their pocket, they're "almost broke," even though they have a nice bank account! Amazing? But it happens so often.

An inventory taken regularly would give a *true* picture of our finances judged by what we have in cash; what's coming in; what we owe; what will come up for payment and when. Another term for a financial inventory is *budget*.

And please pardon us for being trite if we remind our reader of the fellow who exclaimed: "I'm rolling in wealth. Look at all the blank checks I've got left!"

5. *In our emotional life*—An *emotional inventory* is very important to the alcoholic. The law of nature tells us that every unit of energy we expend must be reclaimed or the time will come when we find ourselves *exhausted* of energy. Doctors call it *nervous exhaustion*. It simply means we *spent* energy which we did not regain either through rest or proper food. And how can we know how much we can afford to spend; and how much time we need in rest to recoup that expended energy? Only by an honest inventory.

In this business of sleep and rest. Why do some people need so much more sleep and rest than others? Because some expend much more energy per hour than the next guy or gal.

One often hears a doctor advise an energetic, active type individual who is getting nervous, and sleepless and jittery to *slow down*. That's impossible in many cases, particularly in the case of the individual who *by nature works, acts and thinks fast.* He *can't* slow down; *but he can get more rest!* And it is *very* true, excluding possible laziness, that these energetic type individuals *do need much more rest* than the average individual.

The most stupid and asinine statement to make to a tired, complaining fellow is: "It's all in your imagination. You don't need more sleep. Look at me, I only get four hours and I feel fine." Trouble is "he ain't you." Or what is a greater show of ignorance is to say: "Look at Edison; he only had three hours sleep a night!"

How to find what we need? By an *inventory of ourselves* and our emotional habits and type of energy expenditures.

6. *In our mental life*—An inventory is the one thing that produces an orderly mind and orderly thought. It will also point out some of the dangerous trash we keep putting in there, and which will ultimately seek an outlet. "As we think, we ultimately act." An inventory will also 'catch" in time those little beginnings of "stinking-thinking"; it will pin-point the worries which have so long masqueraded as *thinking;* and it will uncover the fact that many of the disturbances, emotionally and even physically, have their roots in those ordinarily hidden attitudes and prejudices. The *finest practice of mental hygiene possible is taking a regular and thorough and an honest inventory.* Such a mind *knows* what it does; and *does* what it *knows* to be necessary; and like a knife blade, is able to cut through all the phoney and false theories and find truth—which is *God.*

7. *In our physical life*—There are so many people who neglect a physical check-up and as a result "crack-up." A prudent inventory of our *whole* physical make-up is the best form of insurance against sickness. Our bodies will function properly and be fit instruments for the soul *if* we keep them that way. And we shall keep them that way only by a regular check-up—an inventory. And that goes for the *whole* body; the eyes, the teeth,

102

the internal mechanism, and the heart and the lungs and the liver—all of it. And when wrong *promptly* correct it! (There may be one exception—our poor hair; but then that's an ornament, not a function!)

8. *In our spiritual life*—It is impossible to lead a spiritual life without a regular inventory. The *whole* personality—in fact *all creation* tends to deteriorate. It is all a result of sin. So the soul—even in the best of people—*tends* toward evil. And without an inventory those little beginnings of evil grow *ever so gradually*, until the day comes when they blossom out into serious wrongdoing. It is only by a regular check, by a regular inventory in the light of grace that will recognize these tendencies and thus be enabled to stunt their growth. Without an inventory we won't even notice them—until too late.

You know—in this old world of ours there are some huge works of nature: the immense mountain ranges; the almost bottomless oceans; the amazing crater which is the Grand Canyon, to mention but a few.

There are also some amazing works of man's hand which are of such huge proportions that they stagger the imagination: the pyramids of Egypt; the Empire State Building; the Golden Gate Bridge of San Francisco. These stand out by their very size.

But there are other amazing things in nature, more influential than even these huge wonders mentioned above. But they are so small that a microscope is needed to visualize their existence. These wonders of creation are the tiny germs and the viruses which at times lay low entire populations even though they themselves are unseen by the naked eye.

A passer-by would hardly miss seeing the great things mentioned; their very size demands attention. But *only the microscope* will bring into view the deadly germ; the deadly virus.

A similar condition exists in the spiritual life. In fact it exists in the total personality of man.

No one fails to notice the broken arm; the maimed back; the sightless eye. No one misses seeing the nervous break-down; the palsied hands; the sudden fear. No one passes by without

103

seeing the *big* crimes; the serious sins; the loss of faith in God. *But* there is only one way to recognize and root out the very *roots* of all these serious conditions—and that is by the microscope of an *inventory* enlightened by the grace of God which alone will notice the small beginnings of physical weakness; of emotional instability; and of the spiritual aridity which *lead* to all the *big* break-downs.

And you know something? You can't miss seeing the guy or the gal who is terribly *drunk;* but only an inventory would have brought to the attention of that drunk all those small beginnings which *led* to the binge.

9. *In our A.A. life*—Here the inventory becomes important lest in a very gradual degree we *graduate* from A.A. It is necessary for *total sobriety* to intelligently lay out all those things which we *must continue to do in A.A. for permanent sobriety:* meetings, twelfth-step activity, the twelve steps, the principles we learned, and all those things we held so dear during our first months or years in A.A. But there is only one way to keep the necessity of those things continually fresh in our mind and convictions; *the continued inventory.*

We shall not at this time go into what causes slips. But we would like to make an observation on slips in their relation to a continued inventory. And this is our observation for what it is worth:

Many A.A.'s stay sober without ever taking a continued inventory; but no A.A. has ever slipped during the time he was taking an honest and regular inventory.

So—take it (the inventory); or leave it (the stinking thinking)!

WE ARE NOT DIFFERENT

"The hair, the eyes, the skin may differ;
all those things we see—
But deep down within no difference lies
between you and you and me!"

Good example in life often is barren in drawing in its wake imitators simply because so many people on seeing it muse to themselves: "Yea, but *I'm* different." Many of the laws of God and the land are not kept because the one breaking the law, does so—and also muses to himself: "Yea, I know it's the law but you see *I'm different.*" Likewise obligations, responsibilities, realities are shunned and pushed aside by countless members of the human race *because* (so they think) *they are different.*

Many, many alcoholics put off doing anything about their drinking because they think they are different from other alcoholics; because *no one* (so they thought) has quite the problem that they have. *They* are *different.* So they are hopeless in their own convictions; and they remain confused, suffering, pitiable drinking alcoholics.

Along the same line of misunderstanding we also find millions, yes millions, of souls who do not even attempt a solution of their problems, moral and otherwise, because they *think they are different*—and therefore are hopeless.

Particularly does the alcoholic tend to think he is different from his fellowman. He is the most abused person in the world; he has the severest temptations of anybody; he has more pains; he has more needs; he has more (or less!) shortcomings; he has more misfortune. There is in fact *no one* in all the world who has anything like the problems that he has. This misconception of life; this excuse—call it what you may—even persists in many alcoholics after they come to A.A. Particularly is this true among the professional people; the medics, the clergy, the attorneys, etc. They have finally admitted they are alcoholic— but *different* and thus in need of special therapy, and of special groups.

On the other hand one of the most basic truths to be aware of and to understand in adjusting to life is the principle: *we are not different.* It is one of the first products of becoming *honest.* And it is very, very necessary if one ever hopes to adjust happily to the circumstances of their life and to the people they meet along life's path. It is a prime ingredient in tolerance, and understanding, and love. Permanent and happy married life is impossible without it; a home but a bedlam unless it is accepted and understood.

When giving our talk on *principles* some years back, we always along with this principle of not being different injected the remark: "Really we are not different. Take that guy or that gal sitting next to you—he or she has the same thoughts, the same feelings, the same temptations and failings that you have." Immediately one could perceive smiles, and hear giggles and see a blush or two here or there! Why? All were thinking to themselves as they stole a glance at their neighbor: "He does?" Yes, he does, because basically we are *not different.* So let us look deep within our own selves and very probably we will have looked into the heart and the soul of our neighbor. *We're not different!*

Even the alcoholics, *outside of the problem of alcohol itself* are not different from the so-called "normal" people in this world Don't believe it? Go to any mixed group of A.A.'s in the world where there are many alcoholics and also many non-alcoholics. Then try to pick 'em out! *If you can't smell 'em you can't tell 'em.*

Now where does this sameness, this similarity come from? It has its origin *in our basic identical humanity.* It has been there ever since man first inhabited this earth and will remain until the last one has left it. We are all the same because we are all *human.* Only *our circumstances differ.* We may have different father and mother; we may have different color of hair, eyes, or skin; we may have different stature; different religion; different homes; different financial status; different states of life; different talents and abilities; different sex external characteristics; different educational backgrounds; different nationalities —*but underneath all of these external characteristics lies the same basic human nature.*

Go back and read carefully the story of man's creation. Read the whole story. Space does not permit its re-telling here. But there we will find *in Adam and Eve* as a product of creation and as a "by-product" of sin *all those human traits and tendencies and capabilities and failings and sufferings, even as in you and me.*

Why is it that youth usually starts out and continues for many years to *change life,* but age alone finally *gives in and adjusts to life*—to both ourselves and others? Because *youth* has yet to learn this basic truth; *we are not different; times indeed change; but the human soul changes very little and almighty God not at all,* which indicates that each succeeding generation —*anyone*—may and should work to *improve* life, but *no one* can change it. *That* will be done only by an eternal God in His eternity.

Let's take a look at this *sameness* of human nature. Let's see what makes us so like other humans in spite of circumstances.

1. *Psychological identity.*
   a—*All* have *intelligence.*
   I—*All* have the ability to *know.*
   II—*All* have the ability to *reason.*
   b—*All* have a *free will.*

2. *Emotional identity*—Wherein *all* have *seven basic tendencies to evil, (Passion).*
   a—*Anger*
   b—*Pride*
   c—*Envy*
   d—*Lust*
   e—*Gluttony*
   f—*Sloth*
   g—*Covetousness*

3. *Physical identity*—all have a *body* which is subject to:
   a—*Pain*
   b—*Sickness*
   c—*Death*

4. *Spiritual identity with the Deity.*

a—*All* have a *soul.*
b—*All* have the *ability to contact the Deity.*
c—*All* have the same *destiny.*
d—*All* were created to the image and likeness of *God.*

Therefore the "persona"—the *human person*—is each identical with each other. All have the *same basic* traits. *Differences* in people are *only accidental—on the surface—external.* It is this principle that we are not different which was responsible for the "human rights" clause in the Declaration of Independence and which declares that *"all men* are created free *and equal."* There would be none of the widespread misunderstanding today over segregation if *all accepted and understood* the principle: *we're not different.*

So let us now re-capitulate and analyze more carefully each of these basic human traits which make all like unto one another. We will then more easily see and more fully understand why it is that so many often "veer" from the so called "normal" in life. We will understand also more fully *all* of our fellowmen and not be so apt to misjudge them.

1. *Psychological identity*—All men are created with *the ability to acquire knowledge* and *to reason.* But if you read the story of creation as we suggested above, you would have learned that because of sin the ability to know and to reason is "darkened" and thus will tend to reach wrong conclusions unless enlightened by God's grace. For this reason humans need *teachers,* —men and women who have already *learned correct conclusions.* For the same reason we all need *discipline of thinking.* The aim of all knowledge and reasoning is to obtain *wisdom.* And wisdom is only a product of long *practice, age*—and the *grace of God.* Wisdom is the knowing *what to do with* the knowledge we acquire. This takes *long* practice and in the meantime necessitates a competent interpreter lest our unenlightened intelligences and darkened powers of reason *misinterpret* truth. It was for this reason that many papers hailed *"the wisdom* of the founding Fathers" who created the Supreme Court as the ultimate interpreter of our national laws and constitution. It would have been the height of folly for them to have left such a document with

112

all of its *potential* interpretations without an authoritative teacher. Even *God* wouldn't do that!

And so it is that even after long years of study and practice of right thinking we still get "screwy thinking" on occasion; "crazy" thoughts; "bad" thoughts. In fact we will *never* achieve *full* control of our mental processes in this world. *We're human.* We will *always* need a *guide* lest we be led astray by the "flights of fancy" which will ever tend to take root in our thought life.

All humans also have a *free will*. And again, if you read the story of creation you would have found that is the one thing we have been given that is truly ours. A *free* will—*weakened* by sin; but *free*. So once again it was for this reason that St. Paul cried out: "In my mind I serve the law of God; in my flesh the law of sin. The good that I will, I do not. The evil that I hate, I do. O miserable man, who will deliver me from the bondage of this death? The grace of God." Man's will is *free;* sin makes it *weak;* grace makes it *strong.* "I can do *all* things in Him Who strengthens me," is the conclusion of St. Paul.

Psychologically the will follows what *seems good to itself.* It will follow therefore whatever the intelligence shows it to be good. But the intelligence is darkened; on occasion it shows to be good what isn't. Then we "goof"; and when through the weakness of our will we follow what is *most desirable* to the will here and now, albeit our intelligence shows it to be *forbidden*, we *sin.* So it is that on occasion *everybody*—and that meant *you and you and you*—and *me*—"goofs" and sins. We are *all* human; we're *not different.*

It would take another entire treatise to go into the influence on the will of *habit*, and of *emotions*, and of *grace.* Nor is it in the scope of our own discussion to do so. Suffice it to realize simply this one conclusion: *psychologically we are not different.*

2. *Emotional identity*—Within *every* human being there are seven *basic "drives"* which constantly impart pressure upon and influence our "feelings," our thinking, and our actions. These drives along with that intricate and complicated part of us called the "nerve system," plus bodily reactions, plus at

times "glandular disturbances," plus certain types of "thinking" produce *emotions:* sadness, fear, joy, elation, etc., etc. The word itself *emotion* comes from two Latin words: "e" and "motus" which literally means a "motion (movement, feeling) from"—*within.* The mind, the body and the soul all usually take part. And it is for this reason they can become so complicated and so disastrous if not properly controlled. Each time they leave a mark *on the body, mind and soul.* (And by *body* we include the *nerve system, the glandular system, the blood vessels, the heart and what have you.*) Emotional control is achieved—albeit slowly and only imperfectly—by keeping within the bonds of reason these seven basic *drives,* which *all of us have and will have until "two days after we're dead."*

Before looking at these "drives" let's bear in mind that they are all basically *good* in themselves. Their *use* is beneficial; their *abuse* only is harmful and sinful. Sometimes they are called *capital sins.* We don't like the term. It is likely to be confusing. It is true that *"capital"* means actually *"sources"* and therefore *capital sins* mean *"sources of sin,"* but we feel it is too open to misunderstanding. In fact we *know* it is because we have had *thousands* come to us who *did* misunderstand their meaning thinking *all* anger, and *all* pride etc., was *sinful.* They seem never to have heard the words of Christ Who said, *"Be angry and sin not."* But most of the time it was the words *"capital sins"* that deceived them. A better name? Well, let's call them *sources* of sin —in fact we could call them *sources of all troubles in life!* Why? Because with a weakened will, and a darkened intellect, they don't have too difficult a time "getting out of control." But call them what you like—they are definitely necessary to life and we *all* have them. Let's take them one by one.

a. *Anger*—Without *anger* there would be little drive to action. For this reason the *more active* person is usually the one who tends the more quickly to anger. The phlegmatic, the slow mover, the *inactive* man does not usually tend so easily to be angry. Anger *controlled by reason* is *good;* and sometimes necessary and useful in maintaining discipline. *But uncontrolled anger,* anger which dictates action without reason, becomes wrong and

114

leads to many other wrongs and sins. So it was that Christ was *justifiably angered* at the money-changers in "His Father's house"; and *justified by reason,* He drove them out of the Temple. The parent likewise who *justifiably* is angered at the wrong-doing or disobedience of the child and *reasonably* and in *full control of that anger punishes* the child is doing a *good;* is practicing *reasonable* and therefore *good discipline.* But the parent who *"flies off the handle"* and in *anger which has shunted all reason aside "whales the daylights"* out of his child is doing wrong—*serious* wrong. It is all very simple: *anger* is *good* if reason *controls it;* it is *bad* if *it controls reason.* And so with all of these "drives."

b. *Pride*—Pride in itself is a good and necessary drive in life. Without it there would be no self-improvement. There would be no family improvement; there would be no work improvement. And thus as long as pride is *reasonable* and *justifiable* it is good. It is *not* wrong therefore to be proud of a job well done; or that we are human beings; or that we are Americans. Such feelings are both reasonable and justified. *But* when this goes beyond the limits of reason and truth—then we have sinful pride as in the refusal to accept our limitations; refusal to admit our faults; refusal to be tolerant of our neighbor; and all of the thousands of other sins that come along in the wake of sinful pride, which in very ordinary language means: assuming or pretending circumstances relating to us or others which "ain't." Humility, the opposite of pride, is assuming "I am what I am"— pride is assuming "I am what I ain't." Then comes egotism, vanity, frustrations, resentments, self-pity, and what have you But it isn't our purpose to consider all of the facets and by-products of pride. We did that in our discussions on *humility* and *honesty.* Now we are only emphasizing the fact that *we all have pride and will tend to become proud—unreasonably proud* all of our life.

c. *Envy*—Envy is sort of a "sadness" over another's success or possessions. But if this basic feeling were not present in man, there would be no competition. And envy, if reasonable, will goad the envious one to emulate the other; to succeed as he has

115

but justly. But when it turns to *unreasonable jealousy* it becomes wrong—it is unreasonable and usually leads to an *unjust* acquiring of the other's success. The difference? Envy begins with a "discontent" with what we have, having noticed what others have; jealousy is a *resentment* against what the other has. So if reason takes over, we shall enter into competition with the other without resentment; if unreasonable we will also enter into competition with the other resentful of him and using any means to emulate him. Unlike *covetousness* which desires what the other has, envy desires to get *ahead of the other,* to have *more* than he has. But once again—*we all tend to be and are at times envious beyond reason, and jealous.* (There is another type who when envy goes beyond reason, instead of trying unjustly to *emulate* the other, tries to destroy what the other has or has achieved— through calumny, and slander, and libel.)

d. *Lust*—Next to self-preservation, the drive of lust is the strongest. Without it there would be no human reproduction and the human race would die out. It is *good* in itself when it is controlled by reason and the laws of God. It is when lust drives humans to break God's laws or to go beyond the dictates of reason that it becomes wrong and so damaging. The act itself is not wrong; it is not damaging; *it is the going contrary to God's laws and reason* that makes it wrong or sinful. So *everyone* has lustful *feelings,* and lustful *thoughts,* and lustful *desires* and *imaginations* and *dreams. But these are not wrong in themselves.* They only tell us one thing—*we're still human and not different from anybody else. Everybody has this tendency.* And *everybody will* have this tendency until they are dead. It doesn't make one *"terrible"* or *"different"* or *"awful."* It becomes sinful only *when we willfully entertain the thought or desire or indulge in the action contrary to God's laws. Control* of sexual drive never hurt anyone—all contentions by psychiatry to the contrary notwithstanding! But *repression* has hurt many people, because repression is the attempt to deny the very existence of this drive within. Whenever a worthwhile psychiatrist says "repression causes neurosis, he is correct; so would the denial of the existence of any natural function cause a neurosis. *But control never caused*

*a neurosis and we challenge anyone to produce a case where it
did.* Of course *"controlling it 'half-way' "* might cause anything!
Likewise we agree with the good psychiatrists when they say that
it is "impossible to stay chaste over a long period of time." But
we must add something they left off: *"Without the grace of God."*
This drive is so strong that it is controlled *only by the grace of
God.* So it is never "we can't help it"—but rather "God and I
can *always* help it." But the important point in this present
discussion again is: *we all, without exception, tend the same
way in this matter.* And we all too without exception need the
grace of God.

e. *Gluttony*—For the alcoholic there is much misunderstanding here. In fact we fear most people have the same misconception; namely that *drunkenness*—and we mean *willful
drunkenness,* is wrong and seriously so *because of the excessive
intake of alcohol;* a sin of gluttony. *It is seriously wrong because
man willfully gives up his use of reason* without sufficient justification. So the act of *"getting drunk"* is judged by its influence
upon the reason of the individual. Excessive intake of alcohol
might be gluttonous; but many do this *but don't get drunk.*

But here we are discussing only the tendency within man to
eat and drink too much. Everyone tends to do this on occasion.
And we always will. But it might be remembered that *there are
thousands of people who drink too much; who drink excessively
and regularly* who do *not* become alcoholics. And in this regard
we might call the reader's attention to the first chapter of *Sobriety
and Beyond* where this part of the alcoholic is discussed thoroughly. For now: *all people tend to eat and drink too much.* Eating
and drinking and enjoying our food and drink *within reason* is
good. Without this desire there would be no self-preservation.
But over-eating and drinking too much is a tendency in all of us.
Lest we forget, *drinking* means *all* liquids, not only alcoholic
beverages.

f. *Sloth*—Here is just plain, downright laziness. The tendency to 'just set" is within *all* of us. But if it weren't who
would bother resting? It is only when this inactivity "drive"

117

interferes with obligations and responsibilities in life that it becomes unreasonable and wrong. But *all* of us will *all* of our lives *too often* like to *just "set* and *think."* (In fact there are a few who would love to just "set"). And incidentally unless someone or the other be misinformed, *everyone hates to and will always hate to get up in the morning.* Even though we *have to do it for years,* we will *still* hate to do so—*all of us.*

g. *Covetousness*—A "tongue-twister," and many have a "twisted" idea of just exactly what *covetousness* is. It is not the same as envy or jealousy. In covetousness we desire the exact thing our neighbor possesses. We desire not a duplicate of what he has—but *what* he has. If it leads us to get what he has *justly* —there is no harm done and it is not wrong. But if it leads us to dally with the desire to or actually to get what he has *unjustly,* then it becomes wrong. Let's take an example. We see a precious stone owned by someone else. We want it. We buy it. We have done no wrong. *But* if we set out to get the stone unfairly or unjustly, or even toy willfully with this idea, then it is wrong. Without covetousness there would be no use for buying or selling. There would be no such things as *rare values.* Nothing is worth much if no one wants it. But there is another kind of *coveting*— that is "our neighbor's wife." Remember? "Thou shalt not *covet* thy neighbor's goods; thou shalt not *covet* thy neighbor's *wife."* But here it is the same as above. To toy with the idea of getting our neighbor's wife would be wrong 'cause "there ain't no *just* and *reasonable"* way of getting or having her. Of course if he *dies;* then it would be perfectly just and reasonable to "go a-courtin." The same holds true for *husbands,* too, ladies! If this tendency in man were only controlled *in its beginning* how many fewer divorces there would be! But all humans *will tend* to illicitly desire what others have—goods and wives (and husbands!) *We're not different.*

In concluding our observations of these seven basic drives of all humans, and the awful fact that they so easily and frequently not only *"tend"* to but do get out of control, we might again and again remind ourselves *we are all without exception just ordinary human beings burdened with this fallen human nature*—

and *"there but for the grace of God, go I,"* no matter *whom* it may be we are referring to.

We're not different.

3. *Physical identity*—Whenever we think about the fact that all humans have basically identical bodies, we always remember the song which was so popular a few seasons back. Remember? "The ankle bone was joined to the leg bone; the leg bone was joined to the thigh bone; etc., etc." How true! Skin, flesh and bones—someday dust! But how important now! For it is a vessel informed by an immortal soul! And what a burden the body is at times to the soul. Remember St. Paul? But so it is with *all of us. We all have aches and pains; all become tired; all are going to die;* and *everyone's body bears upon and weighs down the soul*—rich man, poor man, beggar man, thief and *saint!* You know it isn't because of people being so physically different that makes a diagnosis for the doctor at times difficult. It is because we're all such big exaggerators (we hesitated to use the term "liars"!)

We're not different.

4. *Spiritual identity*—All have a soul created "to the Image and likeness of God," which means it is *spiritual* and *immortal—* having intelligence, reason and will. Our spiritual identity also means that we *all* can contact this God anytime, any place—at *our* discretion. But even more than the above, our all being spiritually identical means that we are *all, without exception, children* of that same God—whether we are black or white; rich or poor; Catholic, Protestant or Jew; we are *not different.*

Externals may differ. We may have different ancestors; different circumstances of living; even many *accidental* differences, but *none* of these *has to make any difference—so no matter what our circumstances may be,—*

We *all* are subject to *temptation and sin;*

We *all* have at times *"screwy" thoughts, "bad" thoughts, "unreasonable" thoughts;*

We *all* have seven basic "drives" *which tend to and do get out of control in the best of us;*

We *all* have *pains* and *aches; sickness;* and *death;*
We *all* have an *immortal soul;*
We *all* have the same *God;*
We *all* have the ability to *pray;*
We *all* have an eternal *destiny.*

So no matter what happens—inside or out—we are not alone; we are not the only ones to whom it happened—for *we are not different!*

Now let us see how this principle can affect and improve all areas of our living.

1. *In our home life*—One of the first results of the understanding and applying of this principle in our homes would be to keep us from "blaming" others so much. We would fully realize that although we have problems, the other members of the family have problems too. We have discouragement; so do they. We are tired; so are they. We are tempted; so are they. The only difficulty is that we do not see *inside* the others. If we did or could, we would see that *they are not different,* neither are we. We would have more sympathy and understanding. We would become much more just *one* big happy family—for being so alike we would so much more easily become *one* with them—their hopes, their fears, their temptations, their efforts, yes, even their faults.

2. *In our social life*—In all of our social contacts, the principle of not being different would give us a deep *"attitude of discernment"* which would enable us to always look beyond the surface. And no matter whom we meet, we would see behind that smile or tear; behind that color or race; behind that money or poverty; behind that health or sickness; behind that religion or lack of it; behind that man or woman—*just another "me."* We're not different.

How much more easy it would be for us to be tolerant; how much more difficult to be critical! How much more clearly would there unfold to our mind's eye *the fatherhood of God and the brotherhood of man* in all of its amazing and beautiful simplicity! How quick would then be our generosity; our patience and our understanding! How much more valid and sensible would be our advice when sought. How seldom would there be an expression of surprise no matter *what* we heard or learned about another! And how much more effective and all-inclusive would be our prayers; and how sincerely and from the heart would come that most perfect of all prayers: *"Our Father, Who art in heaven, hallowed be Thy name. . . . "!*

Why? Because we learned once and for all that underneath it all we are *not different.*

3. *In our business life*—The finest and most productive competition in business comes from the fact that there is *equal opportunity for all.* How many foreign-born citizen have attested to this great factor of American democracy and the democratic and Christian way of life. Business failure often stems from the feeling of *being different.* Such a fellow hasn't really got a chance because he *thinks* he hasn't got a chance nor had equal opportunity.

4. *In our financial affairs*—Security does not come from the number of dollars we have but *from the faith in God we have.* And this is everybody's for the asking. "God *will* provide." On the other hand the world's most wealthy person *could* lose all of his money—and quickly. Witness the stock-market panic of 1929.

So, financial condition has practically *nothing* to do with whether we are the same as our fellow man or not. The least differential is the difference of finance.

Perhaps it would be well at this point to repeat the oft-told story of the world's nine most successful business men. It carries with it such a powerful lesson, and goes like this:

In 1923 nine of the most successful business men in the world held a meeting in a hotel in a midwestern city. They were:

1) The President of the largest independent steel company—a millionaire;

2) The President of the largest public utilities company—a millionaire;

3) The President of the largest gas company—a millionaire;

4) The greatest wheat speculator—a millionaire;

121

5) The President of the New York Stock Exchange—a millionaire;

6) A member of the Cabinet of the President of the United States—a millionaire;

7) The greatest "bear" on Wall Street—a millionaire;

8) The President of the Bank of International Settlements —a millionaire;

9) The head of the world's largest monopoly—a millionaire.

Nine men who, we feel sure would have been the envy of everyone not understanding the principle of ultimate equality, or that they, like us, were human—very, very human, and that in the over-all picture of life *all of us—everyone without exception,* had equal opportunity with them to succeed in and to adjust to *life.* In fact it sorta looks like our own chances were even better than theirs—*for*

In 1952—just twenty-nine years later, these nine of the world's great and wealthy men gave the following amazing picture:

1) The President of the largest independent steel company —Charles Schwab—*died bankrupt* and had to live on borrowed money for five years before his untimely death!

2) The President of the largest public utilities company— Samuel Insull—died *penniless* and in a foreign land!

3) The President of the largest gas company—Howard Hopson—went *insane* before his death!

4) The greatest wheat speculator—Arthur Cutten—died abroad *insolvent!*

5) The President of the New York Stock Exchange— Richard Whitney—was sent to Sing Sing *prison* before his death!

6) The member of the President's Cabinet—Albert Fall— was pardoned from *prison* only so he could die at home!

7) The greatest "bear" on Wall Street—Jesse Livermore— died a *suicide!*

8) The President of the Bank of International Settlements— Leon Fraser—died a *suicide!*

9) The head of the world's largest monopoly—Ivan Krueger —died a *suicide*.

Remarkable?

But it happened to them in spite of their great wealth. And *we're not different*—it *could* happen to *you*—it *could* happen to *me!*

In the area of finance even the gambler has a better chance and is a better gambler if he begins with the conviction that he *has at least equal chance.*

5. *In our emotional life*—It is very difficult to differentiate in life between the neurotic and the non-neurotic. Emotional disturbances and upsets are a part and parcel of everyone. And you know something? The true neurotic usually becomes that way *because he or she thinks they are different!* The result: flight from reality.

All people have "nerves" and sleepless nights and jittery days and "fear" and "funny-feelings"; but the neurotic doesn't think so, so he pampers his own and they grow and grow and grow into a well-fashioned and full-bloomed neurosis. Thus he *is* different; but he doesn't have to be—once he ever gets to the conviction that basically he "ain't."

In the same way scrupulous person is convinced that he or she is different. Although conceding that others can live without serious sin; and that others will be saved; they are *positive* that they are always sinning and haven't got a chance for salvation. They see wrong in everything. They are sick people, and one of the things they need more than anything else is the conviction that *they are not different*—spiritually.

We had opportunity recently to witness a rather dramatic example in the emotional area of one who had come to the very verge of despair and hopelessness and morbid fear *simply because she thought that she was different.* She had taken the shock treatments. And although people recover rather consistently from the shock treatments someone had convinced her that *she was different*, that *she would not*, that the shock treatment *had only proven her insanity* and that it was *only a question of time until she "cracked-up" completely.*

When she came to us she was the most frightened individual we had ever seen. There was positively stark fear and terror written all over her face and her eyes veritably bulged with fright. The reason she had come to us is that having been introduced to A.A. she had heard us speak and had heard that we had the shock treatments some years previously.

When she came to us, we tried in a very simple way to first explain the mechanics of the shock treatments and to point out that no one ever went "insane" as a result of them, but that most people who had taken them ended up with a much clearer and a sharper mind than ever; and that the worst that could happen as far as damage was concerned was on occasion a broken bone gotten in the convulsion but even this danger had been eradicated in later years in most cases.

We could almost see the veil of terror lift from her face and flee from her eyes; we could see relaxation enter into her whole personality; we saw a different person *because we had convinced her that in reality she wasn't different from others.*

Then too, in this matter of the emotions—let's not expect too much in this day and age of pressure and hurried living. *More than ever in history* everybody is "on edge." Let's allow for it—in others and in ourselves: *God does.* And *we're not different.*

6. *In our mental life*—Success in study, in mental endeavor of any kind, *must* be predicated upon the fact that *we're not different.* Some have a "slower" mentality; but that only means it will take them a bit longer.

The successful student in school is the one who sees his chances of success in his classes as equal to the rest of the students. In fact the one who fares the worst in school is the so-called "bright" boy who thinks he is different in being *better* than the rest. He usually leaves school with less—because he did not study enough. He didn't think he had to; wasn't he different? He was and he is—but he didn't have to be. *We're not different.*

7. *In our physical life*—The principle of not being different would lead us to use our bodies and not to abuse them—regard-

less of accidental differences as to size, form, color or what have you. We can *all* have an efficiently working body *if we want to*, even though we be ill, or crippled, or even blind. The tremendous and amazing accomplishments of such ill people, and of the blind, and of the lame bear eloquent testimony that deep down within *there is no difference.*

In fact, we find that many, many sex difficulties in married life arise from the thinking that one is different. Any doctor or psychiatrist will bear testimony to this. The man thinks he is different from the rest of men; the woman is sure she is; comes shame, and fear, and guilt-complexes—and failure as man and wife. The happily married couple are the ones who are convinced without shame or doubt that they are no different from anyone else and therefore use this instrument of God in the reproduction of children and of citizens for here and for heaven. They accept sex as a matter of course, as a gift from God and use it accordingly with modesty but without shame; with reverence but without fear; with humility but without a guilt-complex. They are few in number—their name should be legion as God really intended. For, you see, *we are not different.*

8. *In our spiritual life*—Here above everything else the failure to realize that we are not different wreaks havoc and keeps many souls from attempting a spiritual life, even a life of sanctity. Mention the saints, and what do we hear? "Yea, we know, *but we're different."* Or "God doesn't expect that of *us.*" Or does He? Weren't His words spoken to *all* men when He said, "Be ye *perfect"?* But if we think we're different, we surely won't try, will we?

But the principle of not being different tells us that we each have a soul, a destiny, the ability to pray and an invitation to be perfect. So *we're* not so different from the saints, are we? So much discouragement comes from thinking we are. We fail to realize that the saints, the great men and women of God down through the ages had *the same temptations, the same tendency toward evil, the same body, the same darkness of intellect and weakness of will that we have—but* they went to *God.* They took Him at His word. They, *through the grace of God, eventually*

125

did reach perfection, but it wasn't because they had no obstacles. They had the same as we do—*we're not different.*

Then again, so many bring up their "awful" past. This makes them different. This excuses them from becoming spiritual; from becoming saints. Yet—who was it named St. Mary Magdalen? An *ex-prostitute!* And St. Augustine? We challenge anyone to match his past. In fact we feel pretty sure that whoever you may be you do not have a much worse past than anyone else—the only difference *you know yours—you* don't know *theirs.*

"We can do *all* things in Him Who strengthens us." And that, chum, has no "unlesses," or "ifs," "buts," "excepts" about it. For when it comes to God—that is one time we *are* not different.

9. *In our A.A. life*—One of the biggest difficulties in A.A. groups and one which stems from ignorance of or lack of realization of the principle that we are not different, is how so many so easily seem to forget that *all the other members of A.A. are alcoholic too*—even as you and I. Whether they have been sober one, ten, or twenty years, they are *still* alcoholic. And that means they need as much as they ever needed in the beginning to stay sober. How often on the other hand we tend to "graduate" others! Particularly do we tend to do this to the old timers. We just seem to forget that they *can* slip even as you and I—because, you see, *we are not different.* Remember? "Once an alcoholic always an alcoholic." *Everyone,* from Bill W. on down the line to the guy who just at this minute is joining A.A. or taking his last "snort," *could slip*—and any of these *will* slip *if* they toy with all those things that are dangerous to one's sobriety.

But an old timer slipping should not bother us in the least, nor should it surprise us. One thing is sure, the writer has never in all of his experience in A.A. ever met or heard of anyone slipping *off* the program. He has seen many *get off* the program —and then sooner or later slip. And being human *anyone* might get off the program. But you won't, bud—not if you remain *honest* and *practice the principles of A.A. in all of your affairs.* And you know something? You won't *accidentally* quit practicing them. If you quit you will do so with your eyes wide open. You might be deceived, *but you'll know it.* So if you are wondering "What if I *accidentally* slip?" just quit wondering. No one else ever has—neither will you, because *we're not different.*

So in conclusion may we wrap it up by saying:

No matter what we think or feel or have happen to us—we can be darn sure that we are not the first one to think such a thought or feel such a feeling or have such a thing happen to us—and we can be sure that most people have at some time or other experienced exactly the same—because we are not different. Times change a great deal—but people—souls—change very little and Almighty God not at all!

I AM AN ALCOHOLIC

*"...and practice these principles in all
of our affairs...."*

We have enumerated the principles[1] which hold a prominent place in the A.A. approach not only to *sobriety*, but also to *contented living*. There are many more. The ones related here are merely the basic ones picked up along the way in our travels in A.A.; in our own experiences; in our discussions with others. We are not quite sure whether our readers will all like them, or use them, but we are *positive of one thing: They work*, they really do! Wide experience tells us they do.

So, now let us take them again—one by one—and let us thoroughly try to analyze each one and see *how* we can *apply and practice* them *in all of our affairs*.

"I am an Alcoholic."

What are the implications and the limits and the advantages and the responsibilities that go along with this simple statement of truth?

"I" am the alcoholic, not the other fellow. Remember when we were drinking? How many "poor" alcoholics we knew—those poor souls who couldn't handle their liquor? Perhaps many had the same experience which the writer had when we first read the big A.A. Book. We immediately recalled to mind *many others* whom A.A. would help. We immediately thought of several of our *relatives* who we felt should join A.A. But *we* were not that bad! *I* an alcoholic? Why, nonsense! Not *I*, never!

But now having *accepted* the truth, we practice it by *retaining* and *renewing that conviction—day in and day out, hour in and hour out, minute in and minute out: that I* am the alcoholic, and therefore that *I* need the program, etc., *not* the other guy. We do even concern ourselves about him. *"I am an alcoholic."*

---

[1] Cf. Sobriety and Beyond.

133

I *am* an alcoholic, not *was* an alcoholic; not an *ex*-alcoholic. And this means that no matter whether we be dry ten, twenty, thirty years and then take *one* drink we cannot guarantee our sobriety. I *am*—always *am*, therefore will remain an alcoholic until the day I die. This is precisely what makes us different from so-called *"normal"* people. (Although in A.A. we oftentimes wonder who's who in this normalcy business!) But, outside of the alcoholic problem itself, there is, as we mentioned above, no difference between the alcoholic and his non-alcoholic fellowman. A very interesting experiment to prove this can be done in any "mixed" crowd of alcoholics and non-alcoholics. Just try to pick them out of such a crowd. "If you can't smell 'em, you can't tell 'em!"

I am an *alcoholic*. And we take this principle in its over-all truth as to what an *alcoholic really is*. Not a moral degenerate, not necessarily a willful drunkard, not even an excessive drinker, *but an alcoholic* with the *compulsive* factor of drinking. It is precisely this *compulsion* that makes the difference. An *alcoholic* therefore is sick, *terribly* sick *bodily, mentally and spiritually. So* we must accept, if we are ever to practice this principle, the term with *all* of its connotations: with its *limits* (we can *never* take one drink; we must avoid certain things in the mental and emotional order, etc., etc.) ; with its *advantages* (there are many chief among them being the fact that we have been given a gift by God of the ability to establish a contact of confidence with another alcoholic, something that is seldom and only rarely given to the non-alcoholic) ; and with its *responsibilities,* (particularly of avoiding those things which might cause us to lose *our* sobriety; and of *giving* our sobriety to other alcoholics).

Now let's *apply* and *practice* this principle *in all of our affairs*. Many in A.A. tend to think that this principle needs acceptance only *once*. But we feel and shall try to show how it must be *practiced*—day in and day out, hour in and hour out, minute in and minute out—*in all of our affairs*.

1. *In our home life*—Here we must daily keep in our consciousness this admission *honestly* less we use it as an endless

excuse to get out of many home responsibilities. First we must realize and practice the truth that being an alcoholic does not imply that *"mere"* sobriety is enough to give to our family. How often do we not hear it said: "What does she expect? I'm *sober*, ain't I?" Yes, but we are no different from others *outside* of sobriety and therefore we *owe* our family the same consideration, kindness, etc., etc., that is part and parcel of *all* family life. *"Mere"* sobriety is *not* enough. And something else: *very* probably it will take a *lifetime of making amends* to our family for all the years of drinking! *"Mere"* sobriety will *never* do this. How many wives today lament: "I sometimes wish he was drinking again; at least he was not so mean so consistently." Practice means *repeat* and *repeat* and *repeat* to our family all those things at least *that we owe them*. And to become *"masters"* of sobriety in our homes, would lead us to give them *not only what we owe, but all of those things, big and little, that would contribute to their happiness. That* is *loving*. and *living, as a grateful recovered alcoholic in the home.*

Practicing this principle in the home also would lead us to adopt the truth of the question whether we should keep and/or serve liquor in our home to others. According to the findings of experience, such will *not* cause difficulty *if* we do so for an honest motive: of charity or social necessity. It is only when we do it so we can *toy* with the presence of liquor, or have it around to *prove* to ourselves or others that we won't take any—to build our "will power," that brings trouble.

Finally, practicing it in the home means neither hiding the fact that we are alcoholics, nor bragging about it—just being *humbly grateful.*

2. *In our social life*—Here we use and *practice* this principle by honestly admitting the fact, not using it as an excuse for any or all aberrations.

We try to become *social* people, instead of remaining *anti-social*, excusing ourselves from all 'irritating" social obligations, *because we are alcoholics.*

We do not use the lie—albeit in some people's minds a

"white" one—that we do not drink "because we have a bad stomach" or some other such untruth. We do not drink for one reason: *we are alcoholics and cannot handle alcohol.*

We remember one instance wherein one of the members of our group some years ago had difficulty with this approach in his social contact. His position made it necessary for him frequently to be in circumstances where someone offered him a drink. For some time he always used that so-called "white lie": "No, thanks, I can't; I have a bad stomach."

However, as he tells it, this never left him at ease. And many times the one who proffered the drink would keep insisting and often came up with, "Oh, don't let that stop you. I had a bad stomach once, too. And you know, it was the keeping on drinking in spite of it that cured me. Come on, have a little drink!"

This would only complicate matters. It would only make the refusal more difficult.

Finally, one day he was talking to his sponsor and told him of his problem. The sponsor then advised him to "tell the truth"; that this was a "program of honesty." This he did from then on. And never has anyone insisted a second time that he take a drink!

"No, thanks, *I am an alcoholic* and found that I simply cannot handle alcohol."

3. *In our business affairs*—In the business world the past of the alcoholic *could* be very damaging and harmful, and at times an obstacle to success, *but it need not be.* And again, it *will* not be, or at least experience has taught us that it will not be, *if we also here use absolute honesty,* admitting the fact that we are alcoholic *freely,* but not bragging. The fact that we are alcoholic, and that we have a rather "rugged" past will usually make little or no difference to people we meet in business *provided they realize we are doing something about it.* There is something about that simple admission without pretense, "*I am an alcoholic,*" that fascinates and attracts people. After all, *truth* is always attractive; *dishonesty* is repulsive.

One time there was a fellow who had to be sobered up in a sanitarium. While there, he came in contact with a lot of A.A. visitors. He was intrigued at first, then attracted, then wanted what A.A. had to offer. One thing frightened him. What was the boss going to say or do when he returned to work? What if the boss would find out that he had been on such a binge? "Don't take a chance on him finding it out," one of the A.A.'s told him, "there is one way in which it will be *impossible* for him to find it out."

"There is?" queried the patient in eager amazement.

"Yea, there is," replied the visitor, "and it is a very simple way and a very sure way. Just go to your boss and tell him that you were on a binge, and that you had to be sobered up in a sanitarium, and that you there learned that you are an alcoholic and that you joined A.A. so you could really do something about it."

"But then he will know!" remonstrated the fellow.

"Sure, he will know, but *he* will not have *found it out*. And our experience is that very probably he will admire you for it, and will appreciate the truth of the matter. This is a program of *honesty*, you know."

Very hesitatingly, and still quite fearful and dubious, our friend went back to work, and told the boss as he had been advised to do. You know what happened? That fellow was made vice-president of the corporation, and today he is president—and still sober and in A.A.!

4. *In our financial affairs*—Being an alcoholic is no reason why one should hoard "*against a possible slip.*" Such thinking is the most fertile field of thought wherein drinking thinking takes its root.

We are alcoholic. But now we are just as secure as the "normal" person *provided* that we are *honestly* working the program. As long as there is honesty within, God's grace will always be a co-worker. So we prudently provide for our financial future as anyone else—all else being in the hands of God.

Then, too, being alcoholic, we *probably* are a bit on the "tight" side. And to balance this tendency, we should *practice giving* and sharing our material goods.

5. *In our emotional life*—All people have emotions. Probably, as an alcoholic, we have a little extra amount. But one thing we must always keep uppermost in our mind, that *we are alcoholics and so cannot permit ourselves to indulge in emotional upsets very frequently or for any prolonged period of time. If we do we will set off that compulsion to drink*—we don't know why, but we do know that it is true. Resentments, self-pity and the like will be constantly gotten rid of *fast* by the one who *practices* the principle that he *is an alcoholic*. This will always be so—day in and day out, hour in and hour out, and minute in and minute out. *We are alcoholics.*

6. *In our physical life*—The A.A. who diligently practices the principle of being an alcoholic will also avoid certain physical reactions that will set off—sometimes automatically—the compulsion to drink. These reactions are: becoming *over-tired,* becoming *over-hungry,* becoming *over-thirsty.* Again, we do not know why, but we do know that such indulgences can cause the alcoholic to crave liquor. And many an otherwise good, sincere A.A. has only begun to practice this principle the hard way—*after a slip brought on through not practicing it.*

The sincere A.A. will also make use of the many physical helps that medicine can provide today to aid the alcoholic in his adjustment on the physical side of the picture. These we should use intelligently as adjuvants to the program, if we need them. A physician *familiar with alcoholism* and the latest findings in its treatment can sometimes be a great boon to the alcoholic especially during the early months of sobriety.

7. *In our thought life*—One of the commonest comments one hears around A.A. circles is: "Well, he is not drinking *yet,* but his thinking is sure stinking, and it won't be long until he's drinking." We are alcoholics. Therefore mental conflicts, indecision, and all negative "stinking" thinking are not for us—i.e., if we value sobriety and want to practice the truth that we are

138

alcoholics. And *practicing* this in our *thought* life means that *all* such be eschewed.

8. *In our spiritual life*—If there is ever a time when we must practice this principle, it is in our approach to God. *We must approach Him as an alcoholic.* If we don't, it matters little how many our prayers or our devotions, it won't be long before we will be like the fellow in the Scriptures who "looked in the mirror and then went his way *forgetting what manner of man he was."* We are *alcoholic.* That means we *must, if* we want to be *sure* of witnessing the setting sun soberly, first and before all else *ask God for the strength of sobriety for these twenty-four hours.* We have seen many stay sober for a time *without* doing this; but we have *never* met a person who slipped after *having done this.*

Particularly A.A.'s with a religious background must get this conviction. They, often realizing the benefits of sobriety at last, and the value of their religion, again say their prayers, avoid evil, do good and in general become good Christians. And then it happens. Without the practice of this principle—day in and day out, hour in and hour out, minute in and minute out—*they forget what manner of men they are.* So it is not long before, *in spite of their numerous prayers, they try it again,* and being alcoholic they end up as they always have and always will end up—*drunk! Let us not forget that even if an alcoholic becomes a saint—and takes that first drink—he will get drunk.* This principle stands out like a sore thumb in the spiritual life of the alcoholic, telling us that *even if we should achieve heroic sanctity and take one drink we will get drunk.* We *are* alcoholic, we are *powerless* over alcohol—*period.*

9. *In our A.A. life*—We are members of A.A., sober members of A.A. Many of us have received almost unbelievable blessings. But we do not brag. We are *humbly* grateful—to God and *by our example* "carry the message" in *all* of our affairs as an A.A.—day in and day out, hour in and hour out, minute in and minute out. *We give to all and always an example of total sobriety,* using *all of the twelve steps* and keeping *all of the twelve traditions.*

139

We are alcoholic—today we are alcoholic. *Tomorrow* we shall *still* be alcoholic. And then a tomorrow will come when we are about to leave this land of sorrows—we shall, like all mortal men, be *dying,* and we shall *die alcoholic—but if we have practiced living as alcoholics and achieved at least a modicum of mastery in sobriety, we shall die as*

1. *Sober alcoholics.*

2. *Courageous alcoholics in spite of death.*

3. *Possibly saintly alcoholics.*

It has happened! And we can certainly have the well-founded hope that in eternity we shall all be together again, *all of us alcoholics!*

THERE BUT FOR THE GRACE
OF GOD GO I

"I am what I am . . . by the grace of God. . . ."

The story is told about Saint Francis. Whether it really had its origin with him or not, we do not know. In fact it makes little difference. But the principle which comes from the story is of paramount importance. Anyhow, the story goes something like this:

One day Saint Francis and one of his good Brothers were walking along the highway. As they sauntered along discussing various things, the good Brother happened to see lying in the road a very drunk individual. He stopped and drew back in horror and to Francis he exclaimed: "Look, Father Francis, at that *horrible* creature!" (Or words to that effect.)

But Francis, with his deep insight both into human nature and into the realm of the Divine, simply smiled, turned towards the Brother, pointed to the one lying in the road and softly said:

"There, Brother, but for the grace of God lies Francis!"

We can imagine the impact upon the good Brother. We can imagine the magnitude of the lesson he learned. We can almost see him taking another big step forward in spiritual growth. And we don't imagine he ever again was horrified *at anyone.* For he had learned one of the most important truths of God, man and grace:

"There, but for the grace of God, go I."

Until we have learned and learned well this fact of the spiritual life, we shall never progress very far spiritually. It is the most important lesson of all of the spiritual life. Without it we can't even begin to love God nor our fellowman. And without love of God and our fellowman, there can be no true spiritual life. *"This is the first and the greatest commandment: That you love God with all your heart ... and your neighbor as yourself."*

Even though the story itself might not have originated with Saint Francis, the truth it enunciates is eternal. It has always existed, and it tells us: *"God gives both the grace to will and to accomplish."*

Way back in the Old Testament we find God severely punishing those who "made fun of Noah lying there drunk with wine." Why? Because, "There but for the grace of God" lay those who were making fun of him.

For this reason the big A.A. book tells us: "We should never look down upon the lowliest of God's creatures nor upon the worst of man's mistakes" ... *because there but for the grace of God go I.*

That is one of the reasons too that Christ so often associated with and defended "such awful people." And in their haughtiness and pride the Pharisees in contradistinction criticized and condemned the actions of Christ. Let's take an example:

There was a woman who had committed adultery. The Pharisees dragged her to the street and were about to stone her. Christ happened along. And to the accusers He said: *"Let the one among you who is without sin cast the first stone."* And then Christ began "to write in the sand." One by one the accusers disappeared. What had Christ written? The Scriptures do not tell us but many scripture scholars say that he began to write the secret sins of the accusers—and they were probably worse than the sin they had brought against the accused. Then Christ said to the woman taken in adultery: "Has any man accused thee?"[1]

"No man, Lord," she replied.

"Then neither do I, go and sin no more."

What a lesson for all proud people! What a truth for all those "holier-than-thou" persons; those "have you heard? Ain't it *awfulers?"*; for *all who sit in judgment of their fellow man no matter what they have done or are doing.* For *"there but for the grace of God, go I."*

Saint Augustine brings out this principle very dramatically and realistically. In his writings he is picturing Christ talking to a soul. He has Christ to say:

[1] This means actually: *"Is there any one accusing you now?"*

146

"If you have not committed adultery, it is because the tempter was wanting: if the tempter was wanting, it is because I so disposed. Or the time or the place were wanting: that they were wanting, I so disposed. Or again the tempter was there, and the time and place were favorable: but that you did not consent I so disposed."

Which in a realistic manner is but another way of saying: *God gives both the grace to will and to accomplish.*

It is the factor of life that caused Matt Talbot to remark: *"I had nothing to do with it, God did it all."* It brought from Samuel B. Morse, as he typed out the first telegraphic message: *"What God has wrought."* It has brought deep from the soul of every saint: *"I am what I am by the grace of God."* It has brought courage to every sinner. It should bring shame to every proud individual who but re-echoes the condemned braggadocio of the Pharisee who stood in the Temple and shouted: *"Thank God I am not like the rest of men"* . . . as they proclaim both to God and to men their virtues and their accomplishments and look askance and condemn the *"awful people"* of this world.

We had a very interesting experience sometime back. Being in A.A. brings us to meet a lot of *"awful people."* (Like when we met you and you met us!) Anyhow we were trying to get a banker to okay a loan for one of these people. We can still hear his words as they came over the phone refusing the loan: "Where in the name of the Lord do you meet such people!" We couldn't help but muse: "Poor fellow—so pietistic and so proud!"

Now does all this mean that we cannot help it when we do wrong? Does this imply that it is God's fault that we sin? Does it mean that it is not up to us to become better and to avoid serious falls and sins? Far from it. In fact it is rather the opposite. We have a free will. We therefore *must want to do what is right, but the time element, the "when" God will give us the grace to accomplish, is entirely up to God. All* we have to do is the foot-work; to keep on trying. It is entirely in the hands of God *when* He will give us success.

It also emphasizes the fact that when we see others who seem not even to have the *will* to do right, we cannot condemn nor

147

judge. *We cannot possibly know whether they are fully responsible or not* for we *cannot see the "heart."* Only one thing can we be sure of: *God permits it,* whether they are responsible or not—just the same as *He* permitted for so long the sins of Magdalen, of Augustine, of the thief on the cross and of all the big sinners down through the ages—even as you and I.

God gives both the grace to will and to accomplish. Our responsibility: *To continue to try; to continue to seek that grace, but it is up to him when He will give it.* And on judgment day He will not ask "whether we won or lost"—whether we sinned or not—but He will ask "how we played the game"—*how much we tried to avoid evil and do good.*

How many surprises there will be on judgment day! We feel there will be three big surprises:

1—We will see so many people there we didn't think had a chance; so many of those *"awful people."*

2—We will find so many *missing* whom we thought surely would be there; so many of the proud and the arrogant and the haughty; so many of those "practicers of pseudo-virtue."

3—And we shall be so surprised that *we* are there!

One more factor we feel should be mentioned in our present discussion. We have long now been convinced of something that we have never heard explained; not even mentioned. Yet we feel sure that it is true and in evidence everywhere. This is the fact that there exists such a thing as *a "cross of sin."* When we see so many of these *"awful people"; so* many of the *"real"* awful people; the prostitutes, the criminals, the "homos," the "cruel people. And when we have the opportunity, as we often have had, to look down deep within their hearts—down "beneath the surface and the show"; it is then that we become convinced, on seeing their "heroic" efforts and attempts to change, that they are carrying in many instances *the cross of sin.* And after all—such a cross is nearest to the cross of Christ! For He too, carried a *cross of sin*—your sins and my sins; these people are carrying a cross of their own sins. And in so many instances we know from experience that to them it is a very heavy cross, and that they are willing to do anything to rid themselves of it—but they do not succeed. And we have found too that once such people become convinced that they are carrying a "cross," behold the weight begins to lift, and improvement, very very slow, but still improvement, begins. Let's take some examples. They are taken from life, but with nothing mentioned to possibly expose their identities. We have been privileged in Providence to encourage many of each.

First there was a prostitute. The story of her life was a long one. Broken home—no security—bad companions: a life of prostitution. Then came alcoholism, and because alcoholism is a *progressive* sickness, it wasn't long before came that point beyond which she could not go—beyond which opened only three doors: death, insanity, or sobriety. Came A.A.; came sobriety; but continued *prostitution.* Then the efforts to extricate herself; heroic efforts but coupled with so much needless and stupid advice and condemnation. And all the time an almost irresistible "Why does this have to happen to me?"

We talked long. Perhaps for the first time in her life it all came out. And perhaps for the first time in her life there was no condemnation. For who were we to condemn? Only one thought ever comes to our minds on such occasions: *there but for the grace of God go I*—a cross of sin! And so it was that patiently we tried to explain all this to her. And to make a long story short, *the next day she returned to her God.* And today she is no longer a prostitute—*she had accepted her cross of sin,* and *in the acceptance God chose to lift it.*

Then there was a criminal—a murderer. His story was much like all the rest: down and down; murder; flight; alcoholism; the "point of no beyond" as mentioned above; A.A.; sobriety. But still remained the fear; the guilt; the inner flight and rebellion.

We also talked into the wee hours of the morning. We spoke of the Good Thief; of God and grace and sin; we spoke of *the cross of sin.* We could almost feel his relief, *as he accepted his cross.* He was once again *free.*

And along came a homosexual.[1] His story was a little different. He was well respected in his community. He was well respected in A.A. He had not even in his drinking days lost his family. But he had come to the "point of beyond" in his drinking. So he joined A.A. But this "bugaboo"; this "phobia"; this "compulsion" kept on *in spite of all his efforts to the contrary.* At times there would be successful control; then sudden relapse. He was confused; afraid; discouraged. And all along he too was asking *"why?"*

We talked long and we talked many times. He was willing to do anything suggested if only he could rid himself of this "burden." We talked about the power of God; the efficacy of prayer; the necessity of sacrifice. But we also talked about *the cross of sin.* And today we have memories of a letter later received from him telling us that much thinking on this *cross of sin* had finally brought him to an acceptance of it and then it was for the first time in his life from boyhood on, there had been real improvement—and along with improvement peace of soul, understanding and renewed love of God Who had permitted this to happen, and how that now, in God's own good time, he had a well-founded hope that he would be completely free—at least in eternity!

There but for the grace of God go I! The cross of sin!

How many people there are in the world today who are "stumbling" along under the burden of secret sins which seem to come back again and again and again in spite of all efforts to the contrary. But they go on trying, and if they only continue to go on trying, some day—sooner or later—*God will free them . . . if* they only *keep on keeping on!*

Then there are in A.A.—and everywhere—quite a number of people who seem to have just *"horrible dispositions."* They can't seem to get along with anyone. They constantly criticize;

---

[1] Contrary to the almost stupid opinion of some psychiatrists who maintain that alcoholism is latent homosexuality, we find very few such in A.A. In fact seldom do we find both problems in the same person. They just don't seem to often exist together. In all our experience with thousands of alcoholics—we have known of only a paltry eight or ten such!

they constantly take exception; they are constantly in the middle of a quarrel. And how we look down upon and condemn these people!

But one of these came to us. He was looked upon in his area as the "enigma of A.A." No one could quite understand how with his seeming lack of tolerance and frequent quarreling and apparent resentments he could stay sober. Yet he had stayed sober—and for years! But there was something we had a chance to see that no one else in his groups did. We had a chance to look *inside* and see there *sincerity*. No one was more conscious of his failings in this regard than he himself. But no matter how he tried, again and again and again he would get into quarrels, become resentful, and be intolerant. All of it to him was a terrible *burden*. And he kept asking himself over and over *why?*

We tried to encourage him. We pointed out that his years of sobriety evidently were an indication of an inner sincerity. We suggested that he simply *keep on trying*. We explained about the possibility of it being *a cross of sin*.

Today he still gets into difficulties, but *not nearly so often*. He *accepted*. He no longer asks *why?* And in this acceptance it has begun to be lifted.

We couldn't help but re-call on this occasion a remark we have often made at meetings, that God puts such people, at least one in every group, for a purpose *to give the rest of the members a chance to practice tolerance and patience and love*. We wonder!

Then there are about 150,000 A.A.'s of all kinds. Men and women who for years struggled along under the burden of alcoholism. Today they are sober. And *when* did that sobriety begin? *On the day they accepted the fact that they were alcoholics, that they were powerless over alcohol. A cross of sin?*

We wonder!

Then there was   Magdalen, and Augustine, and Peter, and the Good Theif, and the lepers (leprosy was considered a *crime* in days gone by), and the tens of thousands—yes, millions, of *sinners*—*big* sinners down through the years who were made the butt of ridicule, but with whom *Christ* associated and with whom He *still* is associating *in eternity: "This day thou shalt be with Me in paradise"* . . . the Good Thief *had accepted his cross of sin!*

So it is that *no matter whom we may be referring to; no matter what they may have done or are doing; no matter what gutter they may be looking up from—*

There but for the grace of God, go I.

And to all of those *awful people* who might somehow chance to read these lines, to them we say—*no matter what their problem or sin may be*—just *keep on keeping on* and *accept.* Then someday, here or hereafter, *God will lift that cross—God will free from sin;* yes, *God Himself will take you into His heaven* because *you bore the cross most like unto His Son's—the cross of sin.*

The same we say to all "slippers" who are still trying albeit without success. Remember, it took Monica, the mother of Augustine, thirty years of prayer. The group perhaps condemns; the world looks down and judges; but *God?* And that is really *all* that matters. Even Christ's own group; the world of His time not only looked down and condemned; they *crucified* Him!

So with all alcoholics and all sinners. To some He will give surcease as he has to you and to me; but to others He will not— why?

Because *there but for the grace of God go you and go I.*

So let's see how this principle can be effectively applied in all of the areas of life.

1. *In our home life*—How much damage is done to the thinking and the lives of children to whom their mother or father keeps insisting again and again "Remember always: *You are a Jones! You are better than others*"! How wrong are parents who are *"shocked"* when John Q. Law comes to the door with little Jonathan P. Jones in tow! How cruel are parents who try to "frighten" their children into good habits (an impossibility) by telling them *"nice boys* (or girls) *never think of such things!"* What fools parents be who insist to their charges that "Uncle Robert married 'trash' "; or that "Aunt Minnie is now beneath us; and we don't associate with her no more!"

It is perfectly all right to keep the children from associating with other children whom we know definitely to be a bad moral influence upon them—but not "blind" condemnation. Rather there should be a thorough indoctrination by word and example of the importance of the accepting the existence of sin *in everyone:* some more, some less. And that the all-important factor is to *begin again no matter what happens.* And that when we see others who seem to be "steeped" in sin; that we should never condemn but rather sympathize and understand and pray for them for *there but for the grace of God would they also be.*

Sin will always be with us. But we should be in this sin business something like a rubber ball—not like a mud ball. The rubber ball, you know, *bounces back* again *no matter how often it falls;* but the mud ball just *splatters* and stays there with no return!

2. *In our social life*—If we were fully conscious of and practiced faithfully the principle that *there but for the grace of God go I* we wouldn't be nearly so apt to "look down" or to "criticize" or to "condemn" others because they are black and not white; or because they are guilty of great sins and we are not; or because they are so ignorant and we are learned; or because they come from one side of the tracks and we came from the other. As the A.A. book states "*We should never* look down on the lowest of God's creatures; nor on the worst of man's mistakes" because

There but for the grace of God go I.

3. *In our business affairs*—Particularly is the realization that there but for the grace of God go I, effective in business personnel relationship. Those in position of authority would be much more tolerant and indulgent to their employees, because after all they would know that if it were not for the grace of God they would be working for others instead of having others working for them. For it was God Who gave the talent, the ability the circumstances—and all that entered into their success in the business world.

The employees too realizing this principle would look down

on none of their fellow-workers whatever their origin, nationality, race, religion or circumstances.

There but for the grace of God go I.

4. *In our financial affairs*—No person in history had a better and deeper conception of the principle under discussion in its relation to finance and material things than did *Job*. He had great wealth. But we feel sure he knew that it came from God. For when he lost everything he gave expression to that great act of humility which indicated his *complete* dependence upon God: "The Lord *gave;* the Lord *took away;* blessed be the name of the Lord." He was so fully aware that "the Holy Spirit breathes where He will." And God gives in *every* area of living *the grace both to will and to accomplish.*

How much worry would this eliminate from our lives—worry about finance; about fear of loss! And how much more willing would we be to *share* and to *share generously* with the beggar, the neighbor who has misfortune—with all those who *have not been so blessed as we have been.*

For in the matter of material things as well as in the spiritual and the moral area, no matter how poverty-stricken may be the one we see—

There but for the grace of God go I.

5. *In our mental life*—Freedom from worry is the finest mental tonic in the world. The man with the acute mind, the logical mind, with the quiet and relaxed mind, is the one who has banished worry. And we feel there is no surer way to banish worry than by getting a deep conviction once and for all *that* the *outcome of everything we do depends upon almighty God; ours* is only the *foot-work.* Realizing for once and for all that it is *God* Who gives the success or Who permits the failure; that being *God* He *knows* what is best for us; that therefore whatever *He* permits *is* best for us—then *what have we to worry about?*

Then too we find that many people are very critical of the mentally retarded or the uneducated. We find a lot of this among alcoholics. Perhaps it is because as a matter of fact alcoholics usually are far above the I.Q. average and as a general rule have a fairly good mind (believe it or not!), better than most people, that they so tend to look down on ignorance and stupidity. But you know something? We never would look down on *anyone* for *any* reason if we fully accept the truth:

There but for the grace of God go I.

6. *In our emotional life*—As we saw above, worry, fear, doubt have no place in the mind of one who is convinced that everything depends upon God. And the person who has rid himself of worry and fear and doubt has gone far in eliminating emotional tension and upsets and "nerves."

But here again, when that "dame" next door irritates us so with her "nerves" and her emotional outbursts—all we need to do is to remind ourselves: *there but for the grace of God go I. It* will give a lot of patience.

And we shall have a lot of patience to *listen* to those long and detailed and drawn out descriptions of all the troubles, real and imaginary, of those neurotics when they approach us and try our patience with their seemingly endless repetitions. For we will realize that the only reason we are doing the listening instead of the endless talking is because of the grace of God. In fact we are fairly sure it has not been so very long ago that we *were* doing the talking instead of the listening!

There but for the grace of God go I.

7. *In our physical life*—It is amazing how many people in this world are not satisfied with the physical make-up with which they were born. "I wish I were taller; I wish I were shorter; I wish I were prettier; I wish I wasn't so pretty" (Honestly!); and on and on. Millions of dollars are spent each year in the endeavor of people to "change" their God-given bodies. On the other hand the truly happy person is the one who is perfectly satisfied with what God has given him—even though his body be crippled, or wracked with sickness; or pain. For, once again: "God gives and God takes away."

And the most despicable person is the one who "looks down"

on those *awful* cripples, or diseased, or "filthy" people. We do not think they ever *heard of there but for the grace of God go I*.

How grateful would we be if we only fully realized the body we have is a gift of God—and that, did He so will, we could be stricken with even worse afflictions than those from which we shy away.

There but for the grace of God go I.

8. *In our spiritual life*—We spoke at length about this in the beginning of this discussion. However let us remind ourselves once again: *our spiritual progress* or *our spiritual stasis* or *our relapses themselves* are in the hands of *God*. He gives the grace *both to will and to accomplish*.

Let us *hate* sin; but let us *love the sinner*. For there but for the grace of God go I. And being a child of God—whether saint or sinner, he needs our love and understanding more, the more of a sinner he is.

And in this spiritual life let us always be very conscious of the advice of Augustine: *"work as if everything depended upon you; trust as if everything depended upon God."* And if we fail again and again and again—let us never quit trying, for there is such a thing as a *cross of sin* and *Christ* carried the *first one*, and that, chum, is *good* Company!

And if in God's goodness we should have a lot of success, let us not be puffed up and look down on *any one*. For it will be then more than any other time that we need to always remember:

There but for the grace of God go I.

9. *In our A.A. life*—Slippers, slippers, slippers! They are like the poor—"we shall always have them with us." But no matter how big a slipper we may have in mind, remember, bud, *there but for the grace of God go I.* If we have never slipped it is only because *God so disposed*—remember? So how can we possibly be critical. "Ah," you say "he ain't ready—or he doesn't want it—or she doesn't try." Now are we sure about that? Have we looked *inside* him or her or those? And even *if* they aren't ready, or don't want it, or really aren't trying—*may we criticize?* We may possibly refuse to pamper them, honestly

156

knowing it isn't really helping them, *but may we criticize and gossip and condemn?* Not if we fully use the principle *there but for the grace of God go I.*

And it is in A.A. circles that we hear so often the knife-like criticisms leveled at the "neurotics"; the "psychotics"; the "bums"; the "worthless ones." Yes, we have even heard A.A.'s here and there speak of a certain type *"awful alcoholic"*—"beneath us"! To them we say: "A rose by any other name is still a rose"—and an alcoholic by any other name is still an alcoholic—yes, and *a man, a human being, by any other name* is still a *human being;* and a *child of God;* and *our brother under God our common Father,* and *whatever name we may attach to him or her or them*—the *truth* is

There but for the grace of God go I.

May we muse a bit? As we write these lines it is Christmas Eve—we are in a little motel as we usually are on Christmas Eve waiting for midnight Mass, traveling to groups and to A.A.s hither and thither and yon—but Christmas Eve so fits what we have been trying so hard to say:

"The air is crisp, and bright and cold
    The night is still and deep;
And over all, the Christmas star
    Keeps watch while we're asleep. . . .
Perhaps it was a night like this,
    When silence wrapped the earth,
That angel voices broke the calm
    To tell of Jesus' birth. . . .
And as the star led wise men then,
    May it now lead us, too—
And may the peace of God's own love
    Be always close to you;
And you—and you—and 'awful' you!"

For, you know something? If it were not for the "awful" ones of this earth—then why did Jesus come?

157

THE TWENTY-FOUR HOUR PROGRAM

"O God, guide these faltering steps today
lest I should fall!
Tomorrow? Ah, tomorrow's far away—
today is all...."

Many members of A.A. are amazed at the simplicity of and the effectiveness of *The twenty-four hour* program, which they seem to hear of for the first time. And it seems to work veritable miracles in those who find it difficult to stay sober the first weeks or months of A.A. Concentrating on the *present*, they find that *anyone can stay sober for one day*—and that is all we have to do, —ever.

However, we know that this principle of living the present and of leaving all of the past in the hands of God's Mercy and the future to His Providence has been the focal point of all Christian living and even of the philosophy extant long before the advent of Christianity.

Because of this, volumes have been written on it and poem after poem has been dedicated to its efficacy. Let's look at a few, —taken from all sorts of sources:

> "O God, guide these faltering steps today,
> Lest I should fall!
> Tomorrow? Ah, tomorrow's far away—
> *Today* is all.
> If I but keep my feet till evening time,
> Night will bring rest;
> Then stronger grown,
> Tomorrow I shall climb with newer zest.
> Oh, may I stoop to no unworthiness, in pain
> or sorrow, nor bear
> From yesterday one bitterness on to
> tomorrow!
> Then O God, help these searching eyes
> today the path to see;
> Be patient with my feebleness,
> The way is steep
> To Thee!"

"Oh Lord, if only for a day,
 I can be really good,
 Be always ready to obey
 And do the things I should
  Just for a day."

"Oh Lord, if only for a day,
 I can be more like You,
 If I can learn to walk Your way,
 And do the things You'd do,
  Just for a day."

"Oh Lord, if only for a day,
 I can take trials or fun
 Or anything that comes, and say,
 Not my will but Thine be done,
  Just for a day."

"Oh Lord, if only for a day,
 I can do this. Oh then,
 When each new morning comes, I'll pray
 For grace to persevere again
  Just for a day."

———————

"This day is mine to mar or make,
 God keep me strong and true;
 Let me no erring by-path take,
 No doubtful action do.

Grant me when the setting sun
 This fleeting day shall end,
 I may rejoice o'er something done,
 By richer by a friend.

Let all meet along the way
 Speak well of me tonight.
 I would not have the humblest say
 I'd hurt him by a slight.

164

Let there be something true and fine,
When night slips down to tell
That I have lived a day at a time
Not selfishly, but well."

"Lord, for tomorrow and its needs,
    I do not pray;
Keep me, my God, from stain of sin,
    Just for today.

Let me both diligently work,
    And duly pray;
Let me be kind in word and deed,
    Just for today.

Let me be slow to do my will,
    Prompt to obey;
Help me to mortify my flesh,
    Just for today.

Let me no wrong or idle word
    Unthinking say;
Set Thou a seal upon my lips,
    Just for today.

Let me in season, Lord, be grave,
    In season gay;
Let me be faithful to Thy grace,
    Just for today.

And if today, my tide of life
    Should ebb away;
Give me Thy grace divine,
    Dear Lord, *today.*

So, for tomorrow and its needs
    I do not pray;
But guide me, guide me, keep me, Lord,
    Just for today.

"Oh, how I love Thee, Jesus!
My soul aspires to Thee—
And yet for one day only my
Simple prayer I pray!
Come reign within my heart,
Smile tenderly on me,
Today, dear Lord, today!

But if I dare take thought of
What the morrow brings,
It fills my fickle heart with
Dreary dull dismay;
I crave, indeed, my God,
The cross and sufferings,
But only for today!

Soon shall I go afar
Among the holy choirs;
Then shall be mine the joy
That knoweth no decay;
And then my lips shall sing
To heaven's angelic lyres
The eternal glad today!"

And we pick at random a couple of musings on this same theme which A.A. groups incorporate into their cards, and pamphlets:

Just for today I will try to live through the day only, not tackling my whole life problem at once. I can do things for twenty-four hours that would appall me if I had to keep them up for a life-time.

Just for today I shall be happy. This assumes that happiness comes from within; it is not a matter of externals and accidental circumstances. I shall be happy therefore in spite of them.

Just for today I will try to adjust myself to *what is,* and not try to force everything to adjust to my own desires.

I will take my family, my business, my circumstances as they come; I'll fit myself to them.

Just for today I will take care of my body; I will exercise my mind, I will read something useful and something spiritual.

Just for today I will exercise my soul by prayer and do at least one act of sacrifice no matter how small. I shall do as least two things I don't want to do. I will keep all of God's laws and perform some small act of love for my neighbor.

Just for today I will try to go out of my way to be kind to someone I meet; I will be courteous; I will refrain from criticism; I will in no way try to change others.

Just for today I will have a program. I will have all set out the things I am to do and when. In this way I shall kill two big pests; hurry and indecision.

Just for today I will have a quiet time of meditation wherein I shall think of God and my neighbor and me. In it I shall relax and seek truth. Having found it I shall make a decision accordingly.

Just for today I shall be unafraid. Particularly I shall be unafraid to be happy, to enjoy what is good, what is beautiful, and what is lovely in life. And I shall—*just for today*—believe that those I love, love me and that God loves me *infinitely!*

There are two days in every week about which we should not worry, two days which should be kept free from fear and apprehension.

One of these days is *yesterday* with its mistakes and cares, its faults and blunders, its aches and pains. *Yesterday* has passed forever beyond our control.

All the money in the world cannot bring back *yesterday*. We cannot undo a single act we performed; we cannot erase a single word we say. *Yesterday* is gone.

The other day we should not worry about is *tomorrow* with its possible adversities, its burdens, its large promise and its poor performance; *tomorrow* is also beyond our immediate control.

Tomorrow's sun will rise, either in splendor or behind a mask of clouds—but it will rise. Until it does, we have no stake in *tomorrow,* for it is as yet unborn.

This leaves only one day—*today*. Any man can fight the battle of just *one day*. It is when you and I add the burdens of those two awful eternities—*yesterday* and *tomorrow* that we break down.

It is not the experience of *today* that drives men mad—it is the remorse or bitterness of something which happened *yesterday* and the dread of what *tomorrow* may bring.

Let us, therefore, live but one day at a time.

All of the above tells us over and over again that in living one day at a time that we thereby *bring life down to a size we can handle*. It is even much more necessary for the alcoholic, because the alcoholic on the average is endowed with a dreaming and planning type personality. For this reason he has *the habit* of re-living the past and of looking to the future. But when troubles and problems and alcoholism came along, his dreaming turned into remorse; and his plans were crystallized into stark fear of the future. Living *today* is his only salvation from insanity—especially in his early days of sobriety.

Even the army axiom emphasizes the value of living only for one day. One of the principles of good military practice is *"Divide and Conquer,"*—in other words *take one at a time*. There is many a man who could "whip" three men—*one at a time,* who wouldn't have a chance against all three at one time.

The same is to be said of problems. So many are frustrated in their attempt to solve their problems *because they try to solve all of them at once. One day at a time; one problem at a time; divide and conquer!*

Along the same line of thought we mentioned in our discussion of *"action"* that *"our future is determined not nearly so much by our plans for tomorrow as by our actions today."* *Today* is the all-important day.

The Scriptures also in many places point out to us the importance of *today.* And over and over again, expressly and between the lines they tell us *"now is the acceptable time."*

And when Christ taught His disciples to pray that most perfect of prayers, He told them to pray:

"Give us *this day* our *daily* bread."

And the past?

"Forgive us our trespasses as we forgive those who trespass against us." He gave us a simple "key" so we could put that *"awful"* past of ours away forever. He indicated in the above words that *"as we forgive"* so we will be forgiven. So if we always forgive everybody, then we can forget our own past— *it is forgiven* as *we have forgiven.*

And so in the Lord's Prayer, Christ wants us to live *today* for *today* accepting *His will today,* and leaving the past to His infinite Mercy and the future to His loving Providence.

So it was expected that A.A. in its endeavor to solve one of the most complicated and serious problems of the age, would incorporate somewhere along the line *the twenty-four hour program,* because the alcoholic more than the average person has been burdened with habits of worry, and fear, and indecision. And the average alcoholic on the day of his initial sobriety has far more (and serious) problems than the so-called "normal" individual. So for him more than for the average man or woman it becomes necessary to *"divide and conquer"*—take *one* problem at a time. And for him the *first* is *sobriety,* for without that solved he won't have a chance to solve any of his other problems anyhow.

For the alcoholic too, in his initial sobriety, it is of paramount importance to *live today,* less he be driven back to the bottle in useless *remorse* or by groundless *fears.*

And as sobriety begins to take shape and to mature, then it still is of prime importance for the alcoholic to practice the *twenty-four hour program* and live for the day in order to achieve and maintain serenity—for with remorse, or fear, or indecision,—there can be *no* serenity except perhaps a bit of the "frantic" variety!

So let us now consider the practical application of this principle and see how living *one day at a time* can influence—and for the better—all the areas of our living.

1. *In our home life*—Instead of worrying about the troubles we caused our family *yesterday,* making big plans for *tomorrow,* or *fearing* a recurrence of these same troubles *tomorrow,* we will *concentrate* on making our family happy *today.* And *one* good turn, one *good* laugh, one "I love you" *today* is worth a thousand protestations of remorse for yesterday and promises of improvement tomorrow.

And the problems of the home. They become so less heavy and burdensome if we take them *each in its turn today.* Even problems with our children become easier to solve and much less complicated if we would try to lead and teach and train *each* child as a separate personality instead of by "blanket" rules, and regulations, and threats, and discipline. *Divide and Conquer!*

Problems between husband and wife can be handled so much more easily and solved so much more surely *if* they are mutually attacked and analyzed and discussed together *one at a time,* and the *basic one first.*

Burdens in the home perhaps caused by the other (and we can't change them, remember?) can be borne more surely and more patiently if we *live one day at a time.* But if we begin to permit ourselves to think about having to *live a life time* with such a hardship it might "break" us. Or if we continually "bring up the past" to the other, there surely will be trouble.

We remember someone remarking many years ago, (he was a bachelor), in answer to why he had not married, "I couldn't quite picture myself living with or looking at the same person for a lifetime!" But he really wouldn't have had to do that—only *one day at a time!*

Now is the acceptable time.

2. *In our social life*—Social responsibilities are often shunned because of their endless "pressure." But actually this too is only a *one day affair*.

We also meet so many people along life's pathway whom we find it very difficult to be "nice" to. And this becomes even more difficult when we find we must come into contact with those same people over a long period of time. But they are the same people. It's that *long period of time* which makes the difficulty more burdensome. And yet it is not very difficult to be kind, and "nice" and tolerant to even the world's most irritating character *just this once*—is it now?

Then there is that "civic" affair which we have been "a-gonna" take part in for so long.

Now is the acceptable time.

3. *In our business affairs*—How few people would continue working at the same job day in and day out, if they permitted themselves to think much about having to do so *for a life-time!* We are convinced that in most cases where an individual quits one job after another the difficulty stems from this "burden" of thinking that he must do the work for a life-time.

The man in business, which he might like very well as far as his own work in it is concerned, would still probably fail if he permitted himself to begin worrying over yesterday's mistakes and losses and fearing tomorrow's problems. It is the business man who concentrates on *today* and the *problems* to be met *today* who is the successful business man.

The failure usually is the one who *borrows tomorrow's* income today and spends it on *tomorrow's* debt and end up with *nothing, today, nor tomorrow;* he's bankrupt.

4. *In our financial affairs*—As we mentioned in several previous discussions, *security* is not in dollars and cents; security is in *Divine Providence* coupled with *our faith* in Divine Providence. And therefore security is *today* even financially.

Let's take for example the one who is constantly worrying (we deliberately refrain from using the term "planning") about how in the world he is going to meet tomorrow's debts. He seems

171

not to realize that debt is not bringing the sheriff to the door today. "But it *might*," such will always answer. Yes, it *might*, but there *is* a *Providence*—and even if there was not, "let us never bid the sheriff good morning until he shows up!"

What does the person practicing the *twenty-four hour program* do under the above circumstances? He "programs" his payment *today;* he contacts his debtors *today;* he draws up his necessary "budget" *today;* then he goes to sleep knowing that there is no *unsolved* financial problem *today.* And how about the *morrow?* "God will provide"—for he knows he has done the foot-work *today.*

The prudent man who lives one day at a time works *today;* and saves *today;* for eventualities of tomorrow—*prudently.* But he does not waste endless hours figuring out how he is "going to make a million *tomorrow*" and thereby neglect the opportunities of *today.*

Now is the acceptable time.

5. *In our mental life*—The ability to *concentrate* is the result of having formed the habit of using our minds to think over *present* problems. It is dreaming of the potential tomorrow and about the attractive past that plays such havoc with concentration power. In such a person the mind, as a result of *habit*, continues to tend to "wander." The same can be said about the fears of tomorrow and the remorse of yesterday. Can we imagine a person filled with remorse *concentrating* on anything? That is the reason the neurotic—who is constantly in the past or the future with his remorses and fears, will tell us that *they can't even read.* Of course they can't. "They ain't here *now!*" The book or the newspaper or the magazine *is.*

If the human mind would expend one-tenth of the energy each day in solving the problems of *today* as it expends trying to find an unobtainable answer for tomorrow or re-hash what "might have been" yesterday—its possessor would be looked upon as a genius. In reality he would be.

The student in school who spends much of his "study" time *wondering what questions* will be asked in the exam, or fearing

172

he won't know the answers in the exam, *won't know the answers.* The student who knows the answers is the one who spends the time allotted for studying *each day* without a thought or care about the exams. He never has to 'cram" for an exam—he has studied it *all—one day at a time.*

And it is the one who takes the future or the past or both to bed with him who lies awake hour after hour in sleeplessness. Wondering, wondering, wondering! Instead of realizing: the day is past; the night is here; *now* is the time for sleep. G'nite! *Now is the acceptable time.*

6. *In our emotional life*—The one ingredient that is always present in every neurosis and which probably contributes more to the neurosis than any other one factor is *fear.* And *fear,* my friend, comes from what might or what will happen *tomorrow!* *Fear* of a *present* existent danger generates courage; but fear of the *future* or the *past* generates a beautiful neurosis. When a *present* danger comes along, in the average individual there is a saving reaction by nature. Adrenalin is poured into the blood; the heart pumps more blood and faster and from this comes more strength, more agility and more courage to act; but *chronic fear* of what might be or what might have been or what has been *depresses* the flow of adrenalin, slows the heart action and thus stymies action. This is why the chronic fearful neurotic seldom is interested in much motion. He just wants to sit—and worry.

So in the mechanics of emotion, it is *living in the present* that saves us from and cures us of neuroses. After all even psychotic "flight from reality" is a form of refusal to face *the present.*

There is no better nerve tonic in all the world than *living one day at a time.* And most nerve tensions come from thinking, consciously or otherwise, of what might be or what ought to be or what has been. The most unbearable tension there is, is remaining in between those two awful eternities: *Yesterday* with all its mistakes, and "goofs" and sins; and *tomorrow* with its threats, and fears—its large promise and poor fulfillment.

So important is this practicing *the twenty-four hour program* and *living one day at a time* in the emotional lives of human

173

beings that it is our sincere opinion that *most neuroses would be cured and/or avoided if everyone lived today—and today only. Now is the acceptable time.*

7. *In our physical life*—Aside from the damage done to the body itself by the neuroses mentioned above, that body is the healthiest which meets its needs *today* each day. In fact, one particular thing plays havoc in the physical lives of most people. And that is " the awful thought" of growing old. They are the ones who *do* age and age fast! But the one who puts living his old age off until his old age comes, by his very concentration on living in the present postpones the advance of age immeasurably.

Likewise the one who goes on and on each day expecting to get proper rest *tomorrow* will suddenly, sooner or later and soon at the latest, come to a time when he *can't* rest, yesterday, today nor tomorrow. He has reached a point of exhaustion and nature rebels. Rest *each* day *today* is what gives rest; and as all medical people will point out, *rest* is the greatest bodily tonic there is—but *regular* rest *each day*.

In a similar way the "work-work-work" fellow who is always taking his vacation and relaxing *tomorrow* also comes to the time when he finds he cannot relax nor even enjoy the finest of vacations.

The hypochondriac who always has a pill or a bottle of medicine at his elbow, got that way from *fearing* that he *might* get sick *tomorrow*. And today, psychosomatic medicine tells us that they have proven that many people *actually catch all the "symptoms"* of a cold or other illness simply because they *feared* catching one so much and *tried so intensely* to avoid it.

The fellow or gal who is in the hospital with a serious accident or sickness, will get well much faster *if* he concentrates on doing *today* all the doctors tell him to do to get well; he will progress much more slowly if he permits himself to *fear* he won't get well or won't get well very soon. Even in incurable cases, it has been found that the *living today* attitude enables him or her to live much longer and much happier than had he been in the "fearing" class of people.

Now is the acceptable time.

174

8. *In our spiritual life*—Guilt-complexes, scrupulosity, weak virtue, and sin all usually follow in the wake of the one who fails to live his spiritual life the best he can *today*.

The "guilt-complex" follows too much attention to that "awful past." Living *today*, on the other hand, would tell such a person the past is *gone* (and *real* gone!) ; God has forgiven it. He is not interested in our past. He is only interested in *how we are trying today*. There is no room for guilt-complexes in the face of that attitude. Let us never forget: God would much rather hear one *"I love You"* than a thousand *"I'm so sorry."* After all, wasn't it about Magdalen who has such a really "awful" past that Christ remarked; "Much is forgiven her because she has *loved* much." He didn't say because she felt so guilty!

Then there's scrupulosity. It is riddled through with *fears*. And fears come from concentrating on the awful past and the fearful future. Its effects upon the personality are devastating. But its cure lies in blindly following the advice of a competent advisor *today*,—each day.

Resolutions to do better so often begin to be burdensome and then break down completely because we attempt to practice virtue or avoid evil *for a "life-time" every day*. That is the reason *never* or *always* are two dangerous words in this resolution business. A resolution taken *today* and re-newed *each day* is so much more easily kept!

Now is the acceptable time.

9. *In our A.A. life*—We have mentioned many times how important for the alcoholic is the *twenty-four hour program.* And right in the beginning of sobriety, few alcoholics can picture a *life-time* without alcohol; but to go without a drink *today*, even the weakest find they can do that.

Matt Talbot was an alcoholic. Before he died, however, he lived for forty years not only sober but lived a saintly life. But he too, in the beginning of his sobriety, tells us that the priest to whom he went to take the pledge advised him to take it only for a short period of time and to then renew it each time. This priest evidently understood the alcoholic. And as we consider the subsequent events in Matt's life and his frequent returns for consultation *on the advice of the priest* we sometimes suspect the priest even knew a little about the A.A. therapy although A.A. was not yet born at the time (1885). But the necessary therapy for arresting alcoholism was known to a few who were perhaps inspired by the Good Lord to help alcoholics all through the centuries. But it took A.A. to crystallize the therapy and to make it known to the world. And one of the principal ingredients of that program for sobriety is the necessity for the alcoholic of *staying sober one day at a time,* especially during the early days— the first year—of his sobriety.

Then in our association in the group. Others wouldn't irritate us nearly so much if we took each meeting—*one at a time,* instead of thinking over all that so-and-so said or did at the meeting throughout the week.

And many of us would not have so many unsolved problems left if we would only begin *today* with the biggest one and solve or accept it *today.*

Now is the acceptable time.

So—let us bring this discussion to a close with what has turned out to be a very thought provoking statement relative to *today.* It is in the form of three questions and we have printed it on the fly-leaf of our Retreat booklet. This is it:

> *And don't forget!*
> *You'll more surely reach your goal*
> *If you rightly answer and with care:*
> *Who am I—today?*
> *Where am I going—today?*
> *What am I doing to get there—today?*

RESENTMENTS

"Whom the gods would destroy...."

In analyzing the various principles of Alcoholics Anonymous we now come to one which has come up for more discussion, and which is at the bottom of more difficulties than any of all the ones listed. This principle is:

"The Danger of Resentment—Self-pity"

In the alcoholic, "frustration begot resentment, resentment begot self-pity, self-pity begot drinking, and drinking begot frustration, and frustration begot resentment, and resentment begot self-pity," and on and on and on—in an unending cycle, until faced with the three-pronged choice: sobriety or insanity or death. And then we chose sobriety in A.A. And we learned the principle that: *If the alcoholic repeated any part of the cycle, the entire cycle would repeat itself, "in toto."*

We learned through the above principle that to the alcoholic, *resentment and self-pity* would always remain his number one twin-enemy—*no matter how long sober.* And this means that, *if he permits himself to indulge in resentment or self-pity too frequently or for too prolonged periods of time, he will automatically set off the compulsion to drink. In short: An alcoholic cannot tolerate resentment.*[1]

If he does, there automatically will begin the old pattern: "stinking-thinking; drinking-thinking; *drinking."* And so also will it be with any part of the cycle above: If the alcoholic takes a drink, he will automatically and ultimately become full of resentment, etc., etc. We do not know *why* this happens, but *we do know from long, long experience that it does happen.*

In fact the experience of the race, although somehow little is ever written or said about it, is that *at the bottom of most troubles*

---

[1] In the writer's opinion self-pity is nothing more than resentment "turned inside out." Self-pity is the coward's type of resentment, and when such a person finds himself frustrated in vindicating his resentment, he turns "inside to himself" and becomes full of self-pity. So from this point on we shall only use the term "resentment" and in it include also "self-pity."

181

in life, including our spiritual life, *is resentment.* So important is this truth that *he who controls resentment* (and by this term we include any of the thousands of degrees of resentment from a mere "dislike" to a positive and malicious "hatred") *controls life here and hereafter.* Ninety-eight percent of all "troubles" in the lives of all people stem in some way, directly or indirectly, from resentments. And, in alcoholics—it is *without exception* the prelude to the bottle.

Now if this be true, then let us try to answer three very pertinent questions: What is resentment? Where does resentment come from? And what are we going to do about resentment?

The answers to all three of these questions are contained in the analysis of the term itself. "Resentment" comes from the Latin words "re" and "sentire". "Sentire" means "to feel" and "re" means "again." Therefore a resentment is born when one "re-feels" any injury to pride, or any "hurt" to one's ego. And so, when anything happens or exists that injures our pride, we are "hurt," "irritated," "angry" but not yet resentful. This injury grows into a resentment only because we "re-feel" it; we "nurse" it; we "mull over" it; we "dig around" it;—in short we "*cultivate*" it. We are injured, and we "infect" the wound because we "re-sentire": we "re-*feel*" it. And once infected, once the resentment has taken hold, then only a "positive antibiotic" will cure it or eliminate the poison. And in the area of hatred, toward which all resentment tends, there is only one antibiotic: that is *love.*

From this short analysis *three very important truths become apparent.*

1. *We get resentments from pride. We will always have this tendency, for pride will be with us until we are dead. But we can minimize this tendency and eliminate many an occasion by the practice of humility*—the opposite of pride.

Many people in this world wrongly think that they can "eliminate" various of their passions, e.g., pride. Or as the story goes, a certain teacher of the spiritual life was teaching her proteges to "slay" one passion a year! This can't be done! We have seven basic passions, seven basic "drives to action," seven basic "human tendencies." It is "the law of the flesh fighting against the law of the spirit" mentioned by Saint Paul. But they *cannot be eliminated.* They are necessary for life, for action. They are *good* in themselves, but *tend* to get out of control. It is our job to *control them.* Closing our eyes to them is what psychiatry calls "repression" and is responsible for many neuroses. Let's take an example or two.

We all have the passion of lust: sex. To deny we have such drive or desire is "repression"—it is not healthy, and leads to neurotic behavior. *But* that does not mean we should therefore *indulge in sex. Sex indulgence never cured a neurosis.* But it does mean that we must *admit consciously that we have the sex drive,* and then *either* 1) use it according to reason in lawful marriage as indicated by our Maker *or* 2) *abstain willfully* in the single state. These two are *"control"*—by 1) reasonable use or by 2) total abstinence. *Both are healthy practices,* for "abstinence" is *not* "repression."

Likewise we all tend to "get angry." (They say there are people in this world who *never* get angry or irritated. But then they also say there are people in this world who are too *dumb* to commit sin! But *we* ain't in that class, bud!) That is a *good* tendency. It gives "drive" and "push" and "initiative" and all those things that go for successful living. *But* when it is *indulged in as a door to frustration, and vindication, and self-pity,* then it has gone "against reason" and also leads to neurosis—and in the alcoholic to *resentment and drinking.*

So we never even try to *rid* ourselves of these "tendencies." They will be with us until we are dead. *But* we can gradually *control and direct them* by *the practice of the opposite virtue.*

We *can by practice of the opposite* virtue achieve at least a modicum of control, minimize or cut down the number of occasions, and in the matter of pride, and "injured pride," which is the seed of resentment, we *can go far in cutting down the number of times and the severity of these "injuries" if we day in and day out practice the opposite* virtue of humility. Let's not forget: *"The greater a guy or gal I think I am, the less it is going to take for someone to dispute that idea!"*

Therefore as a practical corollary to the above truth, we learn that *we cut down the number of chances of becoming resentful in direct ratio to how much true humility we acquire.*

2. *Resentments take hold and grow within us by "re-feeling" the injuries.* Therefore *they cannot remain or grow if we "let go" of them and refuse to think about them, refuse to mull over them, refuse to "re-feel" the irritation.*

Most irritations would evaporate quickly if on every occasion of being "angered" or "hurt" all parties involved would immediately *dismiss the incident from their minds.* But how often is it not the opposite? Instead of dismissing the injury at once, we hold on—we think it over—we "re-feel" it . . . over and over again. Then in twenty-four hours what was only a "scratch" has become a deep, dark, dangerous *resentment.* "What was that he said?" "Why, he meant. . . ." "The so-and-so!" "I'll get even!" And—then "resentment begot. . . .!" Remember?

What to do? *Let it go!* He said thus-and-thus. So what? Refuse to re-feel"!

You know sumpin'? If someone calls us a "so-and-so," we either are or we aren't! If we are, that's that! If we aren't, then why become one by "getting 'mad' about it"?

3. *We eliminate those resentments already contracted not by wishing them away, but only by the practice of positive actions of love.*

We must *do* good to those whom we resent. We must speak *well* of those whom we resent. We must practice some positive *action* for love of them—*and love is the willingness to do for.* Otherwise we will continue to resent, we will continue to dislike,[1] we will continue to hate—no matter how long or how deeply we might *wish* we didn't resent or dislike or hate.

And here again, the more consistent our *habit* of love is in our daily lives, the less chance for resentments to take hold; and

---

[1] There is a form of emotional "dislike" which is not from injured pride, but simply a reaction of nature's law of attraction and repulsion. It is like the positive and negative poles in the inanimate world. So certain people we like; but a certain few we will not "like," no matter what we do. What to do? Just don't try to "like them"—love them!

also the more easily and quickly will they disappear when they do, on occasion, crop up.

In A.A. we find, especially in the beginning of our sobriety, that we are not very adept at the practice of humility and love. We have lived for so long with our drinking pattern that we have picked up pathological habits of pride and hatred and resentment. We are "loaded" with them. And now we find that we can use a few extra "natural" helps to sorta "protect" our touchy, alcohol-tenderized natures until we are more able to pursue a stable course along the path of virtue, particularly until we are more able to "control" our hurts more consistently. And so we picked up various helps which we like to call "gimmicks"—which are nothing more than wise little sayings which if ingrained into our consciousness will serve as a suit of armor against "the slings and arrows of outrageous fortune."

The first of these "gimmicks" which we throw out for your perusal is:

Expect criticism—No matter who we may be, no matter how important or competent we may be, no matter how good either we or our motives are, *if we do anything in life we will be criticised. But* any criticism is in no way a measure of the value, sincerity or morality of our actions. Now, if we meet each day in life *expecting criticism,* then, when it comes (and it *will!*) we will not be surprised, nor hurt, because we were *looking* for it—and we can even reach a state of mind wherein we so look for these criticisms that rather than upsetting us or irritating us *we enjoy them.*

The writer learned this first "gimmick" in the early days of his speaking and writing. And, altho for some time criticisms here or there did "irritate," he now so looks for them in every area that he enjoys them, like the funny papers on Sunday morning! He would almost feel "lost" without criticisms levelled at him.

"Gimmick" number two: *There is in every group of human endeavor at least one who is against everything and everybody. God puts them there—to give all of the rest of the group a chance to practice tolerance, and patience, and kindness, and understanding, and love.*

With this knowledge, it will be a pushover to tolerate and overlook all the diatribes of that "guy" or "gal" in your group who is *always* "agin" everything and who never lets anyone's work go by unchallenged, and who, in short, just doesn't seem to like anybody (including himself). They are to be pitied, not blamed. They are "psychopathic." But they are filling their "niche" in life which demands *all* parts to make the machine of life go on: yes, even the "nuts," and the bolts—and the ubiquitous "crank"!

One such fellow died. At his wake there was overheard the following remark: "Poor John (his name was John Doe) he won't like God."

The next "gimmick" to help protect that "tender" ego of ours is:

Let the other fellow get mad—We are in A.A. (at least we presume most of us are) primarily to stay sober and secondarily to achieve and maintain happiness. Both sobriety and happiness are dependent one on the other. We can't be happy unless we stay sober; we won't stay sober unless we are happy. *Therefore* when someone "irritates" us, or criticises us or talks about us, *let the other fellow get mad.* He is unhappy. All people who criticise or gossip or slander are basically very unhappy people. We, on the other hand, want to be happy. So let's stay happy. Let them get upset or talk or what have you. We simply ignore it. We stay happy. We avoid resentment.

Some years ago when the writer arrived to speak at a large A.A. Conference, someone came "a-running" with the report that "someone was talking *awful* about us" and the "reporter" thought *we* should do something about it. We replied:

"*We* do something about it? Why should we? We're *happy,* and we are going to stay that way. He's unhappy. *Let him get mad.*" (Which he *did*!)

Another "gimmick":

Words can never hurt nor change us if we don't let them. And we won't let them if we are more concerned about what and how we are doing instead of what people are saying—for God alone can approve or disapprove, absolve or condemn.

186

What was that saying we heard in our early school days? "Sticks and stones may break our bones but words can never hurt us." Someone has criticised? Okay, what is that to us? *Let them criticise*, we will simply pursue our way of living happily and soberly and completely oblivious of any verbal ammunition that may be hurled our way. *Words* aimed our way will remain a mere "mirage" provided we neither run towards nor from their vocalizer.

"Gimmick" number five:

Know thyself—An honest inventory of our own shortcomings will go far in eliminating that tendency to "take up" everything that is said about us; or to "strike back" at critics. For if we are honest, we are pretty sure to accept *all* things in life more passively and readily. Like the story goes which tells of a fellow in tatters and rags, sitting on the curbstone, a "leetle" bit drunk, who was heard to mutter in a flash of honesty, as a very successful and wealthy gentleman passed in his limousine, *"There but for me go I."* We think he's got something there!

We will content ourselves with one more "gimmick," and one that will go far in encouraging anyone to keep on doing things *no matter who says what*, for:

If we get a kick in the pants it can mean only one thing—we are still in front!

Someone said: "Criticism is the unconscious tribute mediocrity and failure pay to success." This explains our "gimmick." There is another way of putting it: "Every knock is a boost." (A school boy misquoted the above to read: "Every knock is a boast." He wasn't far wrong at that!). Get angry? How silly. Rather take a bow!

And now we shall give you a bag to keep all your "anti-resentment gimmicks" in. It consists of a bag and string to tie them all together. It belongs to each. Maybe we could call it a "gimmick-chorus." But anyway here it is, stolen from "Easy Does It."

How important can it be?

And if you want to see what we mean, just quietly sit down and think over all the irritations and resentments that have taken hold on you for the past month or so. *Most of them were over something that actually disappears when exposed to the importance of the over-all picture of living happily and soberly and justly—day in and day out.*

So in *all our affairs* we *practice:* 1) *humility* in order to *avoid* irritations; 2) *refusing to "re-feel" any irritation to avoid resentment; and* 3) *love—actions of love to eliminate resentments.*

1. *In our home life*—Humility would tell us that we are *not* the most important guy or gal in our home relationship. Wisdom would tell us that being alcoholic we simply *cannot tolerate resentment.* Therefore we positively will *refuse to "re-feel"* any hurt, apparent or real, from the other members of the family. And love *demands* practice—*actions of love,* day in and day out.

The attitude of humility will avoid many "hurts" or "irritations" for others in the family. The smaller our "ego" the less chance there is for it being "hit"—therefore the fewer upsets, irritations, etc. But being human and since it is impossible to "eliminate" the ego there will be irritations, and fusses, and hurt feelings. The family who is free from these just doesn't exist! It is part and parcel of life but we do not *have to nurse these hurts.*

To avoid resentments? *We simply refuse to "re-feel"* any hurt, or irritation, or slight, or whatever may be directed towards us—actually or apparently. And a conscientious regular inventory of our own selves will help immensely toward accomplishing this ability to "overlook" whatever is said or done to or about us. Then, no "re-sentire" . . . no "re-feel"—*no resentment!*

To eliminate those resentments already picked up? *We simply must practice love!* There just "ain't" no other way. And love means *doing for the* other—*love does not mean "making love."* This latter, this indulgence in passionate loving, in sex *is the reward of love and an expression of love, only if indulged in to please or increase the happiness of, or to satisfy the other in marriage.* Sex pleasure, sex satisfaction is the *human, fleshly* part of love placed there by the Creator to bind *"two in one flesh."* But when this is indulged in a selfish way—because *we want it,* it will ever so gradually sap the vitality of both attraction and love. But if indulged in because the *other wants it,* it will be the icing on the cake, ever so gradually making one's love more and more attractive and beautiful.

But like the cake itself which provides that on which the icing is able to exist so attractively, *you* "gotta" have cake or the icing will fall to pieces and have nothing on which to exist. So with love: unless there is "cake," unless there is *giving, doing for—day in and day out*—there just won't be any icing because there is nothing upon which to have it. And this "cake" of love consists in *actions done for the other for no other reason than to please them or simply because you love them.* They who practice this *giving* regularly will never be troubled with many resentments—neither with those that are already there, nor with those which might try to creep in. Okay, lad or lassy, *just how long has it been since you actually did something for your husband, or wife, or children just because you loved them?* Well, then, what do you expect ? ? ?

Let's always remember, relative to *resentments* in the home: Passion without actions of love, *will, whether one likes it or not, gradually dissipate both love and passion; but actions of love faithfully practiced, day in and day out, will continually replenish and cultivate and perfect, as far as possible in this vale of tears, both passion and love.* Try it!

2. *In our social life*—Here again the attitude of humility will tell us that we are not the most important, or even a "little important" person among our acquaintances—and no matter who we are *we must expect criticism,* and use all the "gimmicks" we can to avoid irritations. So for our social intermingling with our fellowman, we will find a "special gimmick" which should help us very much to avoid those "hurts," etc., which seem to constantly try to upset our sensitive natures. This "gimmick" is: *always do the best we can, never expecting praise or gratitude.* Why? Well, humans being what they are, you just won't get much of either—so no disappointment, no "upset." Remember, what the Lord once said, "I will repay." So, let's *not expect much from people.* (They are all too expecting from you!) A good conscience and the approval of God will be the never-failing result of the habit of looking to God instead of to people. Even though "the best of men likes a wee bit of praise now and again."

189

There was one individual who claimed he had reached this habitual practice of never looking for praise—claiming that all such "ran off him like water off a duck's back." One time after a rather successful and well-accomplished action, a little old lady came to heap praises upon him.

"Madam," he said, "all that runs off just like water off a duck's back."

"Yes, I know," replied the lady, "but oh, how the duck likes it!"

To refuse to *look* for it is possible; to refuse to *"like"* it is impossible. We are human.

Yet how many resentments begin with those so-called "slights" in not being praised or being thanked. How often we hear: "And to think they *didn't even thank me!*

"Don't expect from people."

And if by chance we *have* already picked up resentments, against certain of our fellow men, then there is only one way to get rid of them: *Do something good for them, or to them or* in short *practice* love—*actions* of love.

3. *In our business affairs*—No man in the business world ever had much business-acumen if resentments clouded his thinking. And in business we will be open to many resentments if we get the idea that we are particular "big-shots" in that business, or in our office. The "bigger" we blow ourselves up to be in our minds, the better the "target" for all with whom we come in contact. We must simply, in business, too, adopt an attitude of humility which would tell us to "work with" others, and for others, and not demand always to work "over" others, not emphasize that we are "boss" or "the one who dictates the policy" or the "one who makes the decisions." Such type people seldom go very far in the business world; and, if alcoholic,they just *won't* go very far in the world of sobriety. The "boss" who lets all the world know he is the boss is a "sitting duck" for criticisms, etc., without end. You know them—*big* name-plates; name always qualified *"in charge," "manager,"* etc., etc.; or unique eye-catching names " J. Jonathan Doe, Esq."

The successful business man? He has an honest knowledge of his limitations, doesn't "brag" about his acumen, but "uses" it instead; he has an *attitude of humility*. One never hears of his success save from somebody else. When he needs advice, he calls in an "expert" realizing his need.

'Words" or "criticisms" cannot throw out of focus what he himself knows of himself. He is seldom irritated.

The "failure"? No matter what actual success he might have had in business, to hear him tell it "day in and day out" *he should have been the most successful!* "Irritations"—"resentment"?— just contradict him and watch the explosion!

And if we are resentful of someone in our business, or office? There is only one answer—actions of love—*do* something *for* them.

4. *In our financial affairs*—Resentments are costly! Remember when we "spent just for spite"? "I'll show 'em, I'll get even, I'll just *spend it all!*" And then just add up the "cost" on that last spree!

Whatever we have financially or materially, we *have it because God gave it to us*. That is honesty—that is an attitude of humility. You say you *worked* for it? Well, then, who gave you the ability, the opportunity, the health, etc., to do so? ? ? Hmmm?

This attitude will keep us from being too upset or irritated or hurt when we "lose" some money or material things. What was it Job said? "The Lord gave, the Lord hath taken away!" No wonder he was so patient—or should we be "mad" at what the Lord does?

Then there is love: which tells us to *share what we have with those who have it not. Give!* That's what God gave it to us for. Particularly to those *whom we resent!* It works!

5. *In our spiritual life—*
Resentments, O resentments, we deplore
If it weren't for resentments, we'd be
So happy and so holy—forever more!

"Lousy" poetry, but one of the greatest truths in the spiritual life, for it is our conviction that 99.99% of all spiritual woes and sins and failures *begin with resentment!* And the more we speak to people with spiritual problems and sins, the more we see the *resentments.* And yet, on analysis we do not ever remember of having heard a talk, or sermon, or retreat conference on *resentments!* That is, until we came to A.A. And as the years pass along, more and more we can see *resentments* as the *cause of* and *occasion of* most spiritual disintegration.

Let's look at a few:

a) Drinking, drunkenness, alcoholism—*usually took hold in the soil of discontentment, resentment.*

b) Philandering, divorce, etc.—*usually began in resentment. Most men (and women) who started an affair with another woman (or man) first became discontented with or resentful towards the other!* It was not usually because some "good looking lass" tempted one to follow. They *first* turned against or away from the wife—then anyone is a pushover for any "dame" that might happen along. Resentments pushed *love out,* and the vacuum drew lust in.

c) Laziness—resentment toward working or working as we must, or just towards life, albeit unconsciously. It is the background of every "loafer," of every neglect of duty, and of every just plain "bum."

d) Gluttony in eating—psychiatrists now tell us, and it is evident to those who have dealt with such, there are many who *over-eat just for spite, or* because of *boredom and discontentment and resentment.*

e) Jealousy—this passion *feeds on resentment. Jealousy* could never get hold without resentment coming first. (We speak not of "normal" jealousy, but of that "extreme type" which spiritual writers would label "sinful jealousy" and which psychiatry would call "abnormal"—it leads to revenge, etc., etc.)

f) Omission of prayers—how many who had such a good start in the spiritual life, gave up their prayers, and of course their spiritual living, *because of resentment....* "God never hears *my* prayers,"—"For other people the birds *sing"!*

192

g) Quitting church—most such cases happen because of "what the pastor said, or did" or "some of the other members of the congregation said or did" ... Resentments!

h) Giving up belief in God—because of the pathological resentments towards life, or men, or God. . . .

All of which brings out into full view and gives a depth of new meaning to that saying of one of the philosophers centuries ago. His name was Plato: *"whom the gods would destroy, they first make mad"!*

The *prime enemy of alcoholics, the prime enemy of all spiritual life—resentments!*

But you know something? We should have known that long, long ago. For it was long, long ago, when the Lord told us: "Thou shalt love the Lord thy God with thy *whole heart* ... this is the *greatest commandment."* Then why should we not have realized that the *opposite of love, which is hate and begins with resentments,* is the *most dangerous enemy to all spiritual life?*

6. *In our emotional life*—We can not tolerate resentments! How many ills and woes of the emotions—begin with resentments! Nervousness, upsets, tension, fears, and phobias of all types come when our emotions turn away from the realities of life and, because of resentments, seek outlandish outlets. The alcoholic? *The outlet,* the bottle! *"Let the other fellow get mad!" "Expect criticism!"* And all the "gimmicks" will rush in to help us attain and preserve an evenness of the emotions, *if* we *use* them, and *practice them*—day in and day out.

And *love?* It is, *when true,* the great leveller of life and emotion. That love which upsets emotion is not love but either infatuation or lust. *Actions* of love will rid our emotions of resentful tendencies—a "hangover" for our drinking days!

7. *In our physical life*—Ulcers and tiredness and migraine and allergies and "pains" in the "neck"—and physical ills of every type, *come from resentment*—either conscious or subconscious. With the advent of psychosomatic medicine, it has been learned that more than 50% of *all* apparent physical distress

193

comes from either known or hidden mental attitudes—mostly resentment. (Many such ills have been found to be from *discontentment—resentment against our role in life:* our profession, social status, nationality, even *our being a "man" or a "woman"!* More and more maladjusted people in marital relations are finding the *cause is resentment against living the role of "man" or "woman" which God has given to us.*)

Many people have actually cured a "pain in the neck" ("wryneck" in medical language) by removing the cause, by changing their job and thus eliminating the boss or fellow worker who had *actually* been a *"pain in the neck."*

Many too, they say, have had heart attacks as a result of resentments. Under date of July 25, 1955, we read:

"Philadelphia—Want to avoid a heart attack... ? 'Avoid resentments,' Dr. David Gelfand stated here today.

"Dr. Gelfand heads the cardiac work evaluation unit at Philadelphia General Hospital and in 3½ years of careful study has examined 438 persons.

"He said 46% of the patients—each examined by a cardiologist, a vocational counsellor, a medical social worker and a psychiatrist have a psychological factor present.

"Resentment that is not expressed or removed goes into the cardiovascular system, where it tightens the blood vessels. Continued insult to blood vessel tissue results in permanent hypertension—and then, a heart attack."

(Well that might be a comfort to us in A.A. Maybe many times those binges prevented a heart attack! ? ?)

In the alcoholic—a "bottle-attack"!

And now speaking of *love*—families who *practice actions of love* are proven to be *healthiest families!* And who usually is healthier than a person in love?

8. *In our thought life*—Mental aberrations, mental illness, forgetfulness, etc., etc., *come from resentments*—which cause retreat from reality. The answer? *Refuse to retain* the *thought.* And now then that *love "business."* "It's those we love we think

194

about"—*lovingly!* No room for negative, resentful thinking! Simple, isn't it? ? ?

9. *In our A.A. life*—Dissension in groups, slips, gossip, slander, splits, and what have you—all stem from *resentments.* To the alcoholic—*resentment retained means drinking*—there is no other answer. But how about those in the groups who seem to thrive on resentment; those who are constantly "mad at" or "against" something or someone? Well, they are "drunks" not alcoholics. They have not the "compulsive" factor of drink. They can remain resentful day in and day out—and stay sober. God bless them—He put them there for the rest who can not tolerate resentment, to have opportunity to practice patience, and kindness, and love—and to use "gimmick" after "gimmick" for protection until one achieves a *habit* of patience and tolerance and love! (Remember, there's at least *one* in every group.)

The alcoholic *cannot* tolerate resentment. That is why so much of the A.A. program is aimed at achieving those attitudes which will protect us from resentment—attitudes or *humility* ("there are no big-shots in A.A., no seniority, no graduation, etc., etc." "Anonymity" is to *give humility*) ; and attitudes of *love* ("this is a *give* program," "you don't have to *like* the "dope," but you can *love* him.")

> *Resentments,* O resentments we deplore—
> If it weren't for resentments, we'd be
> So happy, and so holy *and so sober forevermore!*

And as a parting "gimmick": *It takes a real man and a real woman to love; any "nincompoop" can hate!*

So, there you have it.

EASY DOES IT

"One step at a time enough for me....
Easy Does It...."

When an alcoholic drank, his day was usually one round of *pressure, speed, stubborn determination, unbending aim, and blind rushing* through life, irrespective of the outcome. And when one begins to flee realities of living, each step is with increasing speed and with each step vision narrows. In A.A. we learn that neither speed nor pressure, nor stubborn determination, nor unbending aim, nor blind rushing *every achieved mastery.* Mastery comes in *easy* stages, *for mastery of the whole is only achieved through mastery of all of its parts.* Even in taking the twelve steps we learn: *one step at a time enough for me—easy does it.* We learned that Life is to be "sipped"—not "gulped" if we wish happiness and sobriety. Our primary job in life is *us, but* we have a lifetime to do it. Mastery is not achieved in an hour, nor in a day, nor in a month, nor in a year. Mastery comes only through long, patient and *repeated* practice—day in and day out, hour in and hour out, minute in and minute out. *Concerted and continued practice without concern* is achieved by applying in *all of our affairs* the next principle:

"Easy Does It."

The principle of *Easy Does It* was probably the first principle we heard in A.A. Remember the first meeting or soon thereafter? We were all "hot and bothered" and anxious about so many things. We wondered about this and we wondered about that. "How long will it take?"; ... "What do I do?" ... "How about my family? My job?" and other queries of the anxious soul—too numerous to mention. Then it was that someone of the group came along and said, "Look, bud, you didn't get drunk overnight, so you won't get sober overnight. You're sober today, so take your time—*Easy Does It!*"

And thus we first heard the principle so necessary to the alcoholic for happy, sober and sane adjustment to life. This is the principle which will enable the sensitive, stubborn and yet perfectionistic alcoholic to learn to handle pressure, and tension and opposition in every day living without alcohol.

Pressure is bad for any human. It wrecks happiness and oftentimes health—witness the *T-V* "stars" falling by the way-side as a result of "pressure of living in front." And there are only *three ways to handle* pressure in life:

1) Flee reality by having yourself a lovely nervous break-down or psychosis.

2) Flee reality *via the bottle in excessive drinking and/or alcoholism.*

3) *Accept reality and in doing so learn to give with the punch through practicing the principle of Easy Does It.* Since some of us have had our share already of number one and two, let's get along and see how we can use and practice—day in and day out—*Easy Does It.*

The principle of *Easy Does It is based on a truth that is age-old.* It is based upon God's own workings in the world and with the world and with us. Axioms arising therefrom are many: "The mills of time grind *slowly . . .*" and "Rome was not built in a day" are but two. So let's see how it works with God and *why* He uses it.

God took seven days, which we now know were actually "eons" or ages, to *create the world—Easy Does It.* He took *centuries to prepare for sending His Son into the world to redeem it—Easy Does It,* and *why?*

Because *God's ultimate purpose is to have man happy with Him eventually in eternity—*and *that,* bud, is *forever!—Easy Does It.* So it matters little to Him about time, or obstacles, or changes in time—*as long as He will attain His end-purpose, His ultimate purpose of all creation—that man be happy with Him— eternally,* no matter *what* be the vicissitudes of time or human failure, or mistake or sin in between—*Easy Does It!*

There exists today another force, another power—of evil— which also proceeds along this self-same principle. The force is *communism. The ultimate purpose is world-domination of all people,* so what difference does a "side-war" mean, or a saving face, or a Geneva, or a few more years to prepare? *Easy does it.* And it matters little whether Stalin, or Malenkov, or Bulganin, or Khrushchev or who have you achieves this avowed purpose—*Easy Does It.*

In all of life's actions and strivings the secret of practicing Easy Does It is to emphasize the ultimate!

How the alcoholic failed in this! All of our drinking days, and with some of us for most of our lives, and with a few of us, all of our lives, we *demanded everything.*

1—*Right now....*
2—*In a hurry....*
3—*Determined to achieve....*
4—*Scheming to win....*
5—*Frantic to accomplish....*
6—*Panicky lest we lose....*
7—*Fearful of the outcome....*

The end-purpose? The ultimate? We had none, much less emphasized it. So we always landed in a mess—we failed—we got drunk—we became alcoholic *but still demanding, determined etc...* and then, at the bottom of failure, we came to A.A., still frantic, and panicky and *full* of fear. And then *we* heard: *Easy Does It*—emphasize the ultimate—*stay sober—all the rest will follow*—in God's time and in His way.

And then we began to learn *patience, and acceptance, and tolerance, and thoroughness,* without hurry and without procrastination, because we learned that the first meaning of *Easy Does It in practice is do it* when it is to be done.

And in order to help both the new ones and the old ones and ourself to achieve more happiness and serenity; in order to help all of us use more effectively this very simple though basic principle of sobriety and happy adjustment to life; and finally to help all to "handle pressure," we have staked out fifteen "road signs" which point and lead down the pathway of the principle of *Easy Does It.*

Here they are:

1. *If you can't go through an obstacle, then go around it.*

The signpost usually means: "You're on the wrong road, bub, better change direction; or take the by-pass, the "main drag's got a parade on it already."

There are many vocations, many avocations, many jobs, many ways to earn a living. So if there is an *obstacle* either in us or our field of endeavor, we are wise, and we will remain much more calm, if we simply *change* instead of being doggedly determined to do what we're doing *no matter who or what gets in the way.* And if we look real close at the "small print" below this signpost, we will read a very, very wise corollary: *"It is not cowardly to quit when you know you're whipped."*[1] A very famous prize fighter, a world's champion, who gave words to that wisdom many years ago, to a chap who had, in the face of a terrific beating, stuck out the full number of rounds. It was before the days of the referee stopping a fight, when one is evidently beaten. The world's champion? It was Benny Leonard. The lad who was the recipient of the advice? A member of A.A. who told the writer of the incident.

Easy Does It.

2. *If you can't solve a problem—accept is.*

How much tension and pressure and anxiety are the end-product of forever trying to solve an unsolvable problem. There are many such in life. To name but a few: "alcoholism," "old age," "loss of a loved one," "all losses," etc., etc. The corollaries to this signpost? "Don't cry over spilt milk," "never indulge in '*if*' thinking"—"if I had done this or that"—the reality is *we didn't.* So—*accept it.*

Easy Does It.

3. *If you can't finish today—there will be a tomorrow—if it be God's will that you do it.*

We have another principle in A.A. which says *"twenty-four hours at a time,"* but that doesn't mean to try to get *everything* finished today! It is never *how much*, but *how well*—for if we

---

[1] We here speak of "methodology" and materially. In the realm of the spiritual life and of sobriety, there is no quitting—no one is *ever* whipped—for God *will* eventually give success—either here or hereafter if we keep trying.

can't finish today—there will always be a tomorrow, if it be God's will that we finish it. And if it be God's will—time will be given. The "fine print" on this post? "God willing" ... Plan? yes, God willing.... Attempt big things? yes, God willing.... Accomplish big things? yes, God willing. So concentrate on doing today, not on finishing....

Easy Does It.

4. *Hurry never produced a masterpiece.*

Every watch an artist, or a sculptor, or writer? It is true they have completely "conceived" their "finished product," but then they very carefully and deliberately work, one by one, on all of its parts—with care, and precision, and giving time, much time to each. Never was a painting "swished out" overnight! Never was a sculpture "hacked out" in a jiffy! Never was a good book written in shorthand! *"Hurry never produced a masterpiece."* Corollary? "Carve, don't hack!"

Easy Does It.

5. *Time can and will solve all problems.*

We spoke about God's ultimate. When that is reached, *all* problems will be solved and ended; all wounds will be healed; all anxiety and tension and pressure will be over. So with patience and persistence—*time will solve and heal.* The corollary here comes from the Scriptures: *"Wait* on me," says the Lord.

Easy Does It.

6. *If you don't succeed at first—try again.*

Robert Bruce supposedly was the originator of this saying. The story narrates how he had been beaten in battle time and again. This time he had sought refuge in a cave. As he lay there, he saw a spider attempting to weave its web across an opening. Each time the little creature would about make it, the web would break. But he kept on—and finally *he made it.* This gave Bruce the idea of trying just once again-*and he too made it and won* the battle. And now comes a most assuring corollary: *"No matter what happens, just keep on keeping on—the next time may be successful."*

Easy Does It.

7. *No case is hopeless.*

And this differs from the previous signpost only in that is refers to others, while the former refers to ourselves. Its verity is predicated on the fact that *God is all powerful*—and *can*, if He so wills it, *cure anything or anyone.* Therefore all psychiatric and medical opinion to the contrary notwithstanding, *there is no* case hopeless. Witness the many, many—very many alcoholics, who after having "kicked it around" for years, slipping all over the place and refusing all help—suddenly not only achieve sobriety, but *solid* sobriety and happiness and stability!

To get a little personal, a very unique evidence of this happened this week. The psychiatrist who told the writer that he was *absolutely hopeless* fifteen years ago—ordered a copy of *"Sobriety and Beyond."*

The corollary: *patience, patience, patience and more patience*—and when one runs out of patience . . . more patience. . . ."

Easy Does It.

8. *No one ever tripped lying down!*

In all sincerity, much tension, and pressure, and nerves, and anxiety stem from nothing else than *lack of rest.* Many doctors and friends will advise one to *slow down lest you trip up.* Mistakenly they fail to realize that certain personalities (and most alcoholics are such) just *can't slow down.* A quick-thinking, quick-acting pace is part and parcel of our nature, and if we try to slow down (we are not speaking physically), we might get into real trouble. *Our problem is to get more rest* which then will renew sufficiently the over-expending of energy of our type of nature. So it is not the corollary to: *"slow down lest you trip,"* but *"lie down, and you won't trip."* In short *"get plenty of rest."*

Easy Does It.

9. *Do it!*

A short road sign, but a very eloquent and very important one. For why do so many things pile up on us and cause pressure? So much unfinished business? So much for the last day of the month; or of the year? *Because we failed to do so many things when we should have done them.* Easy Does It means *do* it when

206

it is supposed to be done. Old man procrastination reared his ugly head too often. And in fine print we read: "Now is the acceptable time."

Easy Does It.

10. *Expect delay.*

"Backward, turn backward O time in thy flight . . .
I need more time to avoid my plight. . . !"

More lousy poetry, but how often are not those our sentiments. We *forgot to allow* for delay . . . delay comes . . . and now we are again under "pressure". . . .

If we expect and allow for delay in everything we do, we will *never* be under pressure, and *if* delay doesn't come, . . . more time for rest! *Easy Does It!* Look at the difference in the fellow who is taking the detour and who *didn't allow for delay,* and the fellow who *did expect and allow for delay!*

The corollary is appended to everything we plan whenever time or distance is involved. It, too, is just two words: "Add one!"

It should take us about three hours to drive to Smithville? "Add one"—allow four. It should take us five days to finish this job? "Add one"—make it six. One thing sure—there will never be pressure; and, after all, an alcoholic who toys with pressure is toying with dynamite!

Easy Does It.

11. *It is the effort, not the results.*

That is the *only* thing that is ours—the *honest effort*—the *honest trying. The results are always in the hands of God.* That is why it was told to us centuries ago on the first Christmas eve: "Peace on earth to men of *good will"* . . . from how much tension and anxiety would we not be free if always we only concerned ourselves with what we are doing—not about what will be produced or accomplished!

Which brings us to a very effective corollary: *"Concentrate on the work at hand"* . . . "Be what you *are"* . . . "Do what you're doing" . . . and emphasize the *ultimate* . . . or as the Latin puts it: "Age quod agis, et respice *finem."*

Easy Does It.

207

12. *How important can it be?*

Most of our upsets and tension and anxiety are "over things that are actually very insignificant." So in order to avoid this it is well always and forever to ask ourselves when we become anxious or tense or upset over some circumstance or happening: *"just how important is this thing I'm stewing about?"* And you know something? When all is said and done there is only *one thing really important: our ultimate.* Don't know what yours is, but mine's *eternity.* Just can't get more ultimate than that! That was the ultimate for all the saints—they went about doing the best they could with the help of God's grace and not very worried or upset or tense about anything. Know why? Their motto was— in everything—*"quid ad aeternitatem?"* which translated means: *"what is this to eternity?"* What bearing has this or that on my eternity? *Most* things that make us anxious, and tense, and put us under pressure look sorta ridiculous in the light of eternity, don't they? If we have to sit here for hours until they let us through the road—"will that affect our eternity?" Ridiculous, isn't it? Just so they open it up in time to answer Gabriel's horn ! ! ! *Easy Does It!* And we shall find, particularly if we are trying to live some sort of a spiritual life, based on spiritual values, that the corollary here mentioned is a "God-sent" to dissipate anxiety and what have you: *What has this got to do with eternity? What will this mean to me in eternity?"*

Easy Does It.

13. *We can't change others—we can change ourselves.*

This guidepost is the one that is the corollary from the serenity prayer: "God grant us the serenity to accept the things we cannot change; the courage to change the things we can; and the wisdom to know the difference." It is the past that points out the *"wisdom to know the difference."* 99.99% of the time *we cannot change things or others but we can change us.*

More wisdom flowing from this point is the realization, that *being alcoholic, whenever we cannot accept,* and trying to accept is *endangering our sobriety,* then the better part of wisdom is to *change us—if not inside then externally by removal.*

A very practical example comes up many, many times in

A.A. Something or someone in the group constantly irritates us and keeps us under pressure or tension. We have tried and tried to change it; then we have tried and tried to accept it, but still we are tense and upset. What to do? Wisdom would tell us: *change to another group.* No other group? then *start one of your own.* Let's always remember: *we're alcoholic,* and therefore *sobriety is paramount.* We cannot change that which threatens it; we cannot accept it. *Therefore—change us.* The corollary also points the same way. It tells us: *"I'm only responsible for me!"* He is the only one we must answer for—really!

Easy Does It.

14. *It is better not to have done a lick of work than to take that first drink!*

This signpost is literally true. For, how many A.A.'s work and work and work—even do extra work—so hard, and then, behold a drink is justified!

Many times the writer has been told when trying to help one "off one" after a slip: *"But I worked so hard!"* So what—you're drunk. It is better to have loafed and be sober than to have worked so hard and be drunk!

The corollary here is a lengthy one but a very important one which is oftentimes missed: "Never work, especially extra work, with the purpose of *proving oneself to one's family or boss or superior*—if we do, that will *justify in our alcoholic thinking mind just a wee drink. . . ."*

An alcoholic should never try to prove himself—we can't and no one has asked us to. When we do, we really are only trying to build up our own ego to ourself. And that's pride, and that is proud accomplishment—and accomplishments call for a "leetle drink."

Don't try to prove anything to anybody—stay sober *today*— for *yourself*—so *take it easy. . . .*

Easy Does It.

15. *Strive toward, but don't look for, perfection in ourselves or others.*

This signpost will have a much more thorough "tearing

apart" in the next chapter of the *Myth of Perfection*. But to help us toward the practice of *Easy does It*, we should always keep in mind that working on ourselves is a *life-time job, so Easy Does It!* And we should also remember that *all people—even the best —are still human*, even as you and I . . . so *Easy Does It.*

The corollary? *Be an "ignoramus."* By that we mean get the habit of *ignoring others' faults*, and even our own—*provided we are honestly trying and doing the best we can*. We should always be surprised that we are not worse!

Easy Does It! Day in and day out—hour in and hour out— minute in and minute out . . . just like the old negress told her master: *"When ah works ah works hard but not fast—when ah sets ah sets loose—and when ah lays mahself down, ah goes right to sleep!"*—*Easy Does It.*

Now let us apply this principle to the various areas of our living:

1. *Our home life*—a) *Easy Does It* will lead us to be *tolerant* with *all* members of the family. And we will not *push any* of the family, nor shall we *expect* perfection in them. On the contrary we shall only by *working on ourselves* endeavor to *lead* them, but not be too concerned whether they follow—*Easy Does It!* We shall even gracefully realize once and for all that even that *perfection* we thought surely was there in courtship was but a human mirage! Don't ever endeavor to re-capture it either—because since it really *wasn't*, it really *ain't*, nor will really *ever be!* But he or she is probably a wonderful guy or gal at that—even though human as all get-out. So, *Easy Does It.*

It is so foolish for parents to constantly tell their "fault-fill-ed-fledglings": "Why do *you* kids have to quarrel? Now there's the Jones boys—you never see *them* quarrel. . . ." You sure don't; they won't *let* you *see* them! Familes are families and human . . . and "quarreling" is a healthy part of every rugged American home. When we try to convince the children that it isn't—then we *are leading them to strive for the impossible!* That's why *you* haven't reached it. *Easy Does It!*

b) Practicing *Easy Does It* will lead one to *leisurely planning* in the home in place of *determined* planning. And all plans shall be qualified by *"God willing." Easy Does It!*

c) The parent who has the attitude and the practice of *Easy Does It* will never *punish in anger*—but only in and by *reason,* calmly and lovingly. *Easy Does It!*

d) There will be *no ruling by fear and threat* in the *Easy Does It* household. "We can't *change* others"—remember? But we *can lead* and *guide* by *love!* Love takes much longer than a threat or anger—*but* it *lasts forever. Easy Does It.*

e) When the wife nags or "yackity-yacks" (which she will!) or the husbands "clam up" or the children "raise the roof" we can use *Easy Does It* very effectively by practicing being an "ignoramus"—*ignoring it. Let it go!* Let the wife "yackity-yack" till the proverbial "cows come home"—let the husband sit "clammed up" until doomsday—let the kids have their fun *at home*—isn't it great she or he or they *are* at *home? Easy Does It!*

The writer has seen the above actually work out to perfection in a home. He has seen the husband *absolutely oblivious of the stream of words*—he has seen the wife *completely ignoring the silence*—*and he has seen the parent even enjoy the kids "tearing up the house"*—both oblivious of the endless noise and racket and messing things up—*Easy Does It!*

We should never forget that the alternative is retaliation—and goodbye! *Easy Does It!*

2. *In our social life*—*Easy Does It* first will lead us *not to expect* everyone to *like us.* It will not lead us to *look for perfection* in *others.* It will keep one from "social climbing." It will lead us to make *real* friends but *not* necessarily *many friends.* And when our neighbor gossips, or criticises or slights us—we shall *ignore it* . . . *Easy Does It.*

And we shall pursue this business of social intermingling *insofar as it helps us toward the ultimate*—what's *your* ultimate? Sobriety here? And hereafter?

Easy Does It.

3. *In our business life*—We will not work the "clock around" if we are practicing *Easy Does It.* We will try to avoid *pressure*

jobs if possible, and if not we will at least try to avoid the pressure *of the job* by *more rest* and *relaxation,* and when we go to our home, we will *leave the job behind.* We will look for jobs and business not gauging the choice by the money to be earned *but by the fitness for it*—and by fitness we mean not capability of intellect and know-how and expertness *but by emotional* fitness—i.e., if we want to stay sober and happy.

Easy Does It.

4. *In our financial affairs—Easy Does It* will not goad us on to get a big fat bank account, or a nice big "sinking fund," or a great big salary—but it will tell us "Sufficient for the day is the evil thereof" . . . We will prudently plan for the contingencies of the day and the future—sufficient! not superfluous! "God willing," tomorrow's needs will be taken care of just as are today's . . . God will provide. . . .

Easy Does It.

5. *In our spiritual life*—We think most alcoholics at some time or other decided to become saints—*right now.* But when night fell—and they "fell," they gave up! *Easy Does It* will lead us to sanctity—*but not tonight!* It will get us there about "two days after we're dead." And in the meantime we must *expect* sins, and failures, and faults *but still trying to avoid sin and do good* . . . day in and day out, realizing that when sin is overcome and virtue is achieved it will be *God* Who gave it—not *our efforts. Easy Does It.*

It will further tell us in this sanctity business to *emphasize the need and role of God*—good will, an honesty try—yes, but *relying on the grace of God to give the success.* "He gives us both the grace to will and to accomplish." *Easy Does It.*

So many falls in the spiritual life are a direct result of *too much haste. . . . Easy Does It!* Witness the poor deluded soul binding himself to say "dozens and dozens and dozens of prayers a day" imagining that this is sanctity!

Meditation is primary among all spiritual practices and it is also the *primary spiritual method of practicing Easy Does It—relaxation with God! Easy Does It!*

6. *In our physical life*—We grow ever so slowly; as do the plants and all life. Even in the mineral kingdom—formations takes years and sometimes centuries. *Easy Does It is primary* in all of Nature's realm of action. It takes but the fraction of a minute to *break* a bone—but the days and weeks it takes to heal! Man—*right* now! Nature—*Easy Does It!*

Doctors tell us that many of the present day's ills are a result of "hypertension." And "hypertension" is a result of "going too fast a pace"—wherefore heart failure, rheumatism, arthritis and what have you. *Easy Does It.*

The Trappist monks have an average life span far in excess of the average of people in general. They are par-excellent in the practice of *Easy Does It*. Eight hours work—eight hours prayer —eight hours sleep—*Easy does It!* They are emphasizing the ultimate. They aren't going anywhere—except to *eternity!* And they average 80 years getting there!

Easy Does It.

7. *In our mental life*—The finest mental hygiene in the world is *Easy does It*. From bad mental hygiene comes getting all "screwed up," all "wound up," "snap" judgment. *But* from good mental hygiene—from the practice of *Easy Does It*—*the habit of taking time out to think things through*—*comes wisdom,* and peace of mind, and sanity and relaxation—*and sleep!*

Easy Does It.

8. *In our emotional life*—*Easy Does It* guides our emotions to use the "road signs" and avoid over-tenseness, and pressure, and anxiety—from such stem irritations, and nervousness, and depressions, and "funny little feelings" of every kind and description! *Easy Does It.* Take the emotional road the signs point out —not the detour.

Most neuroses come as a result of long continued *over-tense doing,* mixed with an abundance of indecision, and anxiety and speed. After all an "acute neurosis" usually means that the "white matter"[1] of the brain is so tensed that the patient of himself is unable to relax it. And in such cases it has been found that the

---

[1] The "white matter" is the connecting tissue between the gray matter (the thinking part) and the nerve system. It's the "PBX."

electro-shock therapy is very effective, because the electrical current "relaxes" the white matter, and is repeated until the ability to remain in a relaxed state is at the beck of the patient. That's why one with an acute neurosis is plagued with so many "crazy" thoughts. His "PBX" is out of whack!—all "mixed" up!

Easy Does It is the finest insurance in the world against a nervous breakdown or emotional upsets. Use the "road signs."

Easy Does It.

9. *In our A.A. life—Easy does It* gives us the following attitude to help us use A.A. for *sobriety and happiness:*

a) We are in A.A. *not* to sober up drunks, or to save souls, or to save the world, or to sell A.A., or to teach—for these all *give concern, and anxiety, and tension, and pressure. But we are in A.A., solely to* maintain our *own* sobriety and *in giving* it to those who *ask,* also achieve *happiness and serenity.*

How many seem to get all "screwed up" because so-and-so won't stay sober! *So what?* Keeping so-and-so sober *is not our job. Our job* is *only keeping us sober.* And we could mention dozens of like incidents: "so-and-so won't go to church, won't accept A.A., or won't use what I tell him!" Remember the corollary to number 13 road sign? *I'm only responsible for me!"*

Easy Does It.

b) We avoid pietism (look up your dictionary); we do not take the other guy's inventory; we give by *attraction* to those *who want it;* we do not "scheme" and "plan" lots of A.A. "work" emulating someone else; and we day in and day out practice *accepting.* After all it takes about 9 to 12 months for the *initial* leveling off of the alcoholic, and it takes about 3 to 5 years for *complete* leveling off—*so take it easy.*

Easy does It! And that, bub, means *do* it, but don't *overdo* it, and all the rest *God will provide.* "Consider the birds of the air, they neither sow nor do they reap nor gather into barns, and yet your Heavenly Father feedeth them."

Well? Doesn't He?

Well? are you?

"Aren't you less than they?"

Once upon a time a Bishop lay awake night after night trying to solve all the difficulties of his large Diocese constantly fearful of the outcome, the debt, the future.

One night as he lay there, he heard a voice in the silence of the room. It spoke softly, yet so reassuringly: "Your Excellency," whispered the Lord, "how about turning over now and going to sleep and let Me do the worrying! Worry is the property of the management, and after all, I do still run this old world including your Diocese."

Including *your* problems, too bud! So why not get a good night's sleep! *Easy Does It!*

G'nite!

THE MYTH OF PERFECTION

"Let us admit our imperfections so we can then begin to grow toward perfection."—St. Augustine.

The next principle of A.A. is one which has always been the writer's "pet." Perhaps it is because we coined it as it is here expressed; perhaps it is because failure of the writer to recognize this principle in his early years, led him to appraise, both in himself and others, as abnormal what was normal, and led him to be a perfectionist of the first order; or perhaps it is our sincere desire to share our findings with the many, many other alcoholic-perfectionists we have met along the pathway of A.A. Be that as it may—we feel the absence of this principle in one's attitudes and actions is responsible for some of the more serious upsets in human nature. This principle is:

"The Myth of Perfection."

In simple "adulterated" English, the *Myth of Perfection means: "There ain't nobody perfect is this world."* No sir, there "ain't"; and thinking there is, is one of us poor humans' biggest trouble makers, and is the thing most responsible for all perfectionism, particularly in alcoholics.

All of our lives we *expected perfection,* and when we again and again found instead imperfection, faults, failings, even serious ones, we became "disillusioned"—which in reality was only a vicarious form of self-pity. So we retreated from reality and kept on looking for the "will-of-the-wisp," the "mirage," the *nonexistent perfection in ourselves and in others. Our motive?* (albeit with many subconscious), a pathological pride that kept demanding the *top* for us and ours—and which was such a barrier in admitting that we were alcoholic. *"We* alcoholic?" "Why, *impossible! That can't* happen to *us!"* Which translated means: *"We're perfect!"* Funny thing though, it *did* and we *"ain't!"*

Remember how we used to *expect* perfection? We first thought our parents were perfect. Then we found out they weren't! Frustration number one. Then we met the gal (or guy) of our dreams! And think we to us—*here* is perfection! And then we married her (or him)! Frustration number two. (So many think their sweetheart is so perfect, so wonderful that they could "eat'em up." Then they marry them and wish they had!) Then along came *our* children. And without doubt they were perfect! "Isn't he the most perfect thing that ever lived?" And then the policeman brought T. Jonathan home one day—in trouble! *Our* child? *Never!* But it *was* our child. More frustration. And then there was ourself. We held on to that mirage to the very last—*we were perfect*, and if you didn't believe it, all you had to do was to ask us!

And then came alcoholism, and down and down—but still we mumbled in "our cups"—"greatesh guy what ever livhed!" Curtains! And then A.A.

The truth? *No one is perfect.* No matter who they are or what position in life they may hold. *No one* and we mean *no one* is perfect. Like a little Scriptural proof? "If anyone among you says he is without sin, he is a *liar* and the truth is not in him." Just a longer way of saying: *There ain't nobody perfect.*

The motive behind perfectionism we said above, is *pride.* God says: "Be ye perfect." but He doesn't say *right now.* He means *aim* at perfection. "We *grow* along spiritual lines." The A.A. Books says, "We are *not* saints." But pride says: *"We (ours) are perfect."* Humility says on the other hand: "We are very imperfect, but *God* will perfect us *in His time, and in His way.* Let us *admit* our imperfection so we may grow *toward* perfection."

This same motive of pride and perfectionistic thinking is responsible for so many refusing to *accept the problem of alcoholism.* Listen!

"An *alcoholic* in *our* family! Preposterous!"

"*My* child an alcoholic? Impossible, he's a Smythe!"

"A doctor an alcoholic! A clergyman an alcoholic! Why they *couldn't* be!"

"*Me* an alcoholic! Why that's ridiculous!"

And on and on and on ... it "can't happen to *me!*"

Some years ago we contacted the mother of a friend of ours in A.A. who was very unhappy in the thought that any of *her* children were alcoholic or needed A.A. When we went to see

224

her, she led off with: "There *never* has been any weakness in *my* family!" When we told her that we were an alcoholic too, she almost fainted!

Another mother told the writer when he and an A.A. called on her very drunk son to give him some help: "My poor Charley, *he* has *never done a wrong thing in all his life!*" And when it was intimated to her that just maybe that very self-same attitude might be responsible for "poor" Charley being drunk, she became very angry! Wonder why?

But in A.A. we learned that *we were alcoholic,* that we were *far,* very *far* from being a perfect guy, and that probably we never would be perfect until we died, *but* that *we* could *begin* to *grow toward it—by starting at the bottom* . . . and admitting *we are powerless*—period. Then, and then alone, from that "cellar of humility," could we ever hope to *grow* along spiritual lines by constantly and humbly *"aiming"* at perfection, by honestly and consistently *trying*, but withal *"awaiting the grace of God."* We learned no longer to ask ourselves "How are we *doing?*," but only "How are we *trying?*," day in and day out.

Now let's apply this principle of the *Myth of Perfection* in *all of our affairs:*

1. *In our home life*—None of our family is perfect *including us.* This will lead us not to be upset or disturbed or irritated by the wife's (or husband's) faults. Our children will not be *the finest in the world*—and *far* from perfect. How many heartaches would mothers and fathers be spared if *they expected* their child to fall, and fail. Then one wouldn't hear that frequent lament: "To think that *my* child did such a thing!" Why not? *Is* your child better than the next one? Now *is* he? Certainly *not* if he is a descendant of Adam. *Your* children, *their* children, *our* children—*all* children *are liable to do anything.* Which brings into focus the great need for prayer that *God will protect them from harm.*

And the fact that our child is a Smythe, or a Jones, or one of the P. Jonathan Whytes makes him not better than any other child in the whole wide world. What a cruel burden to place on the poor child! "Always remember, young man, that *you are a*

"Smythe!" So he's a *"Smythe,"* so he gets *drunk,* so what? The poor guy was too busy remembering he was a *"Smythe"* to keep count of the drinks!

Let's let our children know *we're human—they're human.* Then they will have *confidence in us.* Who wants to confide in a person self-placed on a pedestal?

Perfection is an *ideal*—to grow *toward*—and *we* are *not* that ideal for our children—no their paragon of virtue. That's why God give us the saints and Himself for them to "strive" to imitate—so *move over!*

You know something? Your kids will love you for it!

2. *In our social life*—Realizing the *Myth of Perfection* we associate with our friends and acquaintances knowing that *neither they nor we are perfect.* We are weak, so are they; we have problems, so have they; we have faults, so have they; *we are doing the best we can with the lights given us, and so are they.*

With this attitude, we will not as likely nor as often *ascribe malicious motives to others.* And amazingly we will find that *most* people are *not* malicious—even in their evil doing, but that for the greater part it stems from ignorance, and misguidance, and thoughtlessness, and that weakness of human nature which is inherent in all of us, and which unaided by Divine grace *might* do anything, but still, with the help of Divine grace, *can* accomplish all things—*if it be God's will and His time to accomplish them in us.*

The attitude arising from a conviction of the *Myth of Perfection* will also teach us what we like to call the *"interdependency"* of human beings. Then we shall be more willing to *help* others —*no matter who* they may be. And we shall also get the conviction that *people need us and we need people—we all need one another.* From this truth grows the basis for the "brotherhood of man."

3. *In our business affairs*—We are *not* the world's greatest business men. This will lead us to *seek advice* in those areas wherein we are not expert in our business. We will be *open-minded* in business, which means *looking* for ways and means unknown to us for improvement instead of proceeding along with a proud

conviction that *we* have *all* the answers in our specialty. Such an attitude as this latter one is what leads many to bankruptcy. And it is also the attitude that leads to the thousands of so-called "white elephants" around the country. And witness the many defectively built schools, and churches, and auditoria—all a result of a pastor thinking *he* was the world's best architect and builder!

The writer was pastor at one time of a very small country church. We had two furnaces: one in the rectory, and one in the church. Thinking we might save on coal, we queried the trustees why we couldn't have *one* furnace for both. "No Father," they replied "we tried that once. We had a furnace in the church but it would never heat the rectory."

Still dubious, and perhaps also goaded on by a bit of laziness, we sought out an expert on the heating business. He suggested a survey of the property. We had one made. And in surveying they found that a furnace in the church would never heat the house, *but* a furnace in the rectory would very effectively heat the church! Why? There was a 30 degree rise in the ground *toward* the church! (We didn't have pumps or blowers in those days.)

The Myth of Perfection!

4. *In our financial affairs—The Myth of Perfection* will lead us to steer clear of that "make a million" crave. It will teach us to be content with a sufficiency instead of always wanting to earn more and more and more— (which so often leads to "slips")—and actually making *less and less.* Slips are *expensive*—or did you know it?

It will also suggest that we *prudently* provide for future contingencies and old age—for since we are *not* perfect, the day will come when we will need such assistance. But we will not hoard. Doing what in ourselves lies, *God will furnish the rest.* Faith and trust in God fills *all* the emptiness left by the imperfection of our nature. God will perfect, and provide, and sanctify—we have only the foot-work—*providing what we can.*

5. *In our emotional life*—With the practice of the principle of the *Myth of Perfection* comes the realization that our emotions

225

will never be *fully* under the control of reason and will, and that they will *always*—for the rest of our lives—be "playing tricks on us." This knowledge should enable us to *ignore* all those "funny little feelings" which are so real but at the same time so elusive.

How many come to us and complain: "I have been trying so long—for years—to control myself and I still get upset, I still get jittery, I still get angry, and I still get nervous!"

Well what did they expect? Perfect control? *Perfection?* We are quite convinced that most people do keep up that vain hope of "reaching an 'even keel.'" Fact is though—*we never will. The Myth of Perfection!* With the alcoholic it is that persistent struggle to reach that "smooth" feeling! Remember? That "permanent"*euphoria*—which *"used to"* come with a few drinks. That is why so many today are taking the "barbitals" by the ton in this country. We want to *always "feel"* good. And with the alcoholic, the increase of intake of the "barbitals" is not far behind—and *addiction.*

We were several times a patient in a sanitarium. In one of these places the psychiatrist to whom we were assigned had a practice which at the time only irritated us, but in recent years it has come back to mind time and time again and we feel it contains lots of wisdom relative to the above "feeling" business.

Each morning we had to report to his office. And each morning the first thing this good doctor would ask us was: "Well, how are you *doing* today?"

We invariably replied: "We *feel* like the 'dickens.'"

And then always came back, but at that time too tame to pierce the padded skull, "I did not ask how you *felt*, I asked you how you were *doing.*"

Think it over. How are you doing?

There are doctors today who claim, that, and we quote one such, "if sedatives are *never taken in sufficient amount to produce euphoria, even though slight, there will never be addiction.*" Well, be that as it may—it certainly opens a door of thought—*but* experience tells us that the alcoholic wants no part of any sedative be it alcohol or barbital *unless there comes therewith euphoria,* which in alcoholic lingo is "feeling no pain." *Perfectionist?*

226

The Myth of Perfection would tell us: there will be days when we will be "feeling" wonderful and there will be days when we will be "feeling lousy"—and there will be days when one is quick to anger and days when nothing upsets—and there will be days when we "feel" "mean" as all get out and days when we "feel" like doing a good turn even for our worst enemy—but then, life, and emotions, are like that—very uneven and *imperfect*—even in the best of men!

6. *In our physical life*—Physically also, *we are not "he" men*—never will be. But proceeding on the false hope of so many people, there is magazine after magazine and "ad" after "ad" *offering to build you into a perfect physique.* (Or, you dear ladies, into a perfect 36 or what have you!) And people by the thousands keep such magazines, and therapies in business "looking for that non-existent *perfection of body.*"

This same perfectionism is responsible for so much medical "clap-trap" that fills the world today. And yet isn't it true—many, far too many, people condemn the ethical doctor who tries to "explode" such false promises. *No* pill, *no* exercise, *no* treatment, *no* "shot" in the world is going to give any of us that *perfect physical body.* No matter what we take or do—we are *still going to carry around with us that old body we were born with*—and even the best of us is going to have a "powerful number of weakness." And something more along this line. That body is going to "weigh heavily upon the spirit" much, very much of the time. The Lord said so.

So the *Myth of Perfection* shows us that we will *always be* subject to sickness, and disease, and aches and pains. In fact the older we grow, bub, the *more aches and pains* are we going to have—day in and day out.

We often hear it said that one should "grow old gracefully." You know who it is that grows old the most gracefully? He or she is the fellow or gal who *accepts* the myth of perfection and *expects* gradual deterioration, and instead of trying to stave *off* the creeping years with pills, and salves, and dyes, and treatments of every kind and sort, *enjoys each day* along with the aches and pains, most of which he becomes oblivious to most of the time, because he no longer concentrates on them by trying futilely to get rid of them.

The *Myth of Perfection!* And finally in the physical world there comes *death*—and disintegration—to dust! Sorta silly to make a lot to do over such a temporary dwelling place, isn't it? Every human's final chapter: *He died!*

7. *In our thought life*—We may live to be a hundred, but we shall still have distractions, and "bad" thoughts, and "screwy" thoughts until we're dead. That's the *Myth of Perfection.*

Yet, so many get very much concerned because they, after many years of trying to concentrate, or pray, or meditate *still have distractions. Perfectionism!* The truth of the matter is that even the great saints—people who have given their entire lives over to prayer and meditation—yes, even after having spent thirty, forty, fifty years in such practice *still had distractions*— and "bad" thoughts and "screwy" thoughts. The solution is to *expect* to have them *but don't pay any attention to them. Ignoring them is the surest way of handling them.* It is like the unwanted visitor at the door. He came there unbidden. He will leave more quickly *if we ignore him; but* he *might get in* if we answer the door and tell him to leave or argue with him. It is a universal panacea for unwanted thoughts: *ignore them.* Practice "good," "positive" thinking.

There is a story told of St. Francis. (Probably never actually happened to him, but it gives a good lesson and he's as good as anyone to have had it happened.) One day as he and one of his brethren were riding horseback down the road, the good brother remarked: "Father Francis, I have reached a state in my meditations where I can now meditate for hours on end without the least distraction."

"Oh, is that right, brother?"

"Yes, Father Francis," the brother replied, "I think I am nearing perfection."

"I wouldn't be too sure of that, brother," Father Francis chided, "but anyway, let's see if it be the truth you are telling. And to do so, I'll tell you what I'm going to do. I'll bet you my

228

horse against your horse that you cannot say the Lord's Prayer without a distraction."

"Why, that's easy, Father Francis."

"Okay," Francis replied, "Let's begin."

"Our Father ... Who art in heaven ... hallowed be Thy Name ... Thy Kingdom come ... Thy Will be done ..."

Right at this juncture the good brother broke in with:

"By the way, Father Francis, does the bridle go with it?"

On occasion, all of our life, in spite of whatever we do—*we will have distractions, and "bad" thoughts, and "screwy" thoughts, and "uncharitable" thoughts....*

The Myth of Perfection!

8. *In our spiritual life*—Here, perhaps more than in any area of living, perfectionism causes untold damage to souls striving to lead a spiritual life. As we mentioned above, we think many alcoholics at one time or other in their lives "started out to be saints." But expecting *perfection and quick,* they just as quickly abandoned their quest with: "It ain't for the likes of me."

The A.A. Book tells us that we are *not saints.* "We become *willing to grow* along spiritual lines." And *growth takes time.* And Almighty God in setting out to us that we should "be perfect" was simply setting a "goal"--an "ideal" to be reached only after a long and arduous pathway reaching from beginning to end of human life.

Discouragement, which more than any other one thing is responsible for giving up the striving for sanctity or perfection, *is a product of perfectionism.* For the myth of perfection tells us that in the spiritual life above all else, burdened with fallen human nature, we will fall and fall and fall again until "two days after we're dead." Remember? "If anyone says he's without sin among you he is a liar and the truth is not in him." Now we're sure there were *all* sorts of people in the crowd to whom the Lord addressed these words—young children, young adults, old adults, men, women, boys, girls, good, bad, and indifferent ... and yet He said *"if anyone...."*

Growth in sanctity means growth toward sanctity—and in simple language that means: anyone who *tries* the *best he can*

229

to do the Will of God in all of his affairs—day in and day out—
and keeps on trying in the face of repeated falls and failures.

The saying that "it makes no difference whether we won or lost, but only how we played the game" certainly contains a pointed axiom for this striving for perfection. *For "God will not ask whether we sinned or not, but how hard we tried . . . to do His Will."*

"Peace on earth to men of *good will"* . . . the one who *honestly tries. . . .*

And a *lot* of discouragement will be side-tracked if only once and for all we would, instead of being *dismayed* by repeated falls, *expect them* albeit always still *trying* to overcome them.

Let us *admit* our *imperfection* so we can then *grow towards perfection.*

Many people also wrongly think that in convents, and monasteries and the like, *friction, sin, faults* are gone! So they refer to such as "heaven on earth." Well, they may be a safe *way* to heaven, *but* they aren't heavens on earth—because there "ain't such." And in the convents, and the monasteries, and the like, one finds the same fault-filled human nature that is present in *all* humans.

This erroneous idea of "heaven on earth" is responsible for the rash accusation made by many that convents and monasteries are "escape mechanisms" and that religion is "an opiate of the people." It also leads many misguided souls to join (for awhile!) a convent or monastery "in order to get away from it all" or "to heal the wound of a former 'love' "! That's why such also soon leave!

There's a story told that might help "congeal" this whole idea of "spiritual perfectionism" into focus: it tells about a very prominent person visiting a Trappist monastery, which is a very strict Order wherein they keep perpetual silence, fast much, pray about eight hours, sleep about eight hours and work about eight hours. "Ah" mused the visitor to himself as the Abbot approached to welcome him, *"here* is perfection—all peace—no friction, a veritable 'heaven on earth.' " And as the Abbot welcomed him, he voiced his thought to him.

"Yes," the Father Abbot replied, "heaven on earth . . . perfect peace . . . no friction. You forget *we are still human and far* from perfection. Now let me give you an example of what I mean. See those two good brothers over there in the field working side by side? Well, just keep watching. They cannot, because of the rule, talk. For necessary things we must use signs. So now just watch. It won't be long before they will be 'making signs at each other' and they won't be 'lovings ones' either!"

The Myth of Perfection!

9. *In our A.A. life*—No *one* in A.A. is perfect. In fact *no one* in A.A. is 100% on the program! And that includes *you* and *me!* And yet isn't it true we hear time and time again "why doesn't he or she *get all the way on the program?"*

The Myth of Perfection is what tells us that in A.A. there will never be "graduation day" except on the day we are dead. Because certainly in the area of sobriety, no matter whether we have been sober forty years, and have done all we could in A.A.—still *one drink*, and that's it, brother. *The Myth of Perfection.* We are alcoholic. And that tells us that we are not only imperfect but in the realm of drinking *we have and always will have a very big defect—and that is the inability to take one drink and guarantee our sobriety.* And that goes for *all alcoholics*—bar none.

The *Myth of Perfection* also will point out to us that *anyone might slip.* Yes, *anyone,* even Bill W., even as you and I. And yet, we hear again and again, "Why, it would be *awful if Bill slipped."* Why, awful? What has *his sobreity* to do with *our* sobriety? The program should be the basis of our sobriety and *it* will still be there *no matter who slips.* Bill is human, your sponsor is human, those "big-shots" in your group are human, you are human, we are human—*so anybody might slip. But if* we practice the *Myth of Perfection* we wouldn't really be surprised *no matter who slipped.*

So why should it be *awful* if a prominent member slips? He undoubtedly will *"feel"* awful (remember?) but *we are sober—* and after all isn't that all we are in A.A. for: to maintain sobriety and to give it to whomsoever asks—and going about our business practicing *these principles in all our affairs* . . . ever conscious of the great need *we* have to *keep on practicing them—day in and day out*—because *we* are still so far, so *very far from perfection.*

The Myth of Perfection!

FIRST THINGS FIRST

". . . and practice these principles . . . in all of our affairs."

We come to the next principle enumerated above. This one we feel rates second to the one just analyzed. And, given sobriety, it is the one that is paramount if we wish ever to achieve mastery of happiness. This principle tells us a truth that *should* have been self-evident. It is:

"First Things First."

When the alcoholic was running in a wild frenzy down the intoxicated pathway (or should we say alleyway?) of life, everything was helter-skelter. *First* things were not necessarily first. The moment and its pleasure were first. Alcohol was first. Money was first. Success was first. We were first, not our welfare, but *our affairs, our will. We wanted what we wanted when we wanted it and if we didn't get what we wanted when we wanted it we were "mad"*—or we got drunk.

We come to A.A. We get sobriety and then we learn that if we are to keep it we *must* maintain serenity in our living, and to maintain it, we must always and at all times try to put *first things first*. We learned that there exists an over-all *set order of things and values in life*. We learned that this over-all order of values, if consulted, would *most* of the time tell us what should be first. And we learned that if always first things were first, and second things second, etc., etc., we would have *order* and not chaos which had seemed to dog us through the years.

What is this order of things? Let us first list them according to value and then proceed to examine their sequence. They are:

1. *God* and His will.
2. The *common good*.
3. *Our* welfare.
4. *Other* individuals.
   a. Our family
   b. Our friends
   c. Our enemies.

God always comes first. We often refer to this in A.A. "Thy will be done." "Praying *only* for knowledge of *His* will and the power to carry that out." This is what gives us the primacy of the spiritual.

So in practicing this principle, when *His* affairs or *His will* is involved, we seek that *first. First* things *first.* We may usually find His will in His expressed laws, the 10 Commandments, our conscience, through prayer and meditation, in our Church if we are a church-member. *God* is *first*—God as we understand Him.

The *common good* comes next in import.[1] This is expressed in the first tradition of A.A.: "Each member of Alcoholics Anonymous is but a small part of a great whole. A.A. must continue to live or most of us will surely die. Hence, *our common welfare comes first.* But individual welfare follows close afterwards."

In our past it was "to heck" with the common good. We had no sense or responsibility. We thus became anti-social. Our wills reigned supreme. But now we seek group interest. We show community interest. Common welfare is second only to God's laws and will.

Then *we* come along—"close afterward." We never in the past really had our *welfare* at heart. If we had, we certainly would not have given ourselves such a beating! But the law of love tells us that we must *love ourselves first, then* our neighbor. So putting first things first means that *we must first take care of ourselves: body, mind and soul.* If we don't, eventually we won't be any good to God, to our neighbor, or to ourselves. So if it is a decision affecting either *our welfare* (*not* feelings!) or our *neighbor's welfare—we come first.* This happens so often: the twelfth-step-call that might throw us, morally or alcoholically; the A.A.

---

[1] In using the term 'good,' 'welfare,' etc., we must bear in mind that in deciding first things first we are presuming that these terms have implied the *same qualifications.* E.g., when we say that our 'welfare' comes before our neighbor's 'welfare,' we mean that our *over-all* welfare comes before his *spiritual* welfare; or our *material* welfare precedes his *material* welfare. But it is not correct to place our *material* welfare before his *spiritual* welfare. The *spiritual* welfare *always* precedes the *material* welfare, regardless of whose *spiritual* welfare. It is the 'primacy of the spiritual'—it is *always first.*

activities that keep us keyed to a dangerous pitch; the person whom we might hurt if we avoid but who is a source of temptation to us—morally or alcoholically. *We come first.*

And then it is *others.* And among the *others* our *family* comes first. So A.A. activities that take us from our family too often, should be eliminated. The *family* comes *first.*

Our *friends* now come in for consideration, *before* our *enemies.* But you know something, our *enemies do* come in—if last.

Now let us *apply and practice* this principle of *first things first* in *all of our affairs.* And *first* let us practice it:

1. *In our home life—First things first.* So—*God,* is He there? No family can ever be happy together as a family without God. Do we consult *His* will in *all* family problems—together? If we do not we are not putting *first things first.*

Then comes the *common good* of the family before *ours!* If the family likes or prefers onions and we hate onions—we should have onions! *First things first,* which is family *solidarity.*

And *ourselves?* First things first. After our family's welfare *we should inspire respect and confidence,* and this we will have *if we practice first things first in all of our own affairs.* We will be putting ourselves in the proper prospectus in the home *if we so live so as to command respect, and not live so as to have to demand respect*—we won't get it!

And *others* come into the home life too—or they *should.* The friends of our children, or husband, or wife should be *welcome* in our home, as long as such do not jeopardize the *welfare* of our family or *our own—welfare,* not feelings or convenience. First things first!

2. *In our social life*—Here again—*God* is first—*Is He there?* Or do we frequently "apologize" for God? Does His will dictate our attitudes and actions in the realm of charity, justice, purity, etc? Or have we again found a good "excuse"? First things first!

Next comes the *common good,* which means that the success of the group *as a whole is* more important than our feelings or convenience in the matter. The group welfare even precedes our *opinion,* as valuable as that might be! And when there is a group project—the success of the project is far ahead of our feelings again. First things first!

But *we* do come along next. And that means that if another individual is a source of damage to us—morally, spiritually, mentally, etc., that *we* come first before the individual's welfare. How often one hears the remark, "Well, I would quit seeing her, but I don't want to *hurt* her!"

Putting ourselves in our place in society, putting first things first, will urge us on to becoming *social* human beings, for this *is for our own welfare.*

And *others.* First things first tells us that in our social life *our family* has first place on the agenda, they also need social living outside the home. We only then will give time to others, and even a bit of our time to our enemies—which becomes a *must* when they *need* us. First things *first.*

3. *In our business affairs*—Yesterday, today and forever, *God* comes first. Is He there? Is our business run on solid justice and rights? Honesty? It should be if we are practicing *first things first.* And if we are *not,* there will be trouble!—conflict, conscience—failure. It has happened. There is a saying in one part of the country in A.A. that any member in a certain type of business will never stay sober, because the business is by nature crooked. Who was going to restore us to sanity? Lots of money? Big business? Or was it God—"we came to believe. . . ." *First things first.*

The *common good* comes next in business. So we must, if we practice this principle, place the common good before our own success in business. So, if our practices, although not in themselves wrong, are hurting the *common good,* we are not practicing this principle.

We must also take care of *ourselves* in business, or in our job. And if the business or job is damaging to *us,* then we better change things, even though we are working *so hard so others will have it nice. We come first.* And if we continue as we are above, there will come a time when *no one* will have it nice, especially those near and dear for whom we are *over-working.* They need it, but *our welfare comes first.* And first things first! ! !

240

After us come *others* in our business, whether they be associates or the help. Their *welfare* might not come before our *welfare*, but their *welfare does come before our greed*. So if we practice first things first, we will, having assured our own *welfare*, see that others have their fair and just compensation. We will be tolerant, and kind, and patient, and charitable. At least we will *not* be *rude* even to our enemies, or competitors.

4. *In our financial affairs*—"Money is the root of all evil." And how many would like to be vegetarians! But money, like all material things in this world is neither good nor evil in itself. Everything has been given to us to be a *means* of drawing nearer to God. For again, *God is first*. So our first financial obligation is to use our money to help draw us to *Him*—by justice, by charity, to His poor, for *His* honor and glory. We all should plan financial security as much as possible, *but* it is always secondary to His Will. So we do the best we can . . . leaving all the future security to Him. God will provide, i.e., *if we do the foot-work*.

Then the *common good* comes before us *if there is true need by the common whole; e.g.,* famine, war, epidemics, etc. But let us not confuse someone's foolish ideas for community improvements with real need and necessity. The former boils down to the individual again, not the *common* good.

And *we* come before others. Reckless spending on others to the neglect of the security of ourselves, and our families is *not* putting first things first. And the motive in such cases is usually pride and vanity, not true charity. First things first!

Among all the *others* in this world we have first an obligation to provide the material needs of our *families*. Then a sharing with *others*, then even a mite to our *enemies*. First things first!

5. *In our emotional life*—We are human. And we shall remain human as long as we live. And that means we will be constantly subject to emotional upsets and disorders. But for a happy emotional life we must practice first things first. And, of course, *God comes first. He* is the primary source of strength and control in *all* emotional difficulties. So above everything else, we can *ask Him first to help us to help ourselves* control our emotions.

241

And if something that is best for the *common good* irritates us, we will just have to be irritated, because the common good comes first. Detours are irritating, aren't they?

But if a certain guy or gal irritates us in spite of ourselves, it is better *for our own welfare* to avoid such a person, for *we* come first, before individuals.

Do circumstances necessitate hurting someone's feelings? Who shall it be? Who is closest to us—family, friends, enemy? Who comes first? If one of them *must* be hurt, then we will first spare our family and friends—first things first.

In our emotional life there is always one question which we should ask when we are upset. Namely, *why* are we so upset? Is that which causes us to be irritated, or angry, or self-pitying, or frightened, or worried so important to us—really now, is it? If it isn't, then being upset is not putting first things first. We drive the car, someone almost hits us—we get *very angry*. Why? *It* was *really* such a *trivial* thing; our *serenity* so *important!* Let it go! First things first!

6. *In our physical life*—We have a *body.* We have a body for a purpose. We have the obligation of taking proper care of it, but only so it can the better *serve God*—because *He* is first. So in all of the affairs of our body—in sickness, in accident, in pain and suffering, in keeping our health, *if the will or law of God is involved, He* comes *first.* Let us take a classical example. Milton was blind. This burden was evidently the Will of God. In his great "Ode To His Blindness" he wrote: "They also serve who only stand and wait." He put first things first. Willfully abusing the body on the other hand is *not* God's Will and therefore we should endeavor, if we can, to *preserve* our health.

Then the *common good* comes next. And as we must give up our bodily life if *God* asks it; so, too, we must if the *common good* demands it, as in war for our country, or in capital punishment for the good of society.

But we come next, and we *don't have to suffer or give up our bodily life for our neighbor*, but we *may if* it is done *out of love*, which is really indirectly placing *God* first, for He tells us:

242

"Greater love than this hath no man, that he lay down his life for his friend."

Then *others'* physical needs come in for our attention, particularly our family and our friends. And we should place our *family's* physical needs *first*. If we bring someone into our home to get well and in the doing cause our own family to suffer ill-health, or disease, that is not putting first things first. This often comes into the decision of whether we are obligated to take in a brother, or a sister, or a mother who has a contagious condition which would endanger the health of our own family. *Our* present family comes first, which means one's wife (or husband) and children precede mother, father, brothers, sisters.

7. *In our thought life*—There is an old saying: "Tell me with whom you go, and I'll tell you what you are." We think there is a better test. "Tell me what you *usually think about* and I'll tell you what you are!" Our thought life is a very important ingredient in both happiness and unhappiness. That is why with truth one can often say, "It is all in your mind." That is the reason too why mental sickness is so devastating. If we think right, we will usually do right, provided we *want* to.

And it is our humble opinion that the one area of living where the principle of *first things first* is all important, is the area of the mind—in *our thought life*. If there is order there, there must be order in our living. For it is from the mind that all thoughts come, and it is from the thoughts that most actions flow.

To practice this principle, therefore, *God* must come first. We are told to "love God above all things." Is it really possible to love someone and not *think* of them? One of the surest indications of love is the frequency the thought of the beloved enters one's mind. But emotional love, as with humans for one another, does not usually take practice *in the beginning*—there is *natural* attraction. Nor does it take practice with the love of God—*in the beginning*—there is *supernatural* attraction. *But all love must be developed and cultivated* and that takes *practice*—day in and day out, hour in and hour out, minute in and minute out. And to keep God *first* in our thoughts, we have a very excellent way—we can improve our thoughts of God through "prayer and meditation." for meditation is basically thinking about God. St. Theresa tells us that when she was a little girl she often sought a quiet spot in the garden so she could "think about God, and heaven, etc." "Now," she writes later on, "I realize that I was *meditating.*"

A.A. gives us the same method. "We sought through prayer an meditation *to improve our conscious contact* (our *thoughts* of, our consciousness of) *with God. . . .*" So, if we practice first things first, our first thoughts will always be *of God and His Will . . .* and *frequently.*

Many do not do anything for the *common good,* because they are so engrossed with their thoughts of self that they never think of the common *need.* They do not practice first things first in their thinking. For, in all of our thought life there should be the order of first things first.

We must first think of God. Then if time permits we must think over the needs of the *common good.* And the needs of *our own welfare* (not selfish desires) must then have place. Many fail *themselves* because they neglect this practice. The needs of *other* individuals then have their proper place in our thoughts. And the needs even of our enemies!

Practicing first things first in our thinking will give us much happiness, serenity and peace of mind. It will also be the best insurance we can get against mental sickness. First things first. (Which by the way, chum, would also rule out all those "evil" thoughts which we know "darn" well God doesn't want us to have there!)

8. *In our spiritual life*—Since this is God's life, we should have no difficulty understanding that *He* comes first. His will is the *essence* of a solid spiritual life. And the spiritual life that is based first on the will of God is the only true spirituality. We can never gauge a man's spirituality or sanctity by the number of his prayers, or the severity or frequency of his penances, or the amount of his almsgiving, or the number of his sacrifice, or the depth of his suffering—none of which in itself gives nor proves sanctity. *But, granted* a person is *doing God's will at all times, to the best of his ability,* that is sanctity, regardless of anything else.

God comes first. So we should approach Him the first thing each day, not only after the day is spent. *First* things *first.*

The *common good* is very important in the spiritual life and comes closely after God and fits in with His will. That is why one who professes to be leading a spiritual life no matter whom he hurts, or what happens to the common good is not putting first things first and in reality is far from being spiritual.

The A.A. who attempts to *cram his* beliefs down everyone's throats, because he is an apostle, is neither spiritual nor an apostle. He is a nuisance!

The one who wears a long face and is a continual kill-joy is certainly not spiritual—he's "cracked." Christ never subdued the joy at Cana, but He made water into wine so *they* would benefit.

The one who insists upon unusual, and numerical, and novel, and odd practices of piety and prayers is far from sanctity, and usually very irritating to the rest of men. "An eccentric saint *ain't* a saint!"

We should pray for the common good, for our country, and for all people. "That they *all* may be one."

But we must not neglect *our own welfare*, spiritually, before another individual's. First things first.

So, in the spiritual life we should pray: 1) To *God;* 2) For *all* men; 3) For *ourselves;* 4) For our *family;* 5) For our *friends;* and 6) For our *enemies.*

So many foolishly remarks: "I *never* pray for myself." But we *should! First things first!*

9. *In our A.A. life*—To keep an even keel in all of our A.A. activities it is also very necessary to practice *first things first.* And the first thing we did after admitting that we were powerless over alcohol and that our lives had become unmanageable, was "Came to believe in a Power greater than ourselves . . ."—a belief in God. And He must remain *first* in A.A. *He* should guide *all* of our A.A. living, both within and without.

God in A.A. is in all the twelve steps. So they must be paramount. Which step first? The *first step first*—the *second step second*—and so on. . . .

Those who minimize God, who apologize for Him both in the groups and on calls are *not* practicing *first things first*. Nor are those members who, although sober, are habitually breaking God's laws in their own lives, putting first things first. It is so difficult to see how these can have any happiness or peace of mind.

After God, *the common good* in A.A. comes next. What's best for the group? What does the group *conscience* want? (We emphatically do not here refer to that common phenomenon often seen in A.A., with a loud voice, a big head, and very little in it, who can aptly be described as the A.A. "knocker"—always attempting to discredit someone or something, and letting on that it is the group's wishes as a whole.) And group *conscience* means the *majority of the group, not* the steering committee which most of the time is far from expressing the group conscience, and which often is the pawn of some "politicking" group-knocker.

Many groups have clubs, and sanitaria and the like. If the *group* wants them, let them have them. First things first.

The same holds good for anything the *group as a whole* wants. The secretary or what have you holds an office of *service,* not censorship! It is ridiculous to hear a "secretary" tell an individual or a group: *"We ain't allowed to* have such and such literature, etc."! Who ain't allowing whom? Or *is* there still the tradition of *autonomy,* which in our opinion is and always will be *the greatest security of A.A.?* Or as expressed by Bill W., our founder, in a letter to the writer some time ago: *"In the future our very existence obviously depends upon our groups remaining free. . . . And it is also one of the glories of A.A. that the individual may make his choice without expecting the least interference or criticism from anyone."*

We follow *closely* the common good, which is the *only* one before *our welfare* save *God.* The common good? The good of A.A. *as a whole.*

Then *others* again, and first among them comes the welfare of our family. *Helping an individual in A.A. should never come before or be permitted to damage our family's welfare.* They come first—and *first things first!*

Then our *friends.* And it is reasonable to take care of our

246

friends *first*, but it is not reasonable to take care of our friends *only*. If possible, we must also help our enemies, even if last!

"*First things first*"—this principle expresses the simplicity of the entire program, for we are in A.A. for one purpose: *To stay sober through the help of* 1) *God and* 2) *the group and make* 3) *ourselves ready to help* 4) *others to gain sobriety when asked——*

All else is secondary.

WEAKNESS IS STRENGTH

"The weak ones of this world God has chosen to confound the strong. . . ."

Once upon a time there were two little rose buds. And they grew and grew and grew. The one had a very hard stalk and became, in blooming, a lovely well-formed rose. But the other one had a stalk that had been weakened and damaged by the weather and bruises. It too bloomed into a lovely rose. In fact the bloom itself was far more beautiful than the other rose. It had a softness and a delicacy and an aroma about it which made it a strikingly beautiful rose.

The gardener came along. Attracted by the beauty and loveliness of this particular rose he came closer the better to see and admire its beauty. Then he noticed the weak stalk. He even saw brown patches on the stalk which he knew might soon spread into the bloom itself. So he got a splint. And he wired the stalk, and he watered it carefully and pruned it. And then a terrible storm arose.

The rose with the healthy stalk was blown and battered by the wind and the rain. Soon the stalk broke and the rose fell heavily to the ground. In a very short time its petals shriveled and withered and turned brown. The rose was dead.

But the rose with the weakened stalk which had now a strong, unbending splint to reinforce it, withstood the gale. And when the storm had passed, and the sun began again to shine— almost perceptibly it turned its beautiful petals to the light and "smiled" more lovely than ever and with an aroma even more delicate than before the storm.

What had happened? In its very *weakness it had found strength*. Of itself it would have been much less able to withstand the onslaughts of the elements than its more hardy neighbor, but the master had, in its very weakness, given to it a protection and a strength not given to the healthy one.

It is always thus with master and servant, between creature and Creator. The servant who finds his security in his master is much more secure than the one who is "on his own," because he draws security and strength from the security and strength of his master; and the creature who is *fully dependent* upon his Creator draws strength and power from Divinity. The creature who is *"on his own"* draws strength only from himself.

All of this was brought out to us in the parable of the house built on sand and the house built on rocks. Then when the storms came, and the wind blew the house on sand was destroyed; the house on the rock remained intact. It was not its own strong structure that saved the house on the rock—it was the *rock*. Although the scriptures do not mention the fact, we wonder whether the house on the rock in its own construction might not have been more poorly constructed than the one on the sand—something like our little rose in the opening discussion?

From all of this comes the principle: *"Weakness is strength."* Just one more of God's amazing paradoxes! So let us take a few examples from the history of the human race and see how this has always been the secret of success in God's great ones.

Moses was an abandoned Jewish child—abandoned in the marsh near the palace of the Egyptains. But not only was he an abandoned child—he grew up to be a "balbutiens": a *stutterer*. Now one would hardly think that anyone would pick a stutterer for the great task of leadership necessary to lead the captive Israelites out of bondage—that is no one except *God*. *He* picks mostly the weaker ones and the sinners and the defective to do His work. There is only one obstacle; *bad* will. Not *weak* will; but *bad* will. God even in His eternal and infinite power never *forces* man's will; else it would not be *free*. But innate and acquired *strength* and *talent*—He doesn't need that; His power has no need of assistance; only freedom of action which is had when there is *willingness* and *cooperation*. So, He chose Moses for the task of leading the Israelites out of Egypt.

But, as we mentioned above, Moses stuttered. So he protested to God that he was unable to accept the task; that he would be unable to forcefully speak to the Israelites. Then God told him to leave that part to Him—that *He* would give the words and phrases and ability of expression necessary for doing His appointed work.

254

And in his very weakness Moses became strong and eloquent *because he had assumed divine power.*

Then remember Daniel? One of God's prophets? He was thrown into the lions' den. Now surely no human flesh would last long when thrown to a band of hungry lions, would it? None but that *protected by God's power.* So Daniel was untouched by the lions. *God's power* had protected him.

Nor let us forget about David. David was a frail child by physical standards. When we read the account of his "tiff" with Goliath we always get the idea that David was a sort of a "Little Lord Fauntelroy-type boy,"—refined, brilliant, but physically far from a burly type child. He was to be King. So his education was directed to that end—not along lines of physical prowess.

Now, you would never choose such a frail, small, gentlemanly little boy to slay a giant, would you? Well, hardly—but *God* not only would; He did. And when the giant, Goliath, saw such a little boy with his sling-shot, we can almost picture the contempt and derision with which he awaited David's approach. But funny thing is: David slew Goliath! By his own strength? But, he had none. However his own weakness became stronger than all the inherent strength of the giant *because David had assumed divine power.*

And somewhere along the years of ancient history there were three other children: Ananiah, Azariah and Misael. The only thing about these three children that would take much to master were their names! So when they were cast into a furnace which had been fired to far above its normal heat, we would hardly expect them to end up anything but a bit of ashes, would we? But *God* did not expect that; in fact He *knew* they wouldn't be burned—even slightly. Which they weren't—*because* they had become "unincinerable" *through the protection of the divine power of God.*

Many years after all the foregoing events happened, Christ came upon earth to establish Christianity. So to do this task assigned by His Father He had a lot of "pickin'" to do. Now, you would imagine He would scout around for the most talented and the most capable and the strongest people He could find, wouldn't

255

you? But He didn't. Let's look at a few He selected. Let's just look at the two He chose for leaders; one to the Jews and one to the Gentiles—Peter and Paul.

Peter was a fisherman. He had no education to speak of; he was a very impulsive individual; had a lot of "braggadocio," mixed with a bit of cowardice. But Christ wasn't looking for strength. He was looking for *willingness*. And Peter had willingness to a point where it was "showing" at almost every turn. His lack of education is very apparent through the entire gospel story. His impulsiveness is also demonstrated on numerous occasions, particularly when he "whacked" off the soldier's ear as they came to apprehend Christ. His,"braggadocio" is exemplified along with the touch of cowardice in his avowal "even if *all* leave You, *I will never*"; then but a few hours later we find him cringing at the accusations of a maid-servant in the courtyard. Again we find him fleeing from Rome and his appointed task of preaching the gospel, returning only when he was confronted with those oft quoted words, *"Quo Vadis?"*

Now who in all the world would even think of choosing such a "character" for such an important job as leader of the Apostles? No one in all the world; but *Someone* in heaven *did*. *God* chose him. And in the end we see Peter with all that lovable sincerity of heart fearlessly going to his death by crucifixion—but in his humility head downwards! *Because God's power had turned Peter's weakness into infinite strength.*

Paul whose name at first was Saul was very educated; a Roman citizen, extremely proud and haughty with a terrific temper; some kind of a bodily weakness; and just a touch of cruelty in his make-up. But, once again, Christ was not looking for strength and character. He was looking for *willingness*. And Paul was perhaps the most willing of those God chose for His apostolate as his later amazing travels, and hardships, and work accomplished bear such eloquent witness. His education is shown by his command of language. His pride and his haughtiness were part and parcel of his being a Roman citizen and his repeated appeal to this fact in his difficulties. His bodily weakness, although we are not sure what it was, is made known to us when he tells us of his "sting of the flesh" which he had asked God three times to remove, but each time was told: "My grace is sufficient for you." Which is but another way of saying. "In infirmity is power made perfect"; *in weakness there is strength.* Paul's cruelty comes to the surface in his avowed hatred of Christians and his cooperation in persecuting them. The scriptures say he was on his way to Damascus *"breathing vengeance* upon the Christians." His temper is evidenced in his "tiffs" with Peter. "I withstood him to his face."

Would any one, even impulsively, select such a personality of complicated "drives" to be the Apostle to the Gentiles? Yes, there is One Who would, and Who *did* and not impulsively. And here again we see the weakness of Paul turned into a tower of strength —fearless, tireless, meek but unyielding to Roman pressure, suffering almost endless "perils on land, perils on sea, perils of hunger, perils of fire"; perils of every type and description. How was this accomplished? *By turning all of his weaknesses over to God and thus becoming but a vessel of divine strength.*

Pages and pages and pages could be written and have been written enumerating tens of thousands of other examples of poor, weak, human beings becoming strong, amazingly strong *in God.* There's Magdalen, and Augustine, and all the thousands and thousands whose names are only known to the great Mind of God—and endless procession all proclaiming and singing along with their Leader, Christ Himself, Who to all external appearances died as the greatest failure of all times; a criminal, a weakling, a Man not even courageous enough to oppose His accusers; singing the *"Hymn of the Conquered"* in that endless procession into eternity:

"Not the jubilant song of victors,
Whom the world has such acclaimed;
But the hymn of the low and the humble,
The weary, the weak—and the maimed;
Whom life had broken, and battered and laughed at,
But who by a Power Supreme,
Have risen glorious, triumphant, true victors—
Courageous, valiant, serene!

For, *speak* history, who *are* life's victors?
Unroll thy long annals and say,—
Are the strong whom the world calls victors,
Who won success of a day?
The martyrs or Nero? The Spartans
Who fell at Thermopylae's tryst?
Or the Persians or Xerxes? His judges or Socrates?
Speaking history! Was it
Pilate?—or was it Christ?"

But we of A.A. do not need to go through the pages of history. We can take a look around any A.A. group and there we shall see hundreds, yes, thousands of examples of *in weakness there is strength.* How? Because we of A.A. have *"admitted that we were powerless over alcohol...that our lives had become unmanageable...and came to believe a power greater than ourselves (the power of God) could restore us...and made a decision to turn our will over to Him,"*—because *power has been made perfect through our very weakness.*

Take a good look into any A.A. group and see there before sobriety, the "psycho"; the "neuros"; the "crack-pots"; the weak and the sinners; even the criminals and the failures—all bearing a striking resemblance to the Man the world saw on the Cross on Calvary 1900 years ago, and Whom the world called: "crack-pot"; criminal; deceiver; magician: corrupter of morals and even blasphemer. (And we feel sure they would have called Him "psycho" and "neuro" had they the terms at the time!)

One similarity is really true: *Both He and every alcoholic before his sobriety could be called, by all external appearances, failures.*

But let us look in on an A.A. group of those who are really on the program—serene, sober and secure. And let's also compare them with a quick glance to that same Man 1900 years ago after Easter had come. What a change! What had wrought it? *The power of God,* both in Him and in us. His weakness was only apparent; ours was real—but *apparent or real* it will always be the same *willingness plus the power of God* which produces a miraculous *transformation*... and in this very weakness men, poor weak sin-laden men become miracles of strength *in Him Who strengthens them.*

And so it is that the really sincere and willing member of A.A. on the average becomes even *more* solid and better adjusted to life and living than his un-erring brothers. And as we ponder this fact we hear echoed and begin to understand the "paradoxes of life": *it is only in the night that we appreciate fully the day; it is only in suffering that we ever hope to understand fully our fellowman;* and *that we must "die to live";* and that there *can be victory even in defeat,* because *in weakness is found strength— and power is made perfect in infirmity!* Life's greatest paradox!

So let us turn to our daily affairs and see how this principle applies in all areas of our living.

1. *In our home life*—We will suggest just three very important facts about our home life which if given thoughtful consideration and used, will demonstrate how effective for good and for happy home life this principle can be.

The first is in regards to something we are afraid that most newly married couples seem to ignore or perhaps not even realize. That is: *in every marriage contract there are three parties involved: the man, the woman—and Almighty God.* If *He* is there the marriage tie will be *strong* with the *strength of God.* If He is absent it will be weak and may waste away and die!

Then we will just repeat a slogan that we feel sure you have heard on the radio and television. It is: *"The family who prays together—stays together."* May we give a corollary of our own wording? *"The family who don't—won't"!*

Thirdly we wish to call attention to a very logical appraisal of home management. It is this: the security of a home will depend to a great degree upon how strong the head of the home is. *So*—who *is* head of our home? Is it *God?* Well, is it?

In weakness is strength—so move over!

2. *In our social life*—Have you ever stopped to consider that the most attractive personality in the world is the one who is permeated through and through with his dependence upon God? We are not referring to the "pietistic" fellows and gals who *talk*

a lot about their great dependence upon God, but those *who actually have built their lives upon a deep faith and a boundless trust and dependence upon God*. When we meet such we can almost *feel* something attractive about them, something deep, a strength beyond the human. And isn't it true that it is usually those who have descended the farthest into the depths, of reversals, and hardships, and sufferings—even of sin, that seem to possess this "touch of Divinity" more than ever?

Make a round of the hospitals, the "poor" farms, the "other side of the track" and listen, long and earnestly, to the words from the lips of such as we find there who are imbued with a deep faith and trust in God.

It is a story written in the hearts of men over and over again:

In weakness there is strength.

3. *In our business affairs*—So many people think bringing God into the business world is very impractical. They never seem to realize that the more spiritual a man becomes, the more practical he becomes. Because the more spiritual he becomes, the more dependent upon God he becomes. The less he depends upon his own unaided intellect—therefore the more he prefaces *all* his thinking, decisions and efforts *with prayer for strength and guidance.*

Then this principle that *in weakness there is strength* leads the wise business man to *admit his own lack of knowledge* when serious problems arise calling for someone having more knowledge than he. So he will seek advice, and then *"two heads"* become so much better and stronger than one.

But the "know-it-all"; the "sufficient-to-himself" fellow never seeks advice even in the face of almost certain bankruptcy—which isn't far behind.

4. *In our financial affairs*—As we mentioned in previous discussions: *Security is not in dollars and cents.* True security comes from an abiding faith and trust in Divine Providence. Many accidental events can completely wipe away even the biggest fortune; but *no* event can wipe away God's Providence for man, a fact which is mentioned again and again in the scriptures:

"Consider the lilies of the field . . . the birds of the air . . . our Heavenly Father feedeth them."

"Can a mother forget her child? But even if she could, I will never forget you, O you of little Faith."

The Little Sisters of the Poor for whom we have such a high admiration and whom we have mentioned many times in our talks and writings as an example of *complete trust* in God and His Providence are striking examples of this principle related to financial security. These good nuns are exactly what their name implies. Poor—and very poor. Each day they, by their rule, seek sufficient for themselves and the many old people for whom they care. Not much money—but security? No one has more security—*for their Heavenly Father feedeth them every day.*

May we again paraphrase our principle? *In weakness there is strength,* and may we also not say *in poverty there is wealth?*

Accepting and practicing this principle financially keeps many from working hours "on end" just to *pile it up for future emergency.* Prudent saving, yes; but *frantic* saving—no.

And might we say that the writer has been amazed at the "turn about" of the General Service Headquarters this past year. After suggesting to all of the groups for fifteen years that we don't need reserve cash, we should never have a "sinking-fund," that God would provide, as the days and the weeks and the months go by; suddenly we find the "powers that be" decide to raise a huge "sinking fund" for the General Service Headquarters! What is not quite clear to our dull mind is what happened to God in the shuffle? And could we label it "irony" that they are faring worse each year?

5. *In our mental life*—All of us have been given varying degrees of mental acumen. But the availability of God's grace to enable us to "know and to understand" sort of evens it all up. And we feel that it is the student who admits his own inadequacy in his search for knowledge and truth who will approach God for the strength and ability to acquire it. And we sort of feel that such a person will acquire more and keep it much longer. St. Thomas Aquinas in school was called the "Dumb Ox." Eventually through sincerity and God's help he became a great "Doctor" of Theology

—in weakness there is strength. But the bright boys, the smart ones, have neither need of thorough study nor of Divine guidance —so they think—and so they acquire little real knowledge; no guidance; and soon lose both.

Then there is the problem of our mental institutions. We have always felt that these institutions administering to sick and weak minds would be so much more effective if they only made room for God in their program of rehabilitation. And to us the phrase *"good"* or *"competent"* psychiatrist applied to one who himself doesn't even believe in God is a "contradiction in terms" and a disgrace to the profession of psychiatry. Have these astute men never heard of: "Ask and you shall receive; seek and you shall find; knock and it shall be opened to you"? Or "Without Me you can do nothing," and Saint Paul crying out for the whole world to hear *"I can do all things in Him Who strengthens me"?*

Psychiatry which follows the Freudian school of psycho-analysis is always looking for the "Id." That's the little fellow in everybody's make-up which is supposed to control our whole personality. We might give them a tip. They wouldn't have to search so long and so laboriously if they would only give their patients a brand new "Id"—a brand new driver; a brand new control tower: *God.* He can and will do so much better a job as any A.A. can testify, particularly we who have run the gamut of psychiatric help for years. In fact, in the second step of the A.A. twelve steps we say as much: "Came to believe that Power greater than ourselves could *restore us to sanity."*

In weakness we found strength,—and sanity.

6. *In our emotional life*—If God is needed in our mental institutions, He is still more needed in our sanataria for nervous troubles. In fact someone once defined a neurotic as *"one who has never made up his mind who is to be the boss—God or himself; his body or his soul."*

We fully realize that neurotics are very sick people, and that there are many *physical* causes for their condition, but we also know that *God is all powerful,* and "nothing means 'nothing' to Him"—*He is all-powerful.*

We also know that an ingredient in many neuroses is a lack of security and we also know that the finest security in the world is Almighty God.

Scrupulosity, which is a form of neurosis in many cases, *stems from fear of our own weakness.* If such could ever be convinced and realize once and for all that *in weakness is strength,* they would be the *happiest* people in the world instead of among the most tortured.

Guilt-complexes stem from a fear *of past wrongs.* Would such people only fully realize that the *worse they were, the more hold they have on God's mercy,* they too could be happy, instead of continuing to be torn apart by useless remorse.

And we feel quite sure that honest sincere prayer, and dependence on God would eliminate a thousand times more "nerves" from this world than all the pills, and barbitals, and "happiness pills" and the bromides and what have you. Nerves come from *weakness; strength* comes from *God.* So—

In weakness there is strength—in God.

7. *In our physical life*—Lest there be any misunderstanding, we are in no way inferring by the foregoing that *God* and *God* alone will always work miracles in curing mental illness, and emotional troubles, etc. We are *not* a faith-healer." We are just a human being with two clay, and very clay, feet. So we believe that God wants us, no matter what the circumstances are, to "do the foot-work." But we do know from His own word, that all that which we cannot attain by our poor human efforts He *will* give it to us if it be witthin the realm of reason and if *it be His will.* So He will give sufficient strength to do what is necessary *always;* and He will also give a superabundance *when it happens to be His will,* and the more honestly we admit our own weakness the more abundantly He will give of His own strength. So we do not claim that God will work endless miracles in the mental hospitals, and sanataria, and hospitals; but we *do maintain that God and the psychiatrist and God and the doctor will achieve much better results* than any psychiatrist or doctor could ever hope to achieve on his own.

So in physical illness, God only works miracles when He so chooses in His Providence. But the sick man or woman who not only follows the doctor's orders but humbly asks God for more strength, admitting his own inadequacy, *will get strength and a lot of it.*

It has always been very difficult for us to imagine an atheistic doctor. Frankly we do not think there are any true atheists. The scriptures say that "only the fool has said in his heart, there is no God." Now, a *fool* is a mighty big liar. *So*—well we have never met a true atheist. We have met a lot of them who *acted* like atheists—until the chips were down! But we have never met a real one.

We do remember one we met in our early years in A.A. It was in New York City. He claimed to be an atheist. But the funny thing about it was that in the same breath he would most emphatically state that "there is no question in my mind that my seven years of sobriety is a *miracle!*"

We do not find nearly so many doctors who maintain they are atheists as we do psychiatrists. We hesitate to analyze why. But our experience has been that by far the vast majority of doctors who treat physical illnesses: diagnosticians, gynecologists, surgeons, and specialists of all types have a deep conviction of both the existence of the Deity and His influence in the healing process. In fact we have had the good fortune to be associated with many who not only had a deep conviction of the existence of the Deity and His influence, but *who sought that divine assistance and daily.* We remember one in particular. His memory will be a very treasured one all the days of our life, for we never met a doctor with a deeper faith and trust in God. And, what is not surprising in light of this deep faith and trust, he had almost unbelievable success in his surgery. He is dead now. But while he lived and practiced he never began an operation without first approaching his God in the hospital chapel asking for strength and guidance. His name? Dr. Irvin Abel of Louisville, Kentucky, who practiced at Saint Joseph Infirmary there as a surgeon and who at one time was President of the American Medical Association. He was a "big" man because he was an "humble" man;

he was a "strong" doctor because he was a "weak" human being. In his very admission of his weakness he sought Divine strength and become a great surgeon.

And where did the stamina come from in all those frail men and women—some even very sickly—who achieved even heroic things in their lives; particularly the blind, and the maimed, and the chronically ill? We mention but one: Helen Keller who achieved such outstanding accomplishments in spite of her blindness.

In weakness there is strength.

8. *In our spiritual life*—One thing should be very clear to the person who is convinced of the truth that *in weakness there is strength.* That is that *weakness is in no way an obstacle to spiritual growth nor sanctity.* God can make a saint out of the world's worst sinner or weakest soul *in an instant* provided that soul is willing. But this does not say that God *does* do this. He usually follows the laws He Himself has set up for progress—something we will discuss in a subsequent chapter wherein we will find out *no one starts at the top.* The laws of progress in human life—spiritual and otherwise—make it so that *all progress is slow.* So likewise when in our admitted weakness we sincerely seek God's strength and help, He will undoubtedly give it *when He chooses* and in so far as we *need it for our salvation,* or for *His work.* And in most cases that is over a period of time. In fact it is one of the great mistakes of many alcoholics who at times in their lives decided to *become a saint—over night!*

So, in the spiritual life our conclusion should be: *God will always give the necessary grace and strength if it is necessary for our own salvation or to do His work.* Other than that maybe He will and maybe He won't *here and now,* but He *always* will *eventually* if we keep on trying.

So let us not hesitate to attempt even the heights of sanctity; but at the same time let us not ever be disappointed if we do not achieve it *right now.*

In weakness there is strength; and in repeated falls from weakness may be found eventually even *more strength:* Humility,

9. *In our A.A. life*—One of the mistaken ideas most alcoholics seemed to have had all their lives is that it was both useful and necessary to be *strong in ourselves*. And achieving a modicum of self-sufficiency we drifted away from dependence on God. We forgot our weaknesses at first; then we denied them, "Me alcoholic?" "Me unmanageable?"—"Why, I can handle my own affairs." Which we did—and what messy affairs they turned out to be!

For many it was only after coming to A.A. and being "forced" by the bottle itself to admit our powerlessness that we learned that great paradox: *In weakness there is strength.*

And many in A.A. slip again, because they again achieve a stage in their "growth" where they have everything under control. They manage their own affairs again. They even manage a little "slip" *on their own.*

There are many occasions in A.A. to call into practice this principle of weakness is strength. When we go on a call. We wonder what to say. May we pass on the advice of our own sponsor given to a group many years ago who had asked the question: "What are we to say on a call?" It was then they turned to him and asked "What do you think about on the way?" He replied, "I don't think; I pray!" *In weakness there is strength.*

The same holds true when we are to talk. What are we going to say? How are we going to say it? What is it the eleventh step tells: "Sought through prayer . . . praying only for knowledge of His will and the *power* to carry it out."

And that, pal, is why we see as a golden thread through all the twelve steps:

"We admitted . . . powerless . . . unmanageable . . . a power . . . restore us . . . our lives . . . to . . . God . . . admitted . . . our wrongs . . . ready . . . have God . . . remove . . . him . . . remove shortcomings . . . willing to make amends . . . made . . . amends . . . wrong . . . admitted it . . . praying . . . for . . . His will . . . power . . . carry out . . . practice . . . all our affairs."

Weakness *is* strength!

266

NO ONE STARTS AT THE TOP

*"Not on Easter, but on through Bethlehem . . .
Egypt . . . Nazareth . . . and Calvary, Christ
became Redeemer."*

Scene: A drinking alcoholic is reading a newspaper. He is a singer of sorts. He reads aloud to himself:

"John Smith, internationally known singer, was given another salary raise by the XYZ Company who sponsors all of his programs. John Smith now has an income of $10,000 a week, which is top salary for his profession."

The alcoholic takes another drink. He beams. Ahhhh—one of these days I too, will be on *top*—*just like that*, when my ship comes in!"Come on, fellows, lesh all drink to the world's greatesht tenor—*Me!*"

Final Scene: A flop house on the Bowery on the lower deck. The lower deck is the floor; the upper deck the bench. Alcoholic is lying on a mess of messy rags on the messy floor in a mess. He mumbles: "Thash me—the world's greatesht shinger,—hic—*just like that!*" Alcoholic passes out—*just like that!* (Curtain).

It's a funny thing about life. *No one ever started at the top.* And yet thousands upon thousands upon thousands *try*—or just *wait.* There is only one place to begin and that is in *the beginning* which for anyone who wishes to reach the top is *at the bottom.* (Our friend above has finally reached the starting line!)

In the spiritual life, in the professions, in the material world, in the social world, in the physical world, in the world of the mind and even in all nature there must always first be the *debut;* the entrance, then painful and slow growth, and then maturity and then just as slow and sometimes even more painful, the decline and finally the exit.

In the spiritual life there must be first the conversion from sin; then the painful examination and purgation and the penance; then slow, ever so slow growth; and God-willing and aiding, a modicum of sanctity and then it is here alone in the area of the spiritual that there can be continuity of growth even into eternity. Like sobriety which is also of the spirit of man—it is *without end.*

In all of the professions there are always the long years of study and training; the debut into the profession by examination; then years of apprenticeship; and then growth into more and more mature and more competent achievement; and the decline; and the exit.

In the material world the huge skyscraper is begun with the foundation; the bank account is begun with a few dollars; and the work of art, the beautiful statue, had to be begun from the crude material and was only fashioned into the masterpiece by strong swift strokes of the brush or the chisel. But as the years and time take their deadly toll, they too eventually disintegrate; and from the world find an exit. (Only *one* of the seven Wonders of the World is still extant,—the Pyramids!)

Even in the land of social prestige, there is the "debut"; the escorting; the formalities of growth—and there too, the decline, the demise.

In the physical world,—in the life of man, there is first the seed planted within the womb of the mother; then come the months of protected growth within the womb; and the painful birth; slow growth and training; manhood and womanhood; maturity; and then begins the decline and finally death.

The little child is born with potential reason and the beginnings of intelligence; but there must then come the slow, painful, wearying hours of study and of discipline; the learning and the constant necessity of re-learning; and then old age; a return in many to childhood fancies. But here again, the mind being in the area of the spiritual will continue—into eternity.

So it is with all. There is no more universal law than *nobody and nothing starts at the top* or at *maturity.* Even the daily journey about the sun; there is the beginning of the day at dawn; the brightening and the lengthening; and only then the zenith; and the sunset; and the disappearance into the west. Even the sun does not *begin at the zenith—at the top.*

In fact there is only one member of all creation that starts at the top—who reaches the top *just like that.* It is perhaps the exception that proves the universal law; it is the *"gad-fly."* You know what a "gad-fly" is? A "gad-fly" is a little moth-like creature hatched on the lakes and the streams mostly in northern climes. These small creatures, once having hatched, immediately *zoom* to great heights over the water—*just like that.* But *just as quickly,* they fall again upon the water—*dead. Just like that* —fish food!

We find the same without exception in other parts of creation. We find that the "sudden star" which flashes in the heavens, just as suddenly disintegrates and disappears. It is the same with the sudden "fame"; the sudden "notoriety"; the sudden "saint"; the sudden acquiring of wealth; the "genius"; yes, even the "sudden" sunrise in the far north finds as its counterpart just as "sudden" a sunset.

And we find the same in A.A. The one who gets the program *just like that* seldom *keeps* the program. In fact it is the writer's opinion that the "harder" the first year the more solid and permanent the sobriety.

Nobody starts at the top. So it is that we find that *anyone* who now occupies a position of importance whether that be in the world of business; finance; the theater; the arts; athletics; government; sobriety or what have you, *invariably spent years,* and *hard years, on the way up—one step at a time.*

Likewise, in A.A. whenever we find one who has really and truly *matured* on the program and in sobriety and serenity, *invariably* also *we will find a person who has gotten there—one step at a time!*

Nobody starts at the top. And that is precisely why we tell the newcomer, "You didn't become an alcoholic *overnight;* so you can not expect to get *fully sober* over night.

Nobody starts at the top.

Oh, the human "wrecks" on the sand of time of poor deluded individuals who reached the bottom *waiting to get on the top— just like that;* waiting for their *ship to come in.* And the alcoholic "wrecks" along the paths and the "by-paths" of A.A. who reached the bottle again waiting for that "sudden flash" of sobriety and serenity—which didn't and doesn't ever come *just like that.* And in those rare cases where it does—watch for sudden relapse, or at best frequent periods of "dry drunks" and aridity of spirit and depression.

We began our discussion of *nobody starts at the top* with a quotation referring to Christ. In it we inferred that even in the business of Redemption *He* did not start at the top. He did not come to earth as the *risen* Savior; but as the *hidden* Savior at Bethlehem. Nor do we find Him "skipping" any of the phases in between. Since Redemption impelled him to "assume human nature," He wished also to follow all of the laws of human nature. His great desire was to teach us that He really wanted to be *exactly* like us—just as *human* as we are. So He *did not start at the top.* He started as every other human being in the womb of His Mother; and was born as is any other human child. And in the same way He went through all the processes of growing up, with all the heartaches and human hardships involved. He was forced to live for a while in Egypt; He settled at Nazareth; He became an adolescent; He reached maturity—even as you and I. He also omitted none of the essence of sacrifice; nor the suffering; nor the pain; not even the death—and then and then alone He became in time what He had been for all eternity our Redeemer— He arose from the dead. He had reached the *top*, but He *didn't start there!*

Only *one* began at the top,—*God,* Who always was and always will be *God.* But humans? And natures? And you and I?

No one starts at the top.

How much discouragement, and frustration, and wasted time, and injustices, and unhappiness would be avoided if *all once and for all* fully realized this principle. Let's take a look at the various areas of living and see how it works out.

1. *In our home life*—Even in the make-up of the family itself nature doesn't begin at the top. First there's a "him"; and then there's a "her"; and then there comes along another him, or her or him and her; and then another, and another. And have you ever stopped to think that we never refer to a married couple without a child as a "family"? We may say they are a happy "couple"; but only after the child comes along do we

usually say "family." So it takes time to have a family even a family of three; and a longer time to get a large family. *We don't start at the top.*

The mother and father in the home would have a lot of worry and anxiety and disappointment if they only would realize that in life *no one starts at the top.* So they would not expect their children to be saints; No one ever does become a saint—*just like that.* So the children—yes, even *your* children will be "devils" most of their growing years. A child "saint" is a true rarity; and only in instances where a special grace of God was operative. Humans do not mature—*just like that.* Neither do saints.

How ridiculous it is for a father or a mother to threaten: "If you *ever* disobey again, I'm going to punish you *very* severely." Poor kid! It's a sure thing he is going to be punished "very severely."

You know, we feel that one great fault of parents is *expecting too much from their children too fast.* They are teaching by example the fallacy that they themselves have probably been deluded by: that they should do this or do that; or achieve this or that; or become a model child—*just like that.* No wonder such children somewhere along the line *quit trying.* Children should be taught over and over again: *life begins at the beginning; each new day is a new beginning; attainment is a result of years of honest effort*—for *no one starts at the top.*

In like manner many parents and families are disappointed because they haven't a home like their parents; but they fail to realize that their parents or older brother or sister *began* at the beginning to gradually acquire such a home.

Likewise many envy the well-disciplined and integrated home of their neighbor; or the well-behaved (humanly speaking) children of their neighbor. To this there can only be one of two answers. Either they do not really *know* what goes on at the neighbors' "behind the scenes"; or they do not realize that behind that well run household *are years of effort and practice, and prayer.* As we mentioned above *no human being is born with a natural tendency* to do what is right. That tendency to evil will

275

always remain; and only concerted effort and discipline plus the grace of God will bring about "control" of these tendencies; and that will be acquired only after years of such effort and discipline. No child *just begins being good.*

No one starts at the top.

2. *In our social life*—Envy, envy, envy. We see people in "high" places; on the screen, on the television, in the newspapers; in the arts; in music; in science and we are "envious." We don't see why we *can't get lucky* and get the recognition like the others have! But we fail to realize that *none* of *these "famous" people got there over-night.* The few exceptions who did, will only remain there about as long as was their "ascent." They are the "flash" stars. Every day in the paper somewhere someone suddenly becomes famous without preceding preparation and effort. But also in every paper there are countless pages filled with other things where the names of these "flash" stars "used to be" for a very short while. Among such we have the ones who become suddenly heirs to fortunes; and then almost as quickly lose it all. We also can think of the thousands upon thousands of "beauty queens" (we can't recall any of their names!) who later got married and lived a very ordinary life—even as you and I, except that for many such there exist a lot more heartaches and disappointments and possible frustrations and discouragement.

There is a well-known television program emanating from Hollywood called "Queen for a Day." We think for once they have named their show perfectly. For it is exactly what it pretends to be: an opportunity for a "gal" to be "queen for a *day*." And we feel sure it leaves less heartache in its wake than any program on the air. It gives the little lady exactly what so many feminine hearts so desire—just to be "queen for *one day*," knowing that they can't be one for always. And the wonder of the program is that almost always, the one selected to be "Queen" is not selected for something a few judges or the vacillating applause of many tell the world she *has;* something the very selection or applause has over-rated in reality; but for some-things usually which she *hasn't got;* loss, hardship, suffering. So we feel this program brings home very dramatically the truth;

*No one starts at the top; anyone might get there for a day, just
like that; but permanent fame and glory and accomplishment are
the product of years of effort.* So "old man" Bailey who is the
"star" of the program—*stays;* but he didn't get there either—
just like that.

No one starts at the top.

3. *In our business affairs*—The man who enters business
convinced that he must work his way up gradually, will work
harder and more efficiently and probably some day actually reach
the top. But the worker who works along "waiting" for the "big
break" or the "sudden beckoning" from the top—will probably
coast along being a half-hearted and discontented worker until
he dies.

Even the father who is now at the top in his business, if
prudent and wise, will not start his own son *at the top.* Such a
business man knows that *no one, even the son of the boss, starts
at the top.* And he further knows that were he to start his son
at the top, the son probably would not stay there—certainly
would not be efficient in the job.

This is the reason that so many one time "famous" organizations or businesses are now gone or bankrupt. Some one at the
top foolishly put his son there to begin; and the business fell
apart. Remember the "gad-fly"?

So every good business man wants his boy to start at the
bottom and to learn the business from the "ground up." *For no
one starts at the top.*

So also the man who begins in business. He *expects* lean
days, and work-filled nights and days; until business grows. He
will reach the top; good days; profit days—but only after perhaps years and years of growth and effort.

We might also mention the professions. These men in a way
are in business. But here too *no one starts at the top.* In fact the
one who begins the practice of his profession (doctor, attorney,
etc.) without the ordinary apprenticeship, but using the fame and
the name of his dad or a relative as his calling card to successful
practice, seldom makes anywhere near the success of his prede-

cessor. This is the reason that in many instances, having a "famous" relative as a precedent in the profession is many times a burden instead of a help.

No one starts at the top.

4. *In our financial affairs*—The first thing the "make-a-million" guy needs to learn and practice is that *no one starts at the top.* With rare exceptions people who have money today—lots or little—got it by persistent hard work and prudent saving. How about the one who is "born" to wealth? Well, someone somewhere way, way back *started at the bottom!*

As we mentioned above in passing, *usually* the one who comes into sudden *"money"* often just as suddenly loses it.

But perhaps the greatest lesson to be learned from this principle; and perhaps the most effective application of it in the area of finance is that *we use present opportunities* and *save bit by bit in the present* instead of wasting what we make or just plain wasting time without making—*until our big opportunity comes along.* Or in "horse" parlance; plug along playing your choice instead of always trying for a "long-shot." But some do insist on the "long-shot" and "some of these days" they are going to make a million—*just like that.* You know something? It would be interesting to know the *odds* against anyone making a million—*just like that. "Millions"* to one!

No one starts at the top.

5. *In our mental life*—A genius is *not* an educated person. Education not only implies "knowledge" but *training.* In fact one of the biggest missing factors today in many of our so-called educational institutions is *training.* There is *"loads"* of knowledge given to all students today; much more than when we went to school. But there is very little training in what to do with the knowledge they acquire. There is little training in *thinking.* So many know all the answers to questions of fact; but haven't the slightest ability to *"think through the mass of facts presented in order to logically reach the correct conclusion as to what to do with the facts.*

278

An educator of the "twenties" already has made the pointed observation about our modern school systems: "Some one somewhere had a dream. All we had to do was to teach *all* of the people and we would have a generation of educated adults avidly devouring the great classics of literature,—*just like that.* So we made every boy go to school. We gave them lots of knowledge. And what did we get? A generation of adults *'glued to the funny papers' "!*

We sort of think he's got something there. We are convinced that education has missed the boat. People know a lot: from school, newspapers, magazines, television etc. But so few—so *very* few know what to do with it and so we have confusion and neurotics and psychotics and criminals and juvenile delinquents. After all, what is a juvenile delinquent? He or she is some one who learned too much *too fast* of the things they haven't the slightest idea what to do with.

It is all something like a fellow who was on a very fast train. The engine was "zooming" through the night at over a hundred miles an hour. He began to wonder. So he called the porter. To the porter he addressed the query: "How fast are we traveling, porter?"

"One hundred and ten miles an hour, suh," the porter replied.

"And how much distance would be required to stop this train with the emergency brake if necessary?"

"A half a mile, suh."

"And how far ahead does the train's spot light pick up an object?"

"A quarter of a mile, suh."

The gentleman returned to his home town on a slower train!

But we have disgressed enough. We hope you pardon us, but we had to write a thesis at post-graduate school on the Philosophy of Education. And we wanted to bring home the point that *true education,* and good *mental hygiene* involve so much more than being a genius or just learning a lot of facts. So, *no one* is born *an educated* person. We are born with all sorts of variance in I.Q. But when it comes to being educated; to mental discipline;

—no one starts at the top—no one begins with it but only acquires it with persistent effort and study and meditation.

After all, animals can exercise memory; but only man *and God* have an intelligence, the power to reason and a free will. But it is given to all—genius or moron—in a *"do it yourself kit,"* from *the beginning.*

No one starts at the top.

6. *In our emotional life*—Ever see someone with excellent emotional control? If you have you can be sure he or she spent many tedious years acquiring that control. Emotional control above all else is not given at birth. It is rather just the opposite. Witness the weeping and wailing and yelling of the baby; the tantrums of children.

Yet there are many people who "coast" through life with the foolish notion that when they grow older they will automatically get rid of their "emotional swings,"—*just like that.* On the contrary emotional "swings" which are not worked on day in and day out just keep on getting a little bit *worse* with approaching age. And, there is nothing more irritating to everybody connected with them, than a "crochety" old man or a "cranky" old woman. People growing old just don't become Whistler's mother type—*just like that.* To be thus in old age—or in adult life—one must *begin at the beginning,* and that is in *childhood.* Even the scriptures tell us that a "young man even to his old age will *not* change *his ways.*" (And that "man" means *human,* including the ladies!)

So if we are fully convinced of all this we will begin *now* at the *beginning* which means *not* trying all at once to control all of our emotional "swings" at one time, but *take each one*—and *one at a time.*

No no starts at the top.

7. *In our physical life*—Neither sickness nor health comes *just like that.* Every healthy individual is such usually because he has "worked at" being healthy; and every "sick" person became ill only over a period of time. Nor does a sick person become well *just like that.*

Realizing this will lead us to avoid "small" breaches of rules of health; and would also lead us to take regularly the medicine prescribed by the doctor, the exercises, the diet, because there is no medicine which will cure us *just like that.* Let us not forget the "star flashes"; the average *sudden cure* is not a permanent cure.

No one starts at the top.

8. *In our spiritual life*—We are really convinced that the average alcoholic is a basically spiritual person. In fact we think most alcoholics would like to be saints *but just like that.* It is the tedium of daily trying that wears us down. In fact it wears all humans down, *unless* we keep on keeping on.

So in practicing this principle in the spiritual life we will first of all realize that *no one ever became a saint over-night;* that the *top* in the spiritual life is in eternity—in union with God and towards that we must grow and painfully grow; and that the usual pattern of growth in the spiritual life is three steps forward and two steps back. It is not only possible for us to achieve that eternal destiny, but it will be probable—in fact certain—*if we keep on trying.* And we will so much more surely keep on trying in the face of hardship and sin and repeated falls if we are fully aware that we won't make it *just like that.* So we will be sure first that we are "good" sinners before we hope to be real saints. We start with sin; not sanctity.

No one starts at the top.

9. *In our A.A. life*—With a deep conviction of this principle of life in our A.A. affairs we will not play up so much that much "over-played" idea of the "sudden flash." We will do a much better job with the newcomer and with ourselves if we emphasize that *we didn't get drunk over-night and we aren't going to sober up over-night.* We can *dry* up over-night; but we cannot *sober* up *just like that. Sobriety* is much more than mere abstinence from alcoholic beverages. *Sobriety is adjustment* and serenity and peace of mind and peace of soul and contentment. And *beyond sobriety* we have seen in the life of the spirit. But sobriety

281

remains an essential part of spiritual living. It remains and will grow along with spiritual growth—into eternity *without end.*

We don't expect, as so many so foolishly do, to be able to intelligently and sincerely practice the last three steps without having first taken the first nine steps and thoroughly.

So many cry around and wonder why they do not seem to have a "spiritual awakening." May we suggest they look very carefully at the twelfth step which mentions this "spiritual awakening"? If they do they will read there that it comes *as a result of these (the first eleven) steps!* We don't *begin* with the "spiritual awakening." The only place we can begin is in the beginning—and that is with the first step,—and then the second —and the third and on *one step at a time.*

For neither in life nor in death; neither in nature nor in super-nature; neither in drinking nor in sobriety does *anyone* start at the top.

No one starts at the top.

THE VALUE OF APOLOGY

"Made direct amends . . . when wrong promptly admitted it."

Apology is for weaklings and cowards. Such was the motto in the drinking days of the alcoholic, or even before his drinking days. In fact there was never anything to apologize for. Wasn't everybody else wrong; and were not we always right?

In A.A. we learn that it is very necessary to be diligent in our mental hygiene; that apology, when apology is in order, is a necessary part of mental keeping house; that to omit it *might,* just *might* cause serious drink cravings even on the level of the subconscious. It has happened.

John Doe hadn't had a drink for six years. He was a member of A.A. Suddenly one day he got a terrific craving for a drink. And in spite of all that he could do and no matter how much or how often he "talked it out" with other members, it still remained —day in and day out, hour in and hour out, minute in and minute out. Frantic and frightened he kept seeking advice. Finally one of the members came up with the question:

"Was there by chance anything or anyone that you deliberately *left out of your making of amends?* Was there anyone to whom you *willfully and knowingly refused to apologize?*"

John thought hard. Suddenly he stammered: "Yes, it was my brother-in-law, the so-and-so, but *he* was to blame! And only two weeks ago he wrote me a letter! Why that ... hey ... two weeks ago,—why that was the day this thing began!"

His friend looked straight at him, grinned, and said, "Well, what are you waiting for? Where does this brother-in-law live?"

It was a long trip. John took a plane. He went to his brother-in-law's office. He apologized asking no corners. And to this day he has had no further craving for a drink. This is a true story!

"When wrong, *promptly* admitted it...."

"Made *direct* amends...."

287

Why apology is looked down upon by so many we do not know. Perhaps it is due to a misunderstanding as to the true nature of apology. However, we feel that the principal reason so many shy away from apology is because genuine apology necessitate genuine humility and genuine humility does not come easy nor is it very attractive to proud human nature.

The word *"apology"* has gone through a transformation in meaning down through the ages to such an extent that the meaning usually attributed to it today is the opposite of its original meaning. It stems from the Greek words "apo" and "logos" meaning "words against"; or more broadly "words in defense of." And for many years the Latin word "apologia" was used to signify "a defense against alleged wrongdoing"; a "justification of one's action." It was sort of a "white paper."

However in recent times the English word "apology" is most times taken to mean just the opposite, ordinarily being used to mean"a verbal admission of responsibility for the purpose of receiving forgiveness." Actually it is an external expression of an honest internal feeling of responsibility or blame. And as such it proves very valuable to the alcoholic for both the mental hygienic value of clearing away all dishonest attitudes and guilt feelings and also for the practicing *external* humility—so necessary to the proud alcoholic; to proud human nature.

So it is that sprinkled throughout the twelve steps of the Alcoholics Anonymous program are repeated suggestions of the practice of apology.

Particularly is this suggested in the ninth step where it is suggested that the alcoholic make *direct* amends. It is not a matter of fulfilling the law of justice and rights, but rather the opportunity for the member to *practice humility* and to *externalize* all of his internal admitted responsibilities in the wrongs of his past. This is the highest type of *moral* and *mental* hygiene.

We feel that many, many members of A.A. miss the most effective therapy of the entire twelve steps in seeking sobriety and serenity by omitting these *direct* amends. They make amends; but anonymously. As a result they lose the whole purpose of the step. They acquire no humility; and they do not *empty* the mind completely. And for sustained serenity it is absolutely necessary to have *both* humility and a clear mind uncluttered by unsolved problems of the past. There is no side-door to sobriety—the only one that opens is *humility.*

We often find alcoholics in A.A. who are consistently trying to stay sober and keep their pride. It just can't be done. This is what is behind the ever recurring effort here and there in starting a so-called "slippers" group. Their *excuse* is that they want to make it *easier for the slipper to come back to the group.* What they are actually doing is trying to give sobriety and protect pride at the same time. Once again, it *can't* be done.

So it is that a question very frequently asked in A.A. circles is *"must* I take the ninth step? *Must* I make *direct* amends?" And the answer is "No, there are no musts in A.A. *But* if you want more than mere abstinence from alcohol; If you want true sobriety—and the serenity beyond, *there ain't no other way of getting it!"* So it isn't a *"must,"* but a heck of a big *"proviso."*

And to *keep* sobriety and serenity, we must say the same for the tenth step wherein "when wrong we promptly admit it," —day in and day out. This is not a sign of a weakling—but evidence of true courage. Anyone in this old world can *refrain* from admitting wrongs; it takes real courage to *do* the admitting. But its payoff is tremendous in continued serenity and sobriety and mental relaxation.

The alcoholic personality is so constituted that we can not tolerate for long emotional upsets, emotional tension. And when the alcoholic refrains from *doing* something about the tensions and the wrongs that come along, this grows inside—and grows— and grows and some day sooner or later and soon at the latest it blossoms and blooms into four beautiful roses!

So therefore *apology*—admitting our wrongs—talking out our upsets is security for sanity—a stepping stone to sanctity— and a safety valve for sobriety—and a soporific for serenity.

"Made *direct* amends . . . when wrong *promptly admitted it."* Cleaned up the past . . . continued to insure the present and the future.

Now let's see how this works out in our daily living, in all of our affairs.

1. *In our home life*—Suspicion, doubt, jealousies, bickering and many other ills of the home life of people come from "hidden" wrongs—hidden from the other. On the other hand the home in which everything is "out in the open and above board"; in which neither mother, father nor children are too proud to admit their faults to the others; and in which "secrets" have no place, is usually a well-adjusted home. Faults? Yes, they have many, but "nobody's letting them bother nobody!"

The reason that "admitting wrongs"; the reason that apology; and the reason that "taking responsibility" in the home is so effective is because it is the finest and surest way to build *humility* in the home.

The monasteries have always been very cognizant of this value in any community life. For this reason many still have what is called "The Chapter of Faults" every day. At this time all the members of the community meet together and all *openly* admit their *faults* to the community. Sin is not under this category. Sin is something very personal and a matter of one's conscience and should be discussed with one's spiritual advisor. Faults are something else. Faults are anything contrary to rule, or custom, or actions which come from our very imperfect human nature but which are not contrary to *the moral* law.

In fact it would be very imprudent to say the least for any member of the home to expect admission of sin or to perhaps even try to force such an admission out of one of the other members of the family. Parents often cause much emotional troubles in their children by uncovering their children's "sin." The same could be said of any group or community.

When we speak of "wrongs" and promptly and directly admitting them, we speak of "wrongs to others." In other words there is a difficulty in the home. Everyone becomes upset. It was *our* fault. We *admit* it; we *apologize*. And in using the term apology, we do not mean constant asking pardon, but *honest* admission of responsibility. And when we speak of "faults" we mean "disruptions of the ordinary course of things in the group caused by *us.*"

So it is that the custom of the "Chapter of Faults" goes far in producing in the members of the community, a deep *habit* of humility. For as we saw before: *humility is truth openly admitted and accepted.*

The home with humility as its foundation is usually a happy and well adjusted home. Why? Because there "ain't anything which isn't known, and accepted and admitted." Under these circumstances there is no room nor reason for doubt, or suspicion, or jealousies, or bickering or "unforgiven" actions.

"Made *direct* amends." "When *wrong* promptly admitted it."

2. *In our social life*—"Standing up for our rights" can always get one into more trouble than "admitting our wrongs." How many times neighbors go for years not speaking, resenting, irritated just because *someone* was too stubborn to admit their responsibility—too proud to apologize.

Have you ever noticed the difference whenever there is a "near" accident, or an irritation between the guy or the gal who immediately starts *demanding* and the guy or the gal who immediately apologizes?

Even the officer of the law becomes a different person to the one who apologizes instead of immediately excusing and rationalizing.

And when there is really a question of our rights or at least probable rights, what is it we say in A.A.? *We don't question whether the other was at fault; we are!*

3. *In our business life*—The first quality necessary in a customer relations official is the ability to *apologize.* And the most substantial basis for a successful business is the attitude that the "customer is always right." This doesn't mean that they *really* are always right, but it does mean, that as far as good solid business practices are concerned, they are.

4. *In our financial affairs*—There are several ways in which this principle can become operative in our financial affairs. First

there is a practice which we feel *most* people don't practice! Let's take an example:

We go to the store. We make a purchase. The store gives us too much change. We pocket it! What happened to "when *wrong* promptly admitted it"? The ninth step of the A.A. program in which we "made *direct* amends" was for the purpose of cleaning up all of the past. The tenth step is to give us a chance to *avoid* having to do the ninth step again. So if we would just stop and take time out and realize that if we *don't* "promptly admit when we are wrong"—particularly in the matter of finance —the day *will* come again when we must again make "*direct* amends."

Also this characteristic is very familiar in the one who stubbornly refuses to buy or sell in face of almost certain disaster. He is determined that *he* is right. Or again in the gambler we see this characteristic crop up. He sticks to his choice *no matter what*, just because it is his choice.

These people know it all; they never seek advice; they are very, very proud, so they can't, in their inflated ego, ever be wrong.

"When *wrong* promptly admitted it."

5. *In our mental life*—"Self-righteousness" is a destructive thing to the personality, but particularly does it play havoc with the mind. Self-righteousness necessitates self-deceit. Self-deceit necessitates a closed mind. A closed mind evolves into flight from reality and ends a victim to phobias, mental illnesses and illusions. On the other hand a mind that *admits* error when there is error, either subjective or objective, remains a simple, united, single substance. It retains open-mindedness and sanity. And in this soil alone will sobriety and serenity blossom and bear fruit. Remember what the A.A. book says: "Willingness, *honesty* and *open-mindedness* are essentials of recovery. *They are indispensable!*"

"When *wrong* promptly admitted it."

6. *In our emotional life*—"And then we lied to get out of the lie we told to get out of the lie we told to get out of the lie

292

we told." The cycle of the drinking alcoholic. Why did we do this? We *never admitted we were wrong!*

So, as a result of this frantic merry-go-round and the constant attempt to cover up, we ended up with tensions, resentments, emotional difficulties of all kinds.

One of the best nerve tonics we can get is the practice of "admitting it when we are wrong." In the alcoholic it is paramount, because as we said above, *if we don't,* all these emotional disturbances sooner or later will seek and obtain an outlet *in alcohol.* It is the same reason that makes *resentment* and *self-pity* mortal enemies of the alcoholic.

And the jitters? Who is more jittery than the fellow or gal who is all of the time fearful someone will find out.

"When *wrong* promptly admitted it."

7. *In our physical life*—Practicing this principle will tend to keep our bodies healthy, not only by eliminating nervous strain, which is the by-product of refusing to admit things and which is so damaging to the entire nervous system and the body, but also because in doing so we will not refuse to recognize "beginnings" of illness, over-tiredness, and other physical ailments and will be able to check them in time.

On the physical side too this principle becomes very valuable to the one who has physical defects. The one who *freely and openly admits* having them is a much more happy and adjusted individual than the one who tries to constantly *hide* them even from himself. Again it is a question of humility. And still we find so many who will not even admit *ordinary* defects to themselves or others; they refuse to wear glasses, to wear a hearing aid, etc., etc.

"When *wrong* promptly admitted it."

8. *In our spiritual life*—Here, of course, more than in any area of living, is this principle so effective. Remember what we said about the one "who sins and *admits* he sins"? He is not nearly so hopeless nor beyond help as the one who *refuses to admit his sins* even to *himself or to God.*

The practice of this principle will suggest that we *have a regular spiritual advisor*. The lack of a spiritual advisor is one of the biggest missing factors of the spiritual life in recent times. For solid spiritual living and growth we need someone to whom we can go with every spiritual trouble. We need someone to whom we can admit those very personal and "hidden" sins and wrongs. It is so necessary to keep our souls from getting cluttered up with "habits" of sin.

In the fifth step we "admitted to ourselves, to God *and to another human being.*" We should do this *regularly,* with our *sins* as well as all other difficulties.

"When wrong *promptly* admitted it."

9. *In our A.A. life*—Here it is very necessary to pin-point all those "wrongs" which have a direct bearing on sobriety. For as we said above, if we do not *promptly* admit and get rid of all these "danger-slip-points," we will not maintain our sobriety even though we may have progressed far in the spiritual life.

And perhaps the "biggest" wrong for us in A.A. to *admit* again and again and again is the one that used to tell us that we could drink normally. In short: that we are *alcoholics;* that we *cannot handle alcohol;* that our lives on our own are unmanageable.

Alcoholics: yesterday, today and tomorrow, and therefore anything contrary to that conviction is *wrong!*

When wrong *promptly* admitted it."

And so an apology is not a matter of repetitive "pardon this and pardon that." That is for the "namby-pambies." But *apology* is for real honest-to-God men and women. It is for men and women of *courage.* It demands courage! It gives *humility.* And it is a necessity for sobriety, and sanity, and sanctity and security —"when *wrong* promptly admitted it."

SEX AND SOBRIETY

*"In the beginning God created man ...
male and female He created them."*

If you opened this book to this chapter first, you need it; if you wanted to open it here first, but didn't, you are virtuous; if you read the table of contents and ignored it, you're a hypocrite; if you read the table of contents and say you didn't even notice it, you're a liar!

We have undertaken to write about the subject of sex for two reasons: first in answer to numerous requests from A.A.s everywhere; and secondly because we feel there is no subject today more discussed and yet less understood than the subject of sex. In fact we are constantly amazed to find so many, even among the so-called educated class, so ignorant of the basic principles of this important human drive.

In the first place let us get straight in our minds that sex is the second most powerful drive in human life. The strongest is the desire for food; for self-preservation. The second greatest and strongest desire is for sex; for self-reproduction. And so with this in mind let us rule out completely that class of pietistic crack-pots who maintain it is a simple matter to *"be mature and just ignore sex."* To their type of mentality one could never hope to get entree; so we won't even discuss their fallacy.

Then let us rule out once and for all that sex is something "evil." *Nothing* God created is evil; it is only *man's abuse of it that is evil.* There is nothing evil in taking money from our own wallet; but *the same act* from someone else's wallet becomes stealing and evil. So the act of sex is not *"per se"* evil; but if it is done *contrary to God's law* it is sinful. Both actions may be identical; but one according to the ordination of the Creator and a good act; the other *contrary* to the ordination of the Creator and therefore sinful.

Actually sex is something beautiful. It in reality is one of the most wonderful and the most beautiful of all powers given to man. It is the one human action in which *God takes part.* It is the action in which husband and wife *become co-creators with God of a new human life.* So sex is not evil; on the contrary it is beautiful and good.

However because of the very power of its drive, it consistently and persistently demands expression either according to the law of God or contrary to His law. And as we mentioned in one of our foregoing discussions, *humanly speaking* it is *impossible to remain chaste*—so great is this drive. *But* with the grace of God it not only becomes possible, but a reality. So the fallacy of many doctors and psychiatrists lies in the fact that they only make a "half" statement. They maintain that sexual abstinence in the sexually mature person is impossible. They would be right *if they added: without the grace of God.*

Now let's throw out another asinine fallacy often heard in medical and psychiatric circles. This is that sexual abstinence in the sexually mature person is harmful. There never was a more "diabolical" lie. Sexual control and willful sexual abstinence not only are *not* damaging, but on the contrary are oftentimes more conducive to good health and mental acumen. We say "willful" continence; because "enforced" continence can easily set up serious conflicts and tensions which might be very damaging to health.

We also use the term "control" in contradistinction to "repression." Control means acknowledging the existence of the sexual tendency and drive, but, assisted by grace, consciously and conscientiously avoiding its use. Repression means the denial of the very existence of the sexual drive or "acting as if it didn't" exist"; or by "not admitting even to ourselves that it exists." Such repression is not only dishonest, but a source of pressure and tension in the subconscious and one which can be very damaging and which can and does cause serious neuroses.

To sum up the above: the healthy attitude toward sex is to accept it and not fear it; to realize that the presence of sexual desires—mental or otherwise tells us only one thing; we are human; to accept the fact that such will be there as long as we are human, which means until death; finally to realize sex was created by God for a good and holy purpose; and therefore we shall not indulge in it in any way except in lawful marriage. With such an attitude there is little chance of getting a "sex-neurosis."

Another fallacy: the bugaboo of being "over-sexed." An over-sexed person is extremely rare. The "Don Juan" type man; and the "nymph" type woman are not over-sexed *physically;* they are over-sexed *mentally.* For this reason there can never be true satisfaction. For psychological demands can not be fulfilled by physiological outlets. So there is immediate recurrence of desire. Many of these people are actually *under-sexed* physically and for this reason their frantic and repeated indulgences deplete the nerve system and bring on nervous, mental and physical disorder. Much of this today is a result of the widespread over-stimulation *mentally:* in the newspapers, magazines, movies, television and what have you.

How about "half-control"? A "little" petting and no more? This is a contradiction in terms. "Half-control" is *no* control. If continence is humanly speaking impossible in the sexually mature adult, we can be darn sure that "half-control" is impossible. And we are even more sure that God isn't about to give the strength to "half-control" sex. We might classify under the "half-controllers" the "petters"; the "dreamers"; and the "readers." In other words all who try to "read" sex-provoking literature; or think sex-provoking thoughts; or do "just a little" sex-provoking actions and at the same time attempt to avoid complete indulgence, are trying the impossible. It's a lot like the alcoholic who would attempt to take "just a couple of 'shots'" and stay sober!

Then there are sex problems between husbands and wives. And to all such problems we have found that there is only one answer. *Both* husband and wife should *together* consult a *competent* advisor and lay it all out "on the table." We have found that this works when countless hours of advice to one or the other or to both separately has not worked. Sexual maladjustment in marriage is not nearly so often a case of actual sex difficulties as it is a failure of having a *meeting of minds.* Mental adjustment is what is needed more than anything else.

One final observation before we proceed to the question of sex and the alcoholic specifically. "Loveless" sex is the most flimsy thing in the world, and nothing dissipates itself more quickly. Love is *giving;* sex is *taking.* Unless there is therefore much giving—much honest love of the other, there "ain't gonna be no sex nor no nothing before long." And you wanta know something? Sex in marriage with the *motive of giving pleasure* to the *other* instead of the motive of *getting* from the *other* would solve *most marriage sex problems!*

Now to *sex and sobriety.* And the first question that comes up is what has sex to do with alcoholism and what has alcoholism to do with sex?

First let us take a good look at *alcohol,* then at *alcoholism,* and then *at sex.* Alcohol is not a stimulant—sex or any other kind. Alcohol is, used normally, a sedative. It sedates the inhibitory factors of the brain and relaxes the blood vessels particularly the capillary system. This is what causes drinkers to apparently blush, or become red-faced. It also in a way contributes to the "alcoholic snozzle." But alcohol is not alcoholism. Alcohol does not cause alcoholism. Alcoholism is an allergy of the body coupled with a compulsion of the mind so that having taken one drink an alcoholic can not guarantee when he will stop. And sex is, as we noted in the beginning of our discussion, a very normal drive existent in all human beings, second only to the drive to self-preservation in intensity. So how do alcohol and alcoholism affect this drive?

We said alcohol *sedates the inhibitory factors of the brain* when used normally. So since sex is a drive which demands in most social circles in this old world, *control,* alcohol in sedating these inhibitory factors, these controls, *seem to enhance* the sex drive. Actually it only *loosens the controls.* It is something like the loosening of the dike on the river. It would enable the water to flow faster, but *it did not cause it to.* So alcohol *enables sex* to more easily assert itself and with less inhibition, but most physicians do not look upon alcohol as an aphrodisiac. Alcohol therefore does not *increase* sex, it *unleashes* it.

But again, alcohol is not alcoholism. And, contrary to popular opinion, when one has entered into chronic alcoholism, he rather than having sex enhanced, loses most sex desires. Why? Because although alcohol taken normally is a sedative to the inhibitory factors of the brain, taken in the manner and to the excess in which the alcoholic indulges, it becomes a *depressant*, and depresses most of the glandular system, including the sex glands. So it is that most alcoholics, in their chronic drinking as alcoholics, were not much interested in sex—period.

Now let's come to the sober alcoholic and sex. Did alcoholism *kill* the sex drive? Strange as it may seem, in most alcoholics the alcohol didn't leave any permanent physical damage. So with the sex drive, once fully sober, he or she is not unlike the rest of men or women.

And here is where many are subject to much misinformation. So many members of A.A. stop drinking. They sober up. They get *"on"* the program. They pray. They want to be good people again. And lo and behold, their craving for alcohol leaves them. *But* lo and behold their sex drive *doesn't*. And they are at a loss wondering why. It is all very simple. *Sex* is a very normal human drive, part and parcel of every man, woman and child. But *alcoholism*, the *craving for alcohol*, is *not*. So to the sincere, God gives surcease for alcoholic craving. *He* expels the compulsion to drink. For this reason in many groups one hears the saying: *"A.A. is the expulsion of a compulsion by a higher power, by Almighty God."* But drinking or sober we are and will always remain *human*, and so the desire for sex will always be with us. But with God's grace, as we saw in the beginning, we *can control it*.

Now for the $64,000 question! Does *sex cause slips?* We have the saying in A.A. in some areas: "The red-headed[1] woman walked in and sobriety walked out." Does this mean that indulging in a *sin* of sex will *cause a slip?* We're sorry, but we will have to say "No." And we have deduced, after talking with several tens of thousands of slippers, that the *sin* will not cause the slip; *but the emotional tension, or the worried conscience, or*

---

[1] We suppose that they use the term "red-headed" because they are so attractive.

the frustrations, or the resentments involved will cause a slip to an alcoholic. And since *most* sexual sins *do* involve emotional tension, and/or a worried conscience, and/or frustrations, and/or resentments, *therefore most* sexual *sins will be the occasion of the slip, not* because it is sinful, *but* because of the above involvements which are always preliminary to any slip. If a person involved in an illicit sex relationship *can possibly* avoid emotional tension, or a worried conscience, or frustrations, or resentments, *he can stay sober.* He probably *won't,* because some of the above will almost inevitably creep in, but he *could.* And there are a few who *do!* So, in relationship to slips, we have reached this conclusion about sex: *an alcoholic indulging in illicit sex could stay sober, but he won't!* (Neither will *she!*)

So in conclusion let us realize that sex is something good in itself; that God created it; that we need only to control it; that such control comes only in answer to prayer, and begins in clean thinking. It begins in the heart. And what was it Christ said in the beatitudes: "Blessed are the clean of heart; for they shall see God." May we add a phrase of our own? They shall see *God* and not *sex* in *everything*!

LIFE IS A SELFISH PROGRAM

*"I have kept thy commandments, O God,
because of the reward."*

A principle that gets "kicked" around A.A. circles quite a bit is: *A.A. is a selfish program.* Many outside of A.A. are a-mazed to hear this; and many inside of A.A. not only are amazed to hear it but confused by it and mostly misunderstanding its true meaning. The primary reason for all this misunderstanding is because so many misunderstand what is meant by the term "selfish." It's something like the "capital" in capital sins. We feel a better term would be *"self-love"* and perhaps a re-phrasing into "A.A. is a program of true "self-love." Be that as it may, we are going to re-phrase it in a different way and state: *life is a selfish program.*

Let's first take a look at the drinking alcoholic. Many a time in his drinking "career," the alcoholic attempted to achieve and maintain sobriety to please his wife, or friend, or boss, or supe-rior. But such type sobriety was usually very short-lived. For just as soon as the wife, or the friend, or the boss or the superior was *pleased,* the *reason* for staying sober disappeared; the motive was gone; the *necessity* was no longer there—so he drank again.

So too many come to A.A. just to *please* someone else or because someone else pressured them to come. They leave A.A., via the bottle, just as soon as the one is *pleased* or just as soon as the pressure is off.

Why does this happen? Because the alcoholic has not yet learned the necessity of true *self-love.* He has never realized that *he must do things in life for himself—because he wants it.* This is the *beginning* of *love* of others and which must start with love of self. It is exactly what God told us when He said: *"Love the Lord above all things; and thy neighbor as thyself."* So we begin to be *unselfish* by practicing self-love—by being "selfish."

In the beginning, for all alcoholics, and for many years for most alcoholics it is the only motive that will work. It is the only thing that stabilizes the pathologically proud alcoholic. He

309

is not *big* enough to stay sober for the sake of someone he loves; he is *small* enough, however, to say sober for *himself.*

So it is that in all of the areas of his living, an alcoholic is best approached from a *selfish* viewpoint which means that he *is doing what he is doing whatever that may be primarily for himself—for his own recognized good.* In fact it is very dangerous for the alcoholic to become *apostolic* in his motive. He can not with his present selfish nature stand the "rarefied" air of that height.

The alcoholic therefore has much more stability and security in his sobriety if he stays sober *for himself;* and he will have much firmer growth in the spiritual life if he continues to operate with this motive for a long, long time.

We practice the twelve steps for *us,* for *our* sobriety; we practice mental hygiene for *us;* we control our emotions for *us;* we do good for others for *us;* we practice virtue for *us;* we do *all things* for *us—in order to* get more sobriety and to keep our sobriety.

Now is this a *new* approach to *life?* Well, hardly. Centuries ago a certain very saintly king said as he approached his death: "I have kept Thy commandments, O Lord, *because of the reward.*" His name was David, and he too had a messy proud past.

Life is a selfish program. This is the reason that all progress in the spiritual life must be prefaced, and for years, with the practice mental hygiene for *us;* we control our emotions for *us;* in order to *gradually* aspire to the higher forms and motives of living—a complete selflessness.

Why is this? It is because the will of man follows what is held out to it by the intellect to be *good.* Therefore man seeks *what he thinks is best for him.* This is true self-love. But this goes haywire when our intellect fools us, or our emotions influence our intellect and discolor the true *good,* and we *seek what seems to us best but what is actually damaging to us.* Behold the alcoholic! At the moment in his beclouded mind and soul and emotions, *alcohol* seems *best.* So he takes it. But this is not self-love —it is self-destruction.

And only when *sobriety appears to him to be good* and

desirable, will he pursue and seek it and maintain it. When he attempted to stay sober for someone else, *to him* that was not what *he wanted nor saw as best for him.* He was still thinking that drinking was better. So his motive was negative, from fear or coercion, and therefore as soon as the fear or the coercion was removed or ceased, he again sought what he thought was the *best* for him—a drink.

So with all sinners. In the beginning, to be secure, they should *seek God because of the reward.* This is why God holds out the idea of reward and punishment. It is usually the only language that people who are not grown up can readily understand. Most people will find this "highway to heaven" one of the lower roads, but there isn't near as much danger of falling off. And one thing sure it is the only *safe* road until one has reached the *"humility* intersection."

And the ultimate objective of all of these seekers is a reward in eternity. However, there come along in life many attractions which seem to us to be *more desirable than an eternal reward,* or which may *seem possible to be had and still get the reward.* We follow this apparent "best"—we "goof," we sin.

To offset this we teach children the *present* rewards of being good; peace of soul, honor, good conscience etc., etc., on the theory that a present reward is more tangible. And this is much more effective than trying to train a child to be "good" to please "mommy" or "daddy." *Very few humans are capable of unselfish love except by direct intervention or grace or after long years in spiritual growth.*

Life is a selfish program. It is a program of love of self in which we do what we do because ultimately and/or presently it will redound to *our good.* Otherwise eventually we would be no good to ourselves, to our neighbor or to our God.

It is thus and thus alone that the soul will ever so gradually (and the more proud a soul is, the more "ever so gradually" will it come about) grow *toward an unselfish love of his neighbor and his God.* That is the *ideal* towards which we strive, *but it will ultimately be accomplished by first taking care of ourselves and our own souls.*

311

In summary then: *"A.A. is a selfish program"* means that *we first and foremost take care of our welfare,* realizing that unless we *do* we will never be any good to anyone else; and also realizing that we are thus insuring against the tumbling off of the "proud seat of pseudo-apostolicity" which is usually the ultimate end of the proud individual's striving to help others for others' sake. Actually proud and vain people are helping others for the glory in it. Want to prove it? Just disagree with them when they are telling how much they do for God and their neighbor! It is only after long prayer and practice of solid virtue that we can venture safely along the royal highway of selfless love.

And likewise *life is a selfish program* means that the same thing holds true in all life. And this is what brought forth one of the most effective spiritual axioms of all times: *"Do what you are doing, and remember the end."* (Age quod agis et respice finem). Or shall we paraphrase: *"Do what you do because it's ultimately for you and your good."*

Let us see how effective these convictions would be in our everyday living.

1. *In our home life*—It might be a paradox, but *if* every member of the family would do good and avoid evil because they *wanted to do so;* because it was *best* for them; because they before all else were concerned about themselves, *what a happy, adjusted* family it would be! Pop would be a "good" father, because he wanted to for *him;* Mommy would be a "good" mother because she wanted to be a good mother for *herself;* all the children would be good and obedient children because they wanted to be thus for *themselves.* Well, what else does a family want? *Love?* With such solid and true love of self, it would eventually overflow all over the place into a rich an selfless love for one another, although to begin with—as a *motive,* their family life is a *selfish program.*

We wouldn't have any of the members of the family being "good" because they feared others; or because they were ashamed into it; or because they wanted to please. They would *be good for their own sake,* and indirectly *would please everybody in the home.*

312

And the more one deals with human nature, one learns more and more that *those who ultimately got into real trouble in life were the ones who did whatever of good they did only because of a motive of pleasing or fearing or they were shamed into it.*

How many wrecked marriages and wrecked professions and wrecked vocations are a direct result of a child getting married or entering into a profession or following a certain vocation *not for themselves,* but because *their parents urged or even demanded it!* In fact one finds that there are thousands of married women, today—terribly unhappy in married life—who entered marriage *only because their friends shamed them into it.* It is our opinion that whoever spread abroad that it is a disgrace for a woman not to be married are guilty of a very heinous crime and have "killed" the very souls of countless women.

But enough of that. Let us only again beseech parents to teach their charges to *choose for themselves;* that *life is a selfish program.* And if children begin asking themselves "What's in it for me?" and are conscious of the fact that "eternity is," we will have much, much better choices,—selfish choices, but secure.

2. *In our social life*—One of the monotonies and one of the burdens of the so-called "elite" of the social world is the fact that *someone did the choosing,* and *they are doing what they are doing because of someone else or out of fear or shame.* That is why so many ultimately *rebel. Life is a selfish program.* And socially therefore we *pick* our friends because *we want them for us;* initially because they please us, but ultimately overflowing into a selfless devotion and love for our friends.

3. *In our business life*—The business man who is successful has entered into his particular business because he *wanted to— for himself.* Because of this *he took a deep interest in its success.* But the one who goes into business *because his dad or mother insisted upon it,* isn't going to care much about the outcome and will probably end up bankrupt.

Life is a selfish program.

4. *In our financial affairs*—True self-love tells us to prudently earn and save for our own security first. With this motive we

will work diligently and be circumspect in our spending. But the one who is *forced* to earn usually becomes bitter and many times ends as a "fugitive from work." Platitudes even about earning money are seldom effective with old human nature. Perhaps that is why God says "Give and *it shall be given to you." Life is a selfish program.*

5. *In our mental life*—When a person realizes that good mental hygiene pays off in their own happiness, they usually then practice it—*for themselves.* When a student studies for *himself* he usually is a good student, but when one studies simply because he *must,* he flunks all along the line.

We taught school for several years a long time ago. It was shortly after the sixteen year old law went into effect under which all children *had* to attend school until they were sixteen. The greatest "headaches" of all the classes were the kids who were in school only waiting until they would be sixteen and then could go to work. They were poor students; intractable many times; and certainly not much interested in studying. It was the student who *wanted* to be in school, who was the real student. He was there *for himself.*

Life is a selfish program.

6. *In our emotional life*—"Helping" others to our own emotional detriment is certainly not well regulated self-love. If the help we give is deleterious to our emotions, we best stop "helping" or else we will be the one in need.

So many people get into awful emotional entanglements and nervous "dithers" *because they must* take part in this or that or the other "charity." We come *first.* Because if we don't soon we will not be any good to ourselves nor anyone else.

Particularly neurotics should *set their sights* on their *own needs first.* It is wise to such to sit down some time and figure out, with competent medical advice if necessary, *just what their emotional needs are:* rest, relaxation, etc. Then *beyond this minimum* they should never go, *no matter who* is *asking.* If they do it will be another "nervous break-down" *because they did not practice sane and sensible self-love.*

Life is a selfish program.

7. *In our physical life*—Many people do not take care of their teeth, or hair, or bodies *because* they never began or learned to do so *for themselves;* for the *intrinsic value* of doing so. This is why so many get "slovenly" and careless about their bodies.

It is an amusing simile, but we see this in the one who diets because of what others say of their being fat. But there are others who diet *because the weight* has become too heavy *for themselves to carry around.* The former often get off their diet and have a very difficult time sticking with it; the latter usually stick with the diet and have an easier time doing it. *They are doing it for themselves.*

8. *In our spiritual life*—As we said in the beginning of this discussion, God Himself uses the idea of *reward* in drawing people to Himself. A step further for the adult should be a realization of the intrinsic *value of a good life,* gradually graduating into the realm of love.

It is the same difference as the time when Christ told the rich young man who asked Him what he must do to save his soul. He was told: "Keep the commandments." Then when the fellow said he had kept the commandments since his youth, Christ added: "If thou will be perfect, go, sell what thou hast and give it to the poor and come follow Me."

The rich man declined. He was not up to the sacrifice for the sake of love. His path had been the path of the commandments and since he was asking about what to do to earn salvation, it looks sorta like he was keeping them *because of the reward.* And he probably kept on keeping them for that reason. It is not a *bad* motive; it is a *good* motive, but not the *perfect* one. It is the securest motive for the average sinner, who still has so much of pride.

We see the same principle come into play when people attend church. Those who do so because they *must* do not usually continue long. But they who do so because of *what they are getting out of it for themselves* usually remain staunch church-members.

Life is a selfish program.

9. *In our A.A. life*—There is no doubt that the members of A.A. who come to and stay on the program *for themselves are the solid members of A.A.* The ones who are there because they in some fashion were influenced to be there against their own wishes, are the slippers. A.A. is *undoubtedly a selfish program.*

It is a *give* program, but a giving in order that we may keep what we have been given: *sobriety.* That is why we call meetings, speaking, calls, etc., *insurance* against a slip. And when one takes out insurance he is taking it out for what he or his will ultimately get out of it.

The difficulty with the alcoholic who even attempts to operate out of a motive of "helping his poor fellowman" is that in him it too easily degenerates into a motive of *vanity.* And we can learn this by denying their good works. They will get "madder" than anything.

A person who really does good out of a motive of true love of God and his fellowman, can be contradicted and despised, but he will not mind. For such a one is *also humble.* We just do not have virtue without *humility.*

A.A. is a selfish program, because thus only can the proud alcoholic securely work for others and succeed in working for himself. *Life is a selfish program,* because thus only will *most sinners* be secure in their striving for spiritual growth *because of the reward.*

"I have kept Thy commandments, O God, because of the reward."

THE LORD'S PRAYER

"Our Father, Who art in heaven...."

Ever since the time about ten years ago when we gave a very short two page analysis of the Lord's Prayer in our first Golden Book we have constantly received requests for a more complete discussion of this prayer which is used in closing practically all A.A. groups throughout the world.[1] So, in answer to these many requests we bring to you our understanding of the *perfect* prayer.

We use the term "perfect" designedly. We call it a *perfect* prayer for two reasons:

1. Because it was composed by Christ Himself.

2. Because it contains *all* possible attitudes the soul would have in approaching its God; and in living its life according to God's will.

Remember the occasion when this beautiful prayer was first endowed with human expression? It was more than 1900 years ago during the time which Christ spent gathering together His first disciples and teaching them the truths He had come to give mankind in Christianity. Christ was walking along the road toward evening with His apostles and disciples. We imagine He had talked with them about many things that day. We imagine He had told them much about His Father and His Father's great love for them. He had on other occasions told them "Ask and you shall receive" . . . "Anything you ask the Father in My Name He will give it to you." He had mentioned the need of prayer. But we know that most of His apostles and disciples were not educated men. So one turned to Him and asked: "Lord, teach us to pray." Then it was that Our Lord first spoke those heaven-composed words:

"Our Father Who art in heaven—hallowed be Thy name— Thy kingdom come—Thy will be done—on earth as it is in

---

[1] There are a very few A.A. groups who do not close their meetings with the Lord's Prayer.

321

heaven—give us this day our daily bread—forgive us our debts[1]
as we forgive our debtors—and lead us not into temptation—but
deliver us from evil."

Here was given to us a prayer veritably pregnant with
principles of living adjusted to our neighbor, to life and to God.
Here was a prayer that gave to us those principles so necessary
for *adjustment.* Here was given to mankind the *answer to* four
thousand years of seeking and questioning.

Here, too, we find those principles which we find basic in the
alcoholic's return to sanity, sobriety, security and serenity. Here
was the perfect prayer.

In this prayer was enunciated the principle of the *fatherhood
of God* and the *brotherhood of man;* the principle of the infinite
beauty and power of *God's name;* the principle of our *eternal
destiny;* the principle of the marvelous effectiveness of *God's
will;* the *twenty-four hour program;* the solution of *guilt;* the
danger of the handling of *temptation;* the *answer to evil.*

Let us take them one by one:

1. *Our Father Who art in heaven*—The very first word *"our"*
indicates to us the equality of *all* men. He did not use the term
"my," because His Father is the God of *every human being without* exception, whether they be black or white, rich or poor, Catholic, Protestant or Jew, drunk or sober, sinners or saints—*all.*

And yet how many do we not find, within even *minutes* of
supposedly having said this prayer, who "look down" on or who
"condemn" or "refuse to associate with" some of their neighbors,
their fellowmen *only because they are* black, and not white, or
poor and not rich, or Catholic and not Protestant, or Protestant
and not Catholic, or Jew and not Christian, or Christian and not
Jew, or drunk and not sober—*or slipping and not staying on the
program!*

The self-same lips which have just pronounced those God-
given words; *"Our* Father" now are used in contempt, or derision, or criticism or intolerance of *another child of God.* For that

---

[1] *All* the latest English translations, Catholic and Protestant, use the
terms *"debts"* and *"debtors"* instead of *"trespasses"* and *"those who trespass
against us."* As we shall see it is much more meaningful.

is the lesson that is given us in that one short phrase: *"Our* Father"; *All* men are equally children of *one* Father Who is *our God,* even as you and I. Let's quit kidding ourselves. It's on both sides of the fence. Just "listen" around; "Who's that new guy in the group?" "Oh, he's one of those——Catholics"! or "He's one of those——Protestants"! And on and on we hear it. In fact it becomes amusing how this "bigotry" and "intolerance" find expression even under dramatic circumstances. They tell the story of a fellow who was going to commit suicide and had decided to jump from the second floor of a building. The good old Irish policeman on the beat was trying to talk him out of it.

"Please, sir, for the sake of your poor old mother, don't jump," the officer begged.

"But my mother's dead," the man replied.

"Then think of your dear wife whom it will disgrace and don't do it," urged the policeman.

"My wife's dead too," the man snarled.

"Then haven't you any children who will be left orphans? Don't do it for their sake," countered the man of the law.

"Naw," shouted the man, "I have no children. I'm gonna jump."

For a moment the policeman didn't know what to say or do. Finally an idea came to his mind, and he stuttered out:

"Well, f-f-f-or the s-s-ake of our B-b-b-lessed Mother, don't do it."

"I'm not a Catholic. I don't believe in that stuff. I'm gonna jump," was the derisive retort.

"Well, then," exploded the exasperated officer, *"jump you— Protestant, jump!"*

We do not know whether he did or not. But we feel that when the candy-coating of humor wears off it will begin to penetrate our minds and hearts how "bigotry" and "intolerance" can disrupt the entire structure of the *brotherhood of man.* Why? Because we haven't fully and honestly accepted the *fatherhood of God.* Which, if we are honest and wish God to listen, we must do when we pray:

Our Father!

"Father"—The impact of that term! He didn't tell us to use *judge*, or *creator*, or *avenger*, or not even *eternal God*, but He told us to use *Father*. You know what a *Father* means? Let's stop a moment and see.

What are the qualities of a good *Father?* What are the qualities that every man who assumes the role of *Father* should have to be worthy of the title?

a. He must have *strength*. There has never existed a small child anywhere who was not convinced that *his* dad could do anything! "My pop can whip *your* pop!" And when the child is confronted with a situation beyond his strength or resources, what is his first thought? *"Dad* can do it!" To every child his *dad*, his *father* is the acme of strength and power.

Now let us look at the One Whom Christ tells us to address as *Father*—God. He is *all*-powerful; He has *all* strength; he can do *all* things; *He is God!* He is the creator of heaven and earth! He is the One Who by a mere act of the Will called into being *all things*. He it is Who gives life; He is the One Who takes life. He is eternal; without beginning and without end. *He is God!* And now Christ tells us that He is also *Our Father*. *"Our Father*—can do *all* things."

Our Father!

b. A good father must *love* his children—*all* without exception and regardless of their qualities. A good father might *agree* that his child should be punished, but in the face of any crime, the father will still realize "This is my son." He will *love* the child *no matter what the child may do.*

And thus it is when Christ told us to call God *Our Father*. He indicated that God *loves us!* How much? With an *infinite love!* "Can a mother forget her child? But even if she *could*, I will never forget thee," is what He tells us. And so mere man, who was only a *creature* of God now becomes through Christ *sons*,— and *heirs to heaven!* Love us? Greater *love no* man has!"

How miserably mistaken are those poor misguided souls who still look upon God as a terrible judge; as Someone up there looking at us with a "spy glass" ready to "pounce" on the slightest infraction of His law or the smallest fault! Can we imagine an earthly father who is holding the hand of his very small child helping it to walk, "batting" it every time it stumbles? And we are still very much very small children in the eyes of *our heavenly Father*. He *knows* we are going to stumble—*all over the place.* But *He loves* us, and wants us only the more tightly to grasp *His* Hand no matter *how often we fall.* It is the *fearful* one who is the more likely to wrench away from the hand of its father; but the child who is fully conscious of its father's *love* will *never* let go and eventually will reach a safe haven *even if his father has to finally take him up into his arms and carry him.*

So with *Our Father* in heaven, a realization of His *infinite love* will but urge us to hold on tighter and to come closer *no matter how often we fall.* The one thing He does not want us ever to do is to *pull away from Him—under any circumstances.* He *loves* us with an *infinite love.*

We should never look upon God as a *hard* man. Most of the difficulties that good people have with being confident in God stem from an internal feeling that God is a hard, grasping man who wants to get everything out of us and give nothing in return. We should try always to realize that above everything else God wants our *love,* and with love comes happiness and contentment in serving God. But we must keep ever in mind the loving Father that God really is. We must always remember that as long as we tread this earthly sphere, God is our *Father,* only in eternity is He our Judge. Realizing how much God really does love us and how lovable He is will go far to make it easy to love Him and to have great confidence in His Providence for us.

From our childhood many of us have been told more of the punishments God has in store for us if we fail to please Him than of the rewards He *wants* to give us when we do please Him. Let's put "first things first." The first thing necessary in loving God is to believe Him lovable. What kind of people do we love? First, they must be easy to get on with. Rather do we not think Him touchy, unapproachable, easily annoyed or offended? Would our father wish us to hang our heads, be shy and shrinking in his presence? How much less so our Heavenly Father! Didn't He tell us that even if a parent would forget its child, He would *never* forget us? He has an almost foolish love for us. *Love* is first; fear a poor second.

Go to God; but go to Him not only as to one who has a human heart, but who is capable of *infinite* Love.

Go to Him as to one who loves us, and if only we understand that a little better, it will explain everything and make everything easy.

Don't think that God requires us to stand on ceremony with Him. We can never be too childlike, too simple, too direct.

Why do we not believe His own words? Why would He say He loves us if He does not do so in fact?

The shortest way to the mind and heart of God is to take Him at His word. A saint is a person who believes God literally, and trusts His promises entirely and always.

What is the explanation of all this?

God Who framed the heavens, has chosen to dwell with man on earth. "God so loved the world. . . ."

Why was His infinite Power attracted by our weakness? Why was His Pity greater than our willfulness? Why was it that the Creator and the creature, Perfection and imperfection, Light and darkness, were thus brought together?

Not by constraint, because no one can constrain God. Not in His Wisdom, nor in His Greatness, nor in His Justice, nor in His Power will we find written the secret—why God created us, and dwells amongst us.

One little word holds it all: The highest, dearest, best of all words; another word for God Himself—*Love? God is love.*

Let's approach Him by love; abide with Him in love. The *love* of God can *fill* our hearts!

Our Father!

c. A good father will also make himself *easy to approach* and not let the children have the idea that *he isn't interested in all their problems—no matter how small.* The good father will listen patiently to any and all the childish troubles of all of his children. To him they are mostly insignificant. But to the child many times *very big* and *important.* So, an earthly father will never make his children stand on ceremony, and bow and scrape, but let them know they may approach him *any time* with *any problem*.

No earthly father, no human being is *more easy to approach* than *God* since He is *Our Father*. We can go to Him *anytime*. *anywhere* with *any* problem. So many make the mistake of thinking that God is not interested in *their* troubles. But *how* do we know that He is? Because He is *Our Father*, and a *Father* is interested in *every* problem of *every one* of His children. How ridiculous to say "I don't want to *bother* God with *my* problems; He just can't possibly be interested in the likes of *me!*" "With *my* past, He just won't forgive, I've done too much!" What was it we mentioned some pages back? The *more* sins we have committed, the *more* right we have to approach God. So the *biggest* sinner should be *first* in line. He is *Our Father* and wants *no* one to stand *aloof*.

Some years ago on our first journey into Mexico, we were quite taken aback on seeing for the first time the absolute lack of formality in their churches. But then we finally realized that *to these people of such simple and deep faith* their church is *their Father's house*, and so they feel perfectly at *home!* It impressed us very deeply. For what was it that Christ once remarked? "Unless you become as little *children....*"

We never need formality to seek God. We never need form to speak to God. He can be approached *any time. any where, in any way*. Just like a child can approach its father. "Unless you become as little children...."

One time many years ago, the writer had accompanied his brother and their family in visiting other relatives. The hour was rather late when we returned. And as we entered the house all of the children made a "bee-line" for bed. It was then their mother called out. "Just a minute; you haven't said your prayers."

Came from one of the younger children without a moment's hesitation: "Good night, Jesus, good night!" and he didn't miss a step!

As a little *child!*

Our Father!

327

d. The fourth quality we would look for in a good father is the assurance that he will *understand.* Not only does the child expect his father to be able to *solve* all of his troubles, he also expects his father to *understand* them no matter what they may be. Otherwise the child will hesitate to approach his dad. And in fact many fathers fail their child in this respect. So when the child does something out of the way, he hesitates—and so we hear so many "teenagers" constantly complain; "I'd have gone to Dad, *but he wouldn't have understood;* he *never* does." What an indictment against parenthood! As a result that child goes instead to his companions who know less about what to do than he; and they give him bad advice; *but they do understand!*

And God? Because He *is God* and at the same time our Father, He has *perfect understanding.* He knows more about us than we do ourselves! There *can* be *no* problems, or difficulty or action which He will not *understand.* He knows *perfectly* the weakness of our human nature; the strength of temptation; the darkness of our intellect; the need of *His* help. *Understand?* He understands us so well that *even if we don't ever go to Him,* He still *understands!*

That is *Our Father!* Just think for a moment what that implies: our *Father*—Who is *in heaven;* Who is *God!*

"*Our* _____ *Father* _____ *who art in heaven* _____ ! ! !

2. *"Hallowed be Thy name"—Hallowed* means *made holy* and therefore to be *reverenced.* The Latin uses "sanctificetur" which means precisely "Let it be made holy." So Christ suggested to His disciples and to us to use God's Name *reverently* at all times. The commandment given to Moses had been very specific relating to the use of God's Name: *"Thou shalt not take the name of the Lord Thy God in vain."* This means we should never disrespectfully nor irreverently nor as a "by-word" use the name: *God.* It refers to *any* of God's names: *God, Jehovah, Eloim, etc.* It also includes the name of His Son: *Christ, Jesus.*

Now this idea of having reverence for someone's name is nothing unusual as some seem to think. It is, in fact, one of the most natural things in life to reverence not only the person of one we love, we instinctively come "to attention," and there passes reverence his name. Every time someone uses the name of one we look up to or love, but to also hold in high esteem and to through our minds at that moment loving thoughts of that person because *we heard his name.* Even the names of ones we hold in high esteem—our national heroes and the like, always seem to arrest our attention and bring from our hearts a feeling of awe and high regard. For example the name *of George Washington, Lincoln*—and what is more apt to touch the heart and to bring a deep feeling of pride and esteem than the word: *America!*

So much more so are we to hold in esteem and to reverence the name of *Our Father: God. "Hallowed be Thy name!"* Wherefore Christ prayed at another time: "Father, I have *glorified* Thy *name* to men...." And again He tells us in the scriptures: "So let your light shine before men that they may see your good works and glorify the *name of God* the Father Who is in heaven."

And many, many times throughout both the Old and the New Testament we find expression given to the necessity of *hallowing* the name of God. A good example is the one hundred and forty-eighth psalm of David:

"Praise ye the Lord from the heavens; praise Him in high places;
Praise Him, all His angels; praise Him, all His hosts;
Praise Him, O sun and moon; praise Him, all you stars and light;
Praise Him, ye heavens of heavens; and let all the waters that are above the heavens praise the name of the Lord;
For He spoke, and they were made; He commanded, and they were created;
He hath established them for ever, and for ages and ages; He hath made a decree, and it shall not pass away;
Praise the Lord from the earth, ye dragons, and all the deeps;
Fire, hail, snow, ice, stormy winds, which fulfill His words;
Mountains and all hills, fruitful trees and all cedars;

329

Beasts and all cattle; serpents and feathered fowl;
Kings of the earth and all people; princes and all judges
of the earth;
Young men and maidens; let the old with the younger,
praise the name of the Lord; for His name alone is
exalted."

And may God grant that in common with all God's people down through the centuries and into eternity, we may be able to say along with Christ: *"Father, I have revealed Thy name to men. . . ."*

"Our Father Who art in heaven—hallowed be Thy name. . . ."

3. *Thy kingdom come*—There are in this old world of ours 1,800,000,000 who admittedly believe in *God.* Of this number only 800,000,000, believe in Christ. Perhaps it is because not enough of us who do believe in Christ have sincerely and often prayed *"Thy kingdom come"*! For, it is in this prayer that we are told to pray to God the Father "that *all* men will come to a knowledge of the truth" . . . to a knowledge of Christ Who said of Himself "I am the way, the truth, and the life." And God the Father has said *"This* is My beloved Son, *hear ye Him."* And Christ Himself thus prayed: "That they *all* may be *one,* as Thou Father in Me and I in You: that *all* may believe that *Thou hast sent Me."*

Let's listen in on a conversation between Christ and Pilate. Pilate is speaking:

"You say that You are a *King?"*

Comes the soft reply: "Thou hast said it" . . . "for this I am come into the world . . . *but My kingdom* is not of this world."

The *kingdom* of *God,* of *Christ,* is *in eternity.* So we find the Good Thief on Calvary asking: "Lord, remember me when You come into Your kingdom." And we hear Christ answer: "This day thou shalt be with Me *in Paradise,"*—In His Father's home—His Father's *kingdom.*

So we pray *"Thy kingdom come"* petitioning the Father to grant and bring *all men into His kingdom*—of grace and belief here on earth; and in His *kingdom* of eternal glory and peace forever hereafter.

"*Our Father Who art in heaven—hallowed be Thy name— Thy kingdom come. . . .*"

4. *Thy will be done*—We spoke of the *will of God* at length in the *Golden Book of the Spiritual Side* and in *Sobriety and Beyond.* However, so deep is this wonderful principle that we could write on forever; we could meditate day after day; we could analyze it again and again, and never fully explore all of its potentialities as it fits into *the perfect prayer*—the Lord's Prayer.

Let us first ask ourselves what do we mean by *the will of God?*

There are two sides to God's *will;* the one is *active,* or *causative;* the other is *passive,* or *permissive.* This means that although God *wills* all things that happen or exist, still when it comes to *evil,* He only *permits* it and in this way can be said to *will it.* So when it is said that whatever happens or is, is God's will, this is true; God either *causes or permits* everything that is. And in this way God's will is *always done.*

This permissive factor in God's will is brought into focus in the following example. We were speaking at a prison group some years ago. We were speaking of the will of God, and had just made the statement that God's will is *always* done. Suddenly one of the inmates jumped up and called "Just a minute—can I ask a question?" There was nothing for us to do but say yes.

"Do you mean to tell me that it is God's will that I'm in this 'dump'?" the inmate queried.

"Better first let me ask you a question," we countered. "Do you believe in God?"

"Sure I do," replied the gentleman. "Have all my life."

"Do you believe that God can do all things?" we asked.

"Sure I do," he replied.

"Then you must admit that God *could,* if He wanted to—if He *willed it*—get you out of this er . . . uh . . . 'dump'?" we smilingly retorted.

331

"Well, a-a-ah I guess He could," he was forced to admit. He sat down!

So in the Lord's Prayer Christ tells us to pray to God— telling Him that *no matter what happens we will accept it as His will*—and be satisfied. So, if we wish to be consistent, we should not be irritated with God when something goes against our will. Because whatever is, is God's will. And if we not only wish to be consistent, but also *honest*, then we just would not ever mind *anything* that happens. For, that is what we have told God so often in this prayer: *Thy will be done.*

From all this we can deduce a very important fact: *All discontentment in life is nothing more nor less than kicking against the will of God.*

Where do we find God's will? We want to do God's will.—Is there a way of finding out ahead of time just *what He wants us to do?* Yes, there is—the Ten Commandments, definitely leave no doubt as to what God wants. And to *all* humans, even those who may not have heard of the Commandments, He has given that "wee" voice which we call *conscience.* This is an inborn something which tells even the pagan that some things are right; others wrong.

Then there are the obligations of our state of life; marriage, doctor, lawyer, clergyman, or whatever may be our state of life. Each has its own obligations. The fulfilling of them *is* definitely the will of God.

And there are obligations arising from the laws of our church; from society; from the civil law. These all point out specifically the will of God.

And in all of those things day in and day out which are not important in themselves and wherein neither law nor obligations are found; those little dilemmas like should we buy this or should we buy that; should we get a new this or that; should we go here or go there; all those that have absolutely *no* bearing on the moral code *are to be decided in whatever way our God-given intelligence decides,* and we can be assured that it *is God's will.* As long as the divine, or the natural, or the ecclesiastical, or the civil law is not involved; as long as there is no question of any moral obligation involved; as long as there is no question of being morally right or wrong; then we are perfectly free to do or not to do as we wish and be sure that it is God's will.

But there is still a much simpler way of being sure of always doing God's will—and also our own! Saint Augustine tells us how: *"Love* God and do what you will"! For if we *really love* God we will never offend Him willfully; nor His children who are identical with our neighbor; nor ever do *anything* contrary to His *will—we won't want to,* i.e., *if* we *love* Him!

And the shortest cut to loving God? By saying over and over again—day in and day out—hour in and hour out—minute in and minute out: *"Thy will be done,"* and *meaning* it.

"On earth as it is in heaven." The will of God is *perfectly* carried out in heaven: His kingdom. We pray that eventually it will be likewise carried out *perfectly* on earth—that *all on earth* will eventually *want His will,* and *not* fight *against it.*

"Our Father who art in heaven—hallowed be Thy name— Thy kingdom come—Thy will be done—on earth as it is in heaven————."

5. *Give us this day our daily bread—A gift* is something given without "strings attached"; without respect to the worthiness or the unworthiness of the recipient. If there are "strings attached" or a question of fulfilling certain "provisos" it no longer falls under the classification of a true *"gift"* of true *"charity,"* but rather under the classification of a *"loan"* or something *"earned"*—earned by the fulfilling of certain requirements.

This difference is strikingly exemplified in the agencies engaged in providing relief in times of disaster. Two examples will bring the difference out very clearly. The Red Cross provides relief in time of disaster *provided the victims fill certain requirements* some of which border on the ridiculous. Actually the Red Cross *gives* "nobody *nothing"*—the victim *earns* everything he or she gets be it food, clothing or shelter. On the other hand the Salvation Army, and many other agencies *give and freely* and *with no questions asked* to *all* who are in *need.* There is never a question in these latter agencies of worthiness or unworthiness

Here is *need*—so they *fill* it. We went through the **great flood of** 1937 on the Ohio River and we saw at first hand the difference between true giving and simulated giving. There is a big difference. One type says, "We *give*."; the latter type says, "We give, *provided*." We think there are many so-called "charitable organizations" who would have a more fitting title if they were named: "wholesale distributors."

So, we are taught in the Lord's Prayer to approach God with the realization that He will *give*—"*whatsoever* you ask the Father in My Name He will *give* it to you." And we do not have to back our petitions to God with a thousand references. Our attitude should always be: here is *God;* here is *Our Father;* here is the *Giver* of *all* things. "All good things come from God, the *Giver* of all gifts."

This attitude will also help us to more and more realize that *all* that we have—*God gave it!* And it will help us to appreciate the many blessings which are *gifts of God*. Finally it will help us to attain that so-necessary "attitude of humility" of which we have spoken so often and which is so eloquently exemplified in the words of Job: "The Lord has *given;* the Lord has taken away; blessed be the name of the Lord."

Finally, it should go far to relieve any possible "guilt-complex" which might tend to wiggle itself in because of our "awful past" and our present unworthiness. All this means nothing to *Our Father*. He says: "*ask*."; and He tells us that He will *give*. "*Give* us this day our daily bread."

"Give *us*"—Wherein He again indicates the value of making *all* of *our* prayers *all-inclusive*. He doesn't say *me;* He says *us*.

"Give us *this day*"—Here Our Lord shows us the need of the *twenty-four hour program*, which we thoroughly analyzed in a previous chapter. We are to live *today;* we are to pray *today;* we are to work *today;* we are to relax *today;* we are to trust *today*. *Tomorrow?* That is entirely in the hands of God's Providence. *Yesterday?* That is to be "lost" in the depths of God's infinite mercy. Remember what is stated in the scriptures so often? "His *mercy* is above *all* of His works." So we are to pray *each day* for *this day*.

"Give us this day *our daily bread"*—Once more He tells us to use *our,* and particularly might we pause and meditate on this truth of making our prayers *all* inclusive when He appends the word *our* to *bread.* For, some time ago Bishop Sheen made a statement on one of his television programs which we feel will give you, dear reader, as it did us,, much food for much thought. He stated: "Two-thirds of the world's population go to bed hungry every night!" Cain it was who said, "Am I *my* brother's keeper?" Remember? Perhaps we should direct the question a little bit differently to our own hearts: "Are *we our* brother's keeper?" Compare the two, chum, and give 'em both a good think.

Give us this day our *daily bread"*—Once again He emphasizes the value of the *twenty-four hour program.* He indicates that we should not be concerned about "laying up for tomorrow," but *each day* ask for what we need *that day—"daily"* bread. Remember what we said about security not being in dollars and cents? There is only *one true security. "Daily"* trust in *God. Nothing* can undermine nor destroy that. Remember the nine V.I.P.s who all were millionaires? And remember the story in the scriptures about the guy who filled his barns with grain against future emergencies? Remember how he even tore those down "to build *bigger* ones"? And remember what happened? *That* night he *died!* So, what is all this business about the *great need* of a sinking fund at GSHQ?

"Give us this day our daily *bread"*—The term *bread* is used to indicate again that we might know that although for reasons known alone to His Divine Intelligence, at times He does not give us what we *ask* He will *always,* without fail, *give us what we need. Bread is* one of the *necessities* of life.

When we pray for *bread* we ask first of all not only for enough to eat; we ask for all the *material* necessities of life: food, drink, shelter, clothing. We ask for freedom from *bodily* harm and from sickness. We ask for the means by which all of these material things may be secured—health, money, employment or the charity of men. For all of these material things we ask when we say, "Give us this day our daily *bread."* But there are other *needs.* For these also we pray. We ask for the needs to satisfy the hunger of the mind; for the *word of God*. We ask too, for the needs of the soul: the *grace of God* and the *"living bread of eternal life."*

"Give us this day our daily *bread"*—Not necessarily the jam, and the jelly, and the cake; but the *bread*. Which simply means that although God may not, as we said above, always give us *what we want;* He will *always* give us *what we need*. "Consider the lilies of the field ..."; "the birds of the air"; "your heavenly *Father* feedeth them."

"Our Father who art in heaven—hallowed be Thy name— Thy kingdom come—Thy will be done—on earth as it is in heaven—give us this day our—daily bread—"

6. *Forgive us our debts, as we forgive our debtors*—To *forgive* means to *dissolve;* to *do away with*. The Latin word is "dimitte" which means *"dismiss"*—forgive and *forget*. So we are told to ask our Father to "dismiss" all of the offenses for which we are or have been responsible. We ask Him to absolutely *do away with them*, and "put us in the black again."

Us—our—we—our—Reemphasizing that there can be no *Fatherhood of God for the individual unless there is also a brotherhood of man*. And even more so is this insisted upon in the essence of this petition, wherein we are told: *we will be forgiven in so far, and only in so far, as we in turn forgive our fellowmen*. "Forgive us—*as we* forgive."

The discussion of sin is never a pleasant topic; many recoil from it. But sin is a universal fact. The scriptures say, "He who says that he is without sin deceiveth himself and the truth is not in him." He is a *liar*. Nor is sin only a universal fact; it also assumes an almost endless variety of form. Sins of thought, word and deed; sins of commission; sins of omission; sins against our own selves; sins against our neighbor; sins committed by the ordinary people; sins committed by the lower classes; and then there are sins which are the pet foibles of the elite. But the common levelling point is the fact that they are *all* against *God*. And it is the common phenomenon in man that each sin leaves a mark, a "sting" of conscience, a "sense of shame and of guilt" which impel us to seek pardon. Of course there are some people in this old world who can sin and remain unaffected—day in and day out. But these are the abnormal; these are the ones who have achieved that almost impossible and disastrous state wherein conscience lies dead—until eternity!

There are usually two ways in which the sense of shame from past or present sin is manifested in the human personality. Some are so over-whelmed by their sense of guilt that they end up with a "guilt-complex" or seek to destroy themselves in suicide (or the bottle). These poor misguided souls have never known or have forgotten the infinite Mercy of a God who is *our Father.* They seem to feel that their sins are too great even for a Merciful, loving and Omnipotent God. They need our pity and our understanding and our encouragement and love. However, the vast majority of humans in their sense of guilt turn to God to ask for mercy and forgiveness. This God expects and wants. *But* He has put a "proviso" on all seeking of forgiveness. And this proviso is given to us in the Lord's Prayer in such a way that we ourselves predicate our forgiveness by God *in so far as we forgive those who have offended us.*

This is one of the basic concepts of all Christianity. It is one of the big departures of Christ from pagan practices; yes, even from the practices of the Old Testament. It is the very *core* of the *Fatherhood of God and the brotherhood of man.* Let's listen to some of His words on this matter.

"You have heard it said: 'An eye for an eye, and a tooth for a tooth'; but I say unto you to *love* one another, to *love those who hate you.*"

And then there was Magdalen. She was forgiven much. Why? Christ tells us: "Much is forgiven her because she has *loved much.*"

How many times must we forgive our neighbor? And Peter asked, "Is it enough to forgive our fellowmen seven times a day" as the Jewish law of the time demanded? The answer? He was told to forgive "seventy times seven."[1]

"He who hates his brother is a murderer!"

---

[1] *Seventy times seven* in the Hebrew meant "without limit"; not 490!

And then there was the parable of the unjust servant. Remember the story? Here it is verbatim:

"The kingdom of heaven is likened to a king, who would take an account of his servants.

"And when he had begun to take the account one was brought to him that owed him ten thousand talents.

"And as he had not wherewith to pay it, his lord commanded that he be sold, and his wife and his children, and all that he had, and that payment should be made.

"But the servant falling down, besought the king saying: 'Have patience with me and I will pay you all.'

"And the lord of the servant being moved with pity, let him go and forgave him the debt.

"But when the servant was gone out, he found one of his fellow-servants who owed him a hundred pence; and laying hold of him, he throttled him, saying: 'Pay what thou owest.'

"And his fellow-servant falling down, besought him saying: 'Have patience with me and I will pay you all.'

"And he would not, but went and cast his fellow-servant into prison until he had paid all the debt.

"Now other fellow-servants, seeing what was done, were very much grieved, and they came and told their lord all that was done.

"Then the lord called the unjust servant and said to him: 'Wicked servant, I forgave you all the debts, because you besought me. Should you not therefore have compassion on your fellow-servant, even as I had compassion on you?'

"And his lord being angry, delivered him to the torturers until he paid all the debt.

"*So also shall My heavenly Father do to you if you forgive not every one his brother from your hearts.*"

Which later on led Christ to exclaim: "This is the first and the greatest commandment, that you should love God with all your heart—and the second is like unto the first 'Thou shalt love thy neighbor as thyself.' "

All of which leaves no other conclusion than:
We are forgiven in direct ratio as we forgive others.

And which gave us the petition of forgiveness in the Lord's Prayer as we have it: *forgive us our debts as we forgive our debtors.*

We have taken this petition a bit more in detail because one of the questions which is asked very frequently of the writer is: "How can I know God has forgiven me?"

In light of the above it is quite simple. Presuming sorrow, (and sorrow is demonstrated best by an improvement in avoiding the serious lapses of the past) *we are forgiven, if we have honestly forgiven others.*

One time many years ago when we were a young lad, we by chance came upon an accident. A switch engine had backed over a switchman and had severed the entire lower part of his body. He was conscious, although he died as they attempted to lift him into the ambulance. But you know the only thing he kept repeating as he lay there in agony? *"God forgive everybody."*

What a beautiful death! *Forgive us our debts as we forgive our debtors!*

"Our Father—Who art in heaven—hallowed be Thy name— Thy kingdom come—Thy will be done—on earth as it is in heaven—give us this day our daily bread—and forgive us our debts as we forgive our debtors—"

7. *Lead us not into temptation*—The word "lead" in this petition of the Lord's Prayer has given many much difficulty. They can't quite understand how God, a *Father*, could *lead* us into temptation. Well, the fact is He doesn't. The original Hebrew phrase used in this petition did not mean *"lead."* The meaning was: "Permit not to befall us any temptation which we cannot overcome."

We must first of all realize that to God, all down through the ages, "temptation" was not the same as we usually take the term today. "Temptation," from the Divine point of view, is a *test, a trial, a proving of oneself, a chance to choose Him* instead of evil. We do the same thing many times. We "try" someone before we hire them; we put someone to the "test"; we make people "prove" themselves. All of these factors come into the broad meaning of the term "temptation" as it is used in the Lord's Prayer.

Many times we tend to forget that life is not meant to be nor can it ever be a continual period of inertia; nor a repetitious period of perfect peacefulness; nor a passive point of no conflict. Life is a warfare—which any human can attest to. It is a constant "pull" between God and evil. God *permits* this so that we can with the aid of His grace *prove ourselves* against all subtle coaxing to abandon Him. All lovers know this "pull"; and all lovers know how much "fidelity" means to the other. So, to God, fidelity to Him is the price of *having Him*, as it is the price of all *love*.

So, "lead us not into temptation" means *"give us the strength and the courage to overcome all trials and temptations and grant further that we may be always faithful to You no matter what temptation or trial may come along life's pathway."*

So in the Lord's Prayer we pray God

a. To shield us from temptations; or

b. If He wills to permit temptations to befall us, that He give us victory in them.

All of which *presumes* that we *will do the foot-work,* and avoid temptations ourselves and not without necessity or serious reasons place ourselves in the occasion of sin. For if we willfully "toy" with temptation and the occasion of falls, our very prayer becomes a mockery. Remember the red-headed woman? "The red-headed woman walked in, and sobriety walked out!"

Or the rationalization a certain member of A.A. gave the writer some years ago. He was in one of our "jitter-joints" drying out. He was crying on his shoulder and ours. And suddenly there came from his lips amazing apparent "dead-end." Said he: "I don't understand why I slipped. I didn't do nothing but pick up a woman and go to a tavern!"

What was the old Roman saying about "Bacchus and Venus"?

We think the Lord had a very urgent reason to put this petition in the Lord's Prayer. *"Lead us not into temptation."*

"Our Father Who art in heaven—hallowed be Thy name —Thy kingdom come—Thy will be done—on earth as it is in heaven—give us this day—our daily bread—and forgive us our debts as we forgive our debtors—lead us not into temptation—"

8. *But deliver us from evil*—It is not our business to define "evil." Philosophers, writers, theologians and thinkers of all ages have discussed the existence of evil and its essence. One thing we are sure of; *evil does exist, and loads of it.* So the Lord included in His perfect prayer a petition that God, Our Father *deliver us from evil.* And this petition points out two truths very clearly:

a. That *only God has the responsibility* to remove *evil* from this world. (Unless we're policemen!) We have the responsibility to *avoid* evil which affects our relationship with God. But *only God* has the responsibility to eliminate *objective evils.* We have only to add our prayers asking Him to do so.

How many troubles would we avoid if we realized this, that we are *not guardians of the morals!* Someone is doing something wrong. That is none of our business. (Again we say unless we're policemen!) Let it go. God *in His own time and way will eliminate it, if it be evil.* And if it be *good,* how foolish to even object to it.

So *"deliver"* means *"to not let evil affect us, nor let it enter into our souls, nor draw us from God."* And *"in Your time, take all evil from us."*

b. *That we should never judge as evil that which God has not judged as such, either Himself or through His spokesmen.* Remember our discussion on *"there but for the grace of God, go I"?* Remember Our Lord asking "Has any man condemned thee?"

Let's take a practical example of the implication of this petition. Someone or some group in A.A. does something. We think it is terrible. We think they are "ruining" A.A. ! ! ! ? ? ? We think they are emasculating our "dear traditions." We get all worked up. We want to *do something about stopping it.*

But we are *not* guardians of the morals—not even of A.A.'s morals. Sure, pray all we wish. But *do* something? And who appointed us in the position of authority and with the *power* to do *anything?*

One time some years ago in our own city there started a project of sanatarium treatment which many of the members at that time thought might be very damaging both to the community and to A.A. We remember well the day when some of these "guardians of the morals" suggested in a meeting that "something be *done* about it." Some suggested going to the civil authorities. After much discussion and after most expressions of condemnation had been made, Dohr S., the founder of A.A. in our town arose. Very softly but with deep conviction he said: "Gentlemen, just a minute. *Who are we that we should either judge or take action against this project. If it is evil, God in His own time and way will eliminate it; and if it perchance be good, God forbid that we interfere. We are not guardians of the morals.*"

The discussion ended. Nothing was done. The project still goes on. Evil or good? That is none of our business; that's God's business. If it is really evil, God will eliminate it in His time and in His way.

Deliver us from evil.

Another time, a group in A.A. did something or other which the *"guardians"* of A.A. in that area thought was evil. So they had a meeting of these *"guardians"* of the groups. And they drew up a very formal and solemn document. Space will not permit its verbatim printing here. In short it said: "We the groups of the fellowship of Alcoholics Anonymous of the_____area, assembled in solemn session, do hereby decree that the_____. Group is no longer an Alcoholics Anonymous Group of this Fellowship. Etc., etc., etc." ! ! ! When we were in that area, they showed it to us. They asked what we thought of it. This was our reply:

"We do not know what this such and such group did. But whatever it did, it couldn't be half as bad as what you have attempted to do. For in your solemn and almost ridiculous proclamation, you have destroyed in your area A.A.'s greatest possession: *Autonomy.*"

We don't think they liked it. But then this is a program of honesty, isn't it?

And *deliver us from evil* is to be addressed to *God, isn't it?*

*"Our Father—Who art in heaven—hallowed be Thy name
—Thy kingdom come—Thy will be done—on earth as it is in
heaven—give us this day—our daily bread—forgive us our
debts as we forgive our debtors—and lead us not into temptation
—but deliver us from evil."*

9. *Amen*—A little word, but a big principle. It comes from
the Hebrew and means: *"so be it."* It is giving the "okay" to
what we have just said: *"as we have prayed, so be it done to us."*
So again we are stating our own promise and *if* our prayer was
sincere; if it was and is always followed by the *foot-work;* if
we have *excluded no one* from our prayer, then we can be sure
that Almighty God, *Our Father,* has not only heard it, but will
answer it in the way we have been considering.

"Amen."

Now there is a little prayer which is appended to the Lord's
Prayer by many in saying it. It goes something like this *"For
Thine is the kingdom, and the power, and the glory forever."*
And since there are members in our group of every denomination,
we feel it might be a good idea to analyze this prayer and en-
deavor to clear up any possible "stinking-thinking" about it.

First let us see some of the "stinking-thinking" that has been
around for years relating to this prayer. Many, far too many,
Catholics have always had the opinion that this was a "Protestant" ending, and that the Protestants put it there just to
aggravate Catholics! And here are many, far too many, Protestants who have thought that the Catholics won't say this prayer
because they're "stubborn," and just to irritate the Protestants!

Funny thing is—they are *both wrong!*

Now let's see how it happened. Although all scriptural
scholars today, both Protestant and Catholic, are agreed that it
was not a part of the *original* Lord's Prayer, it is not certain just
whence it came. Most think it happened when one of the "scrip-
tors" were transcribing the scriptures in the early centuries.
They did not have printing presses, nor mechanical means of
making new copies, so they had to do it by hand using quill
and parchment. So, probably some pious "scriptor" thought that

"For Thine is the kingdom, and the power, and the glory" would make a nice *doxology*[1] for the Lord's Prayer. And he put it on the margin of his new copy. Then another "scriptor" came along and perhaps thought to himself, "My, the other guy must have forgot to put that in the text." So, he put it in the text. Anyhow, somewhere along the line we ended up with two manuscripts of the scriptures. One had "For Thine is the kingdom, and the power, and the glory" with the Lord's Prayer, and one manuscript didn't. From one of these different originals was printed the Douay (Catholic) version; and from another the King James (Protestant) version of the scriptures. For years the one printed a Bible with it; the other without it. But in recent years, those scriptural students who were making a new translation of the King James version first put in as a footnote explaining that it is doubtful whether this prayer was a part of the original Lord's Prayer; and in its more recent edition, they have entirely omitted it from the scriptures.

But you know something, *no real scriptural scholar* nor theologian ever said it was not a beautiful prayer and a lovely doxology for the Lord's Prayer. In fact, and this will "shock" many, the Catholic Church used it as a doxology with the Lord's Prayer in the Mass, and even to this day several of the Catholic Church's Rites *still* use it as a doxology in the Mass![2] The priest says or sings the Lord's Prayer and the people answer: *"For Thine is the kingdom and the power and the glory."*

And how about in closing an A.A. meeting? Well, in A.A., everybody does what he thinks he should do and so there is no discussion. Everybody does what he wants to. If one feels like saying it, he does; if he doesn't feel like saying it he doesn't.

And after all of these years!

Our Father Who art in heaven
Hallowed be Thy name
Thy kingdom come

---

[1] A *doxology* is an ending of praise added to a prayer to give it more solemnity. V.gr. "Glory be to the Father, etc.," added to the psalms.

[2] V.gr. The Coptic Rite. And any Catholic *may* use it to close the Lord's Prayer in private or in a public meeting which is non-religious.

Thy will be done on earth as it is in heaven
give us this day our daily bread
forgive us our debts as we forgive our debtors
lead us not into temptation
but deliver us from evil—
For Thine is the kingdom and the power and the glory for-
ever.

Amen.

THE PRIMACY OF THE SPIRITUAL

"Praying *only* for knowledge of *His will for* us and *the power to carry that out.*"

When we discussed *first things first* we learned that there exists in life an over-all set order of things and values. And first and before all else came *God* and *His will*. We learned that thus and thus alone would we ever be able to bring *order* out of the *chaos* of our lives. So it is that we express this very clearly in the eleventh step of the A.A. program: "Praying *only* for knowledge of *His will* and the power to carry that out." From this we derive another principle of sobriety and sanity and serenity, namely *the primacy of the spiritual*.

During our drinking days most alcoholics did not or could not judge spiritual values. Or at most we held to a very confused set of spiritual values. And almost always *material* values predominated our thinking and our actions. Seldom was the spiritual value of things first in our living.

But then we sobered up. We sobered up not only physically but also mentally and spiritually. We not only ceased drinking, but we achieved *sobriety*—yes, and *beyond* sobriety, a definite conviction that *spiritual values are paramount;* that there is such a thing in life as *the primacy of the spiritual*.

Now just what is this *primacy?* It is a truth telling us that *nothing in this old world really matters except God and His will; that surrender to God's will could and would solve all problems; that the only real problems were those that ran contrary to His will; that conflict was inevitable if we refuse to follow His will; but that true peace was not only possible, but could be a reality if we did follow God's will in all things; that all discontentment in life is nothing more nor less than kicking against the will of God; and that ultimate victory would come only through unconditional surrender to God's will; and that the only true primacy of value in life is the primacy of the spiritual.*

So we "prayed only for knowledge of His will for us." We surrendered, and pursuant to this step *surrender to God became our ideal; our work; our very life.*

And what does that make us? It makes us *idealists* in the truest sense of the term. But it also makes us *realists.* We live not in the dream-land of wishful thinking and possibilities but in a world of solid reality. We take things as they *are* and not as we or others think they should be. Wherever God places us we stand with both feet and do *His* bidding. We no longer build air-castles. We are not troubled with useless cares about the past and the future. We are very much dealing only with the things of the present twenty-four hours. We get from those everything that can be wrested from them as God wills it. Our life and living require not only one percent or one-quarter of one percent of our personal *cooperation,* leaving ninety-nine and three-quarters percent to God. We have learned the hard way that human actions in order to have full human value require both a hundred percent of our effort and a hundred percent of God's work and grace. "We work as if everything depends on us; but we trust as if everything depends on God." We accept the reality of the present, refusing none of the joys and pleasures God may grant us. We *enjoy* them—it is *His* will. We also do not refuse *any* cross He may choose to lay upon our shoulders—it is *His* will. We also face the realities of the visible world in which we live and work and pray, and we will not be outdone by the most astute child of this world in a realistic handling of our worldly affairs. Nor on the other hand shall we ever be outdone by any fantastic idealist in striving for the *highest* of possessions: *God.*

In this very real way, our own personal character retains its identity and can better develop itself according to its *own* talents. We thus are *individualists.* No man can possibly develop his own individuality and attain a mature personality, who is pulled and pushed in various directions. The *fewer the laws and the rules and the precepts,* the *better the educator.* A multiplicity of rules is only a sign of pedantry, of narrow-mindedness and of very insecure people. Too many laws kill freedom and life. And in proportion to the number of rules, the personal life of men is limited and externalized, and all of their actions rendered void of any true value. They do what they are doing only because "they gotta." And *no human* can realize more than *one* ideal; nor can any *human* serve more than *one* master; nor can any *human* strive toward more than one objective. Those who do, as we know so well from our past, become nests of chaos and conflict.

It is true that we must observe certain laws, human and divine. Yet even here God has merged them all into one command; into one great commandment; the "one thing necessary." And He tells us that in this *one thing necessary* is fulfilled *all* laws. It is the commandment of *love: "this is the greatest commandment—to love God."* Its execution is *willing and glad surrender to God's will.* All else is subordinated to this and must serve and promote its fulfillment. We need not *impose nor bear more nor greater burdens than God has placed on us.*

To much method and system also weigh down the soul and absorb too much of its energy. A number of directions may be good and necessary *for the beginner.* But once maturity is approached these "external scaffoldings" should be removed. The more energy a machine is able to convert into actual work, the better is it considered. In the modern automobile language we call this "torque." But we also know that the greater the number of wheels, transmissions, and levers involved, the less "torque" will the power-source deliver. So too, if our God-given job of sanctification were as complicated as many let on, God would never have demanded it in such general terms: "Be ye perfect." God's demands are profound, *but simple.* They are *never* complicated. They fit every state and vocation, every sex and age, every situation of life and condition of soul, every person of every time and every circumstance. What He asks of *all* is only *one thing*—the *"unum necessarium"*—and one thing which *all* may give irrespective of his age, condition, sex, religion, color, race or circumstances of life: *surrender to His will for them.* It is as simple as all that. It is the *primacy of the spiritual.* It makes all who follow it the greatest individualists in all the world, because it enhances what is *theirs* adjusting all to what is *His* and not forcing any to conform to what is *another's.*

Let's see how this works. In the *primacy of the spiritual* we have only the *one* great commandment; and the *one* fulfillment: *love God—do His will.* This is the same *for all,* and yet in the fulfillment a different objective achievement in the life of each one. No one is forced into hard and stereotyped grooves. There are no *systems,* nor *methods* that have to be followed *of necessity.* Everyone lives and *individual life—his or her own,* according to God's will. We "as the stars differing from stars" proceed in the way and only in the way in which "grace" draws us. And in the spiritual life we grow along the way in which *God* has determined for us from eternity, just as our body grows according to the innate powers given to it. If the life of the simplest of cells is for us a mystery, how can we dream of laying out for the even more subtle soul an intricate network of roads for God to travel? "The Spirit of God breathes were He wills"; so in giving our wills over to God we give up *nothing* of our normal and natural self.

Growth in the spiritual life—sanctity—completes, not lessens, our manhood or our womanhood. And we shall attain to sanctity; we shall become saints *only by being completely human.*

This is the reason that flaws and faults in our human nature *hinder* our spiritual life, because nature is not providing a substantial *basis* for the supernatural. The supernatural grace of God does not build its structures on empty space. It is the *reverse* of the alcoholic cycle which dragged us down and away so far from God; wherein each regression begot a further regression. Sanctity *demands* humanity; and paradoxically humanity is only made possible by growth toward sanctity. For it is only in the growth towards sanctity that the faults of human nature are gotten rid of—not by the negative process of suppression, but *by the positive* upbuilding of positive virtue achieved through the surrender to God's will day in and day out. It is the *primacy of the spiritual.*

Once having realized this, the execution of the command to *love* by the glad following of God's will ushers us into a world of *complete freedom* as children of God. As Saint Augustine says: "Love God, then do what you will." Do the will of God and we have *perfect freedom,* because the will of God is *always done* as we have seen on several occasions in previous discussions. "Where the *spirit of the Lord* is there is *liberty.*" "We are not children of the *bond* woman, but of the *free.*" And we no longer consider things as pleasant or unpleasant to nature, but as being according to or against Our Father's will. Our life is no longer determined by the pleasure or the displeasure of men, but by the *will of God.* We are independent of the judgment of men. We go our way. We heed *only God's will.* "Praying *only* for knowledge of His will and the power to carry it out." We heed only God. And we learn more and more each day that *to serve God is to rule.* It is the *primacy of the spiritual.*

Really are there greater individualists than we? We maintain our God-given personal rights, and yet are fully animated with a very strong community and group spirit and consciousness. We derive our very life; our very insurance; from the group. We have all of our things in common. Not perhaps our earthly things, but all of our spiritual goods are our common possession in a very special manner. We give; and we get. We are part of the whole. In our very first tradition we say: "Each member of Alcoholics Anonymous is but a part of a great whole." We "lose" ourselves in the group only to find ourselves again as true people and true personalities. We are all active as if we had to do the whole work; and we are all passive, all resigned to do the will of God—praying *only for knowledge of His will* and the *power to carry it out!*" It is the *primacy of the spiritual.*

Through this surrender of self we give God the strongest and loveliest powers of our soul; our will and our love. And God gives us in return the one thing human nature seeks; *"peace which surpasseth all understanding"*—serenity. "And on earth peace to men of *good will";* and *good* will is *God's* will. We then realize once and for all that no matter what the struggle or the sacrifice, eventually there will be victory for *nothing* can separate us from God and that "for those who love God *all things* co-operate *unto good."* It is the *primacy of the spiritual.*

As we saw in the beginning of this volume, many talk about *peace,* but few find it. "Peace, peace and there is no peace." But to us who seek God's will is *given* this *true peace.* The past we have sunk in the bottomless ocean of His mercy. We have no present cares—"we have cast them upon the Lord" with the psalmist. The future we have placed confidently in the hands of a loving, all-powerful, all-knowing Father. We trust all to Him Who knows better than we what we need. We are *no longer afraid.*

Once upon a time a certain very anxious person whose soul was continually fluctuating between hope and fear, came to God overwhelmed with anguish. And from the depth of his anxious soul there came again and again: "O that I knew that I should persevere."

Immediately he heard a voice, the voice of God, and thus it spoke: "And what would you do, if you were *positive* that you would persevere? That *do* and you *will* persevere."

His anxiety left. His fears disappeared. His anguish was assuaged. *Trust in God and surrender to His will drive out fear.* And in its place? *"Peace* which surpasseth all understanding." That "peace in which we shall rest and sleep." It is the *primacy of the spiritual.*

And so it is that our confident surrender to God's will and His Providence *must* result in inward *peace* and *serenity* and in outward joy and gladness. There is no sadness in *God,* nor in those close to Him. "Always *rejoice,* again I say *rejoice."* For there is only *one thing necessary—God's will,* and that being accomplished in us, we *have everything.*

It is the *primacy of the spiritual.*

Now let us take a look and see how all of this works out in every area of living.

1. *In our home life*—The household which is built upon the *will of God* is a household of *peace.* It is a *real home.* And a home that practices the *primacy of the spiritual* will always bring *God* into everything.

In the marriage itself there shall be a third party to the contract—*Almighty God.*

In their love, husband and wife shall accept each other in all things as coming from *God.*

Into the hearts of the children, father and mother shall first and before all else instill a knowledge and a love of *God*—their *Heavenly Father*. And the first words taught to be spoken shall be words of *prayer*.

Into their sorrows shall come the comforting Hand of God; and each sorrow shall be lightened by accepting it as being placed there by or permitted to come from the Hand of God—it being *His will*.

Into every joy and hope and gladness shall be injected a depth of gratitude and thanksgiving to the Father Who gives us all good things.

Meals shall be preceded and followed by prayer; the day shall begin in prayer; the night shall end in *gratitude* to God—the *master of the house*.

It is the *primacy of the spiritual*.

2. *In our social life*—In our relationship with our fellowman, we shall place *principles above personalities*. This too is because of the *primacy of the spiritual*.

Being convinced of the *primacy of the spiritual* it won't make much difference into what state God has placed us; it won't matter a lot whether we are materially successful or not; it will not make any difference whether we are first in line or last; it will matter only: *is it God's will?*

We shall never look down on *anyone*—God hasn't, has He? "Has any man accused you?" Remember?

The color of our neighbor will not bother us. His religion will not irritate us; nor his financial condition; his race. Well, will it? *Not if we really want God's will*—praying "only for knowledge of His will and the power to carry that out." That comes before color or race or condition or creed—*it is the primacy of the spiritual*.

What anyone says about us won't mean much at all; nor what others think of us; only what *God thinks of us*. That is the *primacy of the spiritual*.

3. *In our business life*—More important than making money shall be the keeping of God's laws of justice and rights, if we

practice the principle of the primacy of the spiritual. No matter what our competitor does, nothing will justify our business practices except what is according to *God's will*.

We will have another partner, too, in our business—*God*.

The truly *big* man in business is the *humble* man. The humble man is the one who depends upon *God* for his success in business as in all else in his living. He practices the *primacy of the spiritual*.

4. *In our financial life*—The primacy of the spiritual will lead us not to depend upon money for security. And it will keep us from being upset over losses. We shall in the words of Job, always have in our hearts: "God gives; God takes away; blessed be the name of the Lord." Praying *only* for knowledge of His will for us and the power to carry that out."

And the future? *God* will provide. He will give *each* day what we need.

Never shall we attempt to *buy happiness*. We can't. We can't even *earn* it. But we *can* get *peace—serenity* from *God* by *doing His will*. It doesn't cost a penny! Just a little effort and a *lot of good will*.

It is the *primacy of the spiritual*.

5. *In our mental life*—The primacy of the spiritual practiced by all men would put psychiatry out of business. Mental illness so often at its beginning has omitted from life the "missing" factor of a deep faith in and trust in God in *everything*. And even when there are cases of true mental disease in one of our loved ones we shall *accept* it as being God's will. Nor shall we *criticize* it in another—it is God's will; He has permitted it.

And you know something? We would have many, many more truly sober members and *sane* members in A.A. because all would give the truth in reality to the second step "Came to believe that a Power greater than ourselves could restore us *to sanity*." And we can't be *restored* to something we "ain't" been away from, can we?

True *sanity* is the *result of the primacy of the spiritual*.

6. *In our emotional life*—Emotional difficulties are usually a result of a *disorder of the personality*. The personality is made up of three things: body, mind and soul. It is partly mental, partly spiritual, and partly physical. And the most important part? *The spiritual*. And if the spiritual part is well adjusted and working smoothly according to God's will one of two things will happen. Either the body and the mind also will be working normally; or whatever of the body or the mind which will not be working normally will *not affect the whole personality much*. There will *not* be many emotional disorders.

So it is that one of the prime factors of a strong and well ordered emotional life is *the primacy of the spiritual*.

7. *In our physical life*—Realizing that it is God's will that we take reasonable care of our body, that we will do, but we will not be too much concerned about the welfare of our physical makeup. We have not as much to say about the condition of our body as we have of our mind and soul and emotions. The latter are possible to ultimately control. But the body is gradually on the down grade. Whether we like it or not it will be subject to sickness, and pain, and death. But it will not disturb us too much —*whatever is, is God's will*. It is the *primacy of the spiritual*.

8. *In our A.A. life*—In life God comes first. This is what we have been speaking of—the *primacy of the spiritual*. In Alcoholics Anonymous God came first, is first and always will be first.

Now let's see if this be so.

Bill W. our founder conceived the beginnings of A.A. when *he first got faith in God*.

In the twelve steps *God* is mentioned specifically or implicitly in every step but the first. And the first would be impossible without humility which also implicitly indicates the existence of a "high Power." If not, we're *stuck* on the first step, because *God* picks us up *off* the first step in the second!

We spoke at length about this "spiritual side" of the program in *Sobriety and Beyond*. Now we are only re-emphasizing that *first, last and always*—without *God,* we couldn't have A.A., nor the *twelve steps, nor sobriety.*

And so at the end of every meeting we once more turn towards *God* as we bow our heads in the humble saying together of the *Lord's Prayer.*

Without the primacy of the spiritual we would not be sober tonight—neither you—nor you—nor you.

And we are *sure* that *we* wouldn't be sober—and we doubt whether we would be alive.

God that we may see!—beyond the perishable things of life to eternity and Your will! Perishable things are after all only symbols faintly reflecting the divine. And if we are really on the A.A. program, the *peace* we enjoy is also but a reflection of the divine. When we *gave,* it was reflected into our hearts from the great Heart of God. This peace will be fully and perfectly unruffled only in eternity. There our prayer—yours—and yours —and ours; our *yes, Father,* will then and then only become an eternal melody—perfect and pure in the fullness of our union forever with *God's will.*

And you know something, pal? If we have practiced surrender to *His* will here in life our loneliness here will be filled with love divine; nor shall we be taken unawares by death, but we shall be always ready to take that *thirteenth* and decisive step from time into eternity just *as* He wills it and just *when* He wills it—for, after all we *expected* it. So when our life ends, and the tears dry, and our last breath has been a soft *yes* to *God's* will, we shall hear the echo of what we heard deep down inside so often in life:

"Rejoice in the Lord always; again I say, *rejoice.* The Lord is nigh. Be nothing solicitous, but in everything by humble prayer and supplication with thanksgiving let your petitions be made known to God. And may *the peace of God which surpasseth all understanding, keep your hearts and minds....* And the God of *peace* shall be with you."

And we shall at last know the truth of the words of Isaias who told us centuries ago: "There shall be no end of *peace!*"

Peace————

        Serenity————

                Sobriety————

                        Without End!

THE TWELVE STEPS

1. We admitted we were powerless over alcohol—that our lives had become unmanageable.

2. Came to believe that a Power greater than ourselves could restore us to sanity.

3. Made a decision to turn our will and our lives over to the care of God *as we understood Him.*

4. Made a searching and fearless moral inventory of ourselves.

5. Admitted to God, to ourselves, and to another human being the exact nature of our wrongs.

6. Were entirely ready to have God remove all these defects of character.

7. Humbly asked Him to remove our shortcomings.

8. Made a list of all persons we had harmed, and became willing to make amends to them all.

9. Made direct amends to such people wherever possible, except when to do so would injure them or others.

10. Continued to take personal inventory and when we were wrong promptly admitted it.

11. Sought through prayer and meditation to improve our conscious contact with God *as we understood Him* praying only for knowledge of His Will for us and the power to carry that out.

12. Having had a spiritual awakening as a result of these steps, we tried to carry this message to alcoholics, and to practice these principles in all our affairs.

Imprimatur:
 ✠ PAUL C. SCHULTE, D.D.
   Archbishop of Indianapolis
March, 1957